LABOR INTENSIVE

LABOR
INTENSIVE

A Nurse's Journal

Natalie Wyler

Library of Congress Control Number: 2016902511
ISBN: Hardcover   978-1-5144-6765-7
                   Softcover   978-1-5144-6764-0
                   eBook   978-1-5144-6763-3

Print information available on the last page.

Rev. date: 03/18/2016

To order additional copies of this book, contact:
Xlibris
1-888-795-4274
www.Xlibris.com
Orders@Xlibris.com
729057

PROLOGUE

A BRUPTLY, DOUBLE DOORS slam open. The emergency room resident, Brigid Tolaro, shouts insistently down the hallway.

"Get the senior resident. We've got a footling breech!"

Seconds later, doctors and nurses in rumpled blue scrubs pour out of labor rooms. Headed by Craig Murphy, the senior resident, now moving at a fast clip, they head toward the staging area for this latest obstetrical emergency. They find the patient, a young, terrified Hispanic teenager, and surround the stretcher, preparing to take their roles in this time-intensive situation.

Dr. Murphy dons gloves and moves in to perform an exam. He pulls back the paper drape and the group stares momentarily at the incongruous sight of tiny feet, smoky-blue in color, protruding from the girl's vaginal opening.

"Any idea how big this Kewpie doll is?" asks Karen Nielsen, the junior resident, as she smears ultrasound gel over the bulging abdomen of their patient.

"No time," Dr. Tolaro responds breathlessly. "The heart rate was bottoming as she arrived in the ER."

Dr. Murphy gets going on his exam. The teenager shrieks, both from the abrupt and unannounced intrusion of his gloved fingers, and from the onset of a killer contraction. One of the nurses quietly moves to the head of the bed and begins to speak in soothing tones to the soon-to-be mother.

The junior resident manages to get a bead on the baby's fluttering heartbeat with the head of the ultrasound scanner. The staff can see the wavelike pulsations of the heart. The rate's not good, about half of what it should be. This little tyke is in trouble, and no one knows how long this oxygen-deficit-producing situation has been going on.

"We're going to have to take her back and liberate this kiddo," Dr. Murphy announces. "Let's move out."

Once in the delivery room, the patient is hurriedly transferred to the delivery table and her legs positioned in metal stirrups. Dr. Murphy pulls on his exam gown and gloves, while nurses open instrument packs and notify the NICU (neonatal intensive care unit) team to run up the stairs to attend this birth. Another nurse flips the switch on the time clock with the intention of capturing how much time is elapsing as the team works to effect this worrisome delivery. No matter what the clock says, each second seems like minutes, with the staff hoping that all their efforts do not end in a tragic loss.

Another strong contraction. The patient screams, and Dr. Murphy sternly demands that she push. The little feet protrude a bit, but contract back once the pain has passed. The senior resident picks up special breech forceps and attempts to insert them. With exasperation, he removes them, not able to seat them to his liking. Within moments, another contraction comes, with equally unproductive results. Sweat begins to bead on Craig Murphy's brow above his mask.

Now the experienced L & D team members are thinking the same thoughts. With those little feet appearing so small, this baby may be a premature one whose head is much bigger in size relative to its trunk and legs. As the girl's cervix opened, there may have been room to extrude the lower extremities and body, but not the head. The awful potential for head entrapment, the cutting off of vital oxygen as the umbilical cord is crushed, is the unspoken prospect facing these doctors and nurses.

"Push, dammit!" shouts Dr. Murphy as he notes the tightening of the teenager's belly, forgetting in his stress that his patient may not understand his English command.

"*Empuje, mamita!*" urges a nurse. "*Con fuerza! Con fuerza!*"

With what seemed at first another futile effort, the patient suddenly emits an agonized and guttural howl, upon which a tiny, very blue baby girl squirts into Dr. Murphy's hands.

No sound except the mother's exhausted and weary sobbing greets the infant's traumatic entrance into the world. Deposited on the newborn exam table, pediatricians surround the baby and begin their practiced resuscitation protocol: drying her with warm towels, softly pumping air into her tiny lungs, and flicking her still-dusky soles. One of the pediatric residents counts the newborn's heart rate with her stethoscope and beats the rhythm on the bedsheet beside the seemingly lifeless baby. It is very slow.

Then almost inaudibly, a weak sound is emitted. Seconds later, a stronger effort. The entire medical and nursing team stops to listen. Then to everyone's profound satisfaction, a forceful, indignant cry cuts the tension in the room. Ahhh! The sweet-sounding, infinitely desirable announcement of life.

This experience is one of an endless array of challenges the staff of the high-risk obstetrical unit faces on a routine basis. As a nurse in one of the busiest such units in the United States, serving an eclectic, diverse, and impoverished population of women, I came to feel that there was a story worth telling. A story not limited merely to the medical situations but one involving the interplay of all characters: doctors, nurses, patients, and families. Beginning at a time when I had four years of experience, I kept my thoughts about my life at work in a journal. Thus, this story is seen through my eyes, for better or worse.

Inevitably, some troubling events occurred. I have not tried to identify or indict anyone concretely given the stressful nature of the work. Men and women described in my journal, including myself, possessed differing strengths and skills when called upon to deal with frequent emergencies and a backbreaking workload. The events happened, but the attributes of the staff are drawn loosely so as to picture the human dynamics rather than stigmatize anyone in particular. The characters are seen through the filter of my impressions—some as difficult personalities, others as colleagues, as friends, as heroes—all struggling with the often battlefield-like conditions.

CHAPTER ONE

". . . my head in a whirl of screaming mothers, demanding doctors, and hair-raising deliveries."

March 1

I GOT THE ASSIGNMENT I was hoping for tonight. Six other night-shift nurses and I were standing around the scarred wooden table in the break room at 11:00 p.m., awaiting report. Most of us were sipping coffee in an attempt to get a spurt of energy for the coming night. Our charge nurse, Merilee, read the assignments for various areas–labor rooms, delivery, recovery, antepartum problems, and nursery. I am going to be the LICU nurse tonight, a role much to my liking.

I walked across the hall to the labor intensive care unit. From all the pregnant women cared for in this complex obstetrical arena, those with the most compelling problems are admitted to this room. If we anticipate that labor will be a particular stressor for a mother or baby, special attention is warranted. The third-year resident is assigned to watch over these patients. This MD works hand in hand with the LICU nurse, and I like this defined team play. Well, almost always.

I started my shift by accepting the narcotics key, then counting the drugs in the locked drawer. Charlotte Ames, the nurse I was relieving, recounted the history of the two women whose care I was assuming. One reason I like my assignment to this room has more to do with the aesthetics than anything else. Our typical four-bed "normal" labor rooms are cramped little boxes. The LICU is a long galley-like room, and there is a bank of windows that lends me a sense of freedom as the hours of the night progress. I can watch the first light of morning spread over the hills in the distance. This always-cheerful spectacle reminds me that even the most taxing night is drawing to a close, and soon a warm bed will be the reward for my efforts.

Nurses assigned to the LICU have only three patients instead of the customary four. Under typical circumstances, these laboring women have complex medical or obstetrical problems that demand careful observation and a bevy of treatments. Making this assignment even more challenging is the unoccupied space near one end of the room. This cubicle is left empty for the unpredictable admission of "red blankets," or emergency OB patients. In the midst of managing the sickest or most problematic patients in the unit, the LICU nurse must drop everything to assist with a tense situation, possibly involving life-or-death issues. This kind of situation can make an already hectic assignment intensely challenging.

OK, not every red blanket is so dramatic. Some of these arrivals are only tense because a woman comes into the ER downstairs on the verge of delivery. She is hurriedly transported up to our unit and deposited in the LICU red blanket cubicle for a quick check before she is trundled off to a delivery room. Since the LICU is the labor room adjacent to the delivery area, this is purely a matter of logistics. This situation is no emergency per se, but the often panicky and anxiety-stricken cries of the mother are reason enough for the ER staff to want to get her to us pronto.

If there is time, an intern checks her, starts an IV, and draws lab work. But if the intern strolls too casually toward the LICU, nature sometimes takes its inevitable course. I have handed many an infant into the world in the LICU, and babies have been born at every point between here and the emergency department three floors below us.

The true red blanket is an entirely different matter. There are some situations in obstetrics that are potentially life threatening for either mom or baby. There is massive bleeding from an abnormally positioned placenta or a placenta that has torn away from the wall of the womb. Pregnancy-induced hypertension, once known as toxemia, has gotten to a critical stage, and the mother has blood pressures that cause dramatic seizures. The bag of water surrounding the baby breaks under pressure, and the umbilical cord washes down ahead of the baby, risking the shutdown of the vital oxygen supply. A patient waits too long to come to the hospital, and by the time she reaches the ER, she is found to have two feet emerging instead of a round little head. These crises demand that the members of the obstetrical team—obstetricians, nurses, anesthesiologists, pediatricians—be prepared to intervene rapidly, surgically if necessary. Sometimes mere minutes separate the delivery of a beautiful, healthy infant from that of a dead or damaged one.

These are the red blankets that always produce an adrenaline rush for anyone involved. We are caring for someone's precious baby, after all, and the life of the mother of a young family. As this is a teaching hospital and one of the busiest in the nation, these episodes provide doctors and nurses in training the opportunity to hone their professional skills. Similar emergencies can and do occur in elegant community hospitals, though much more infrequently. Staff must know how to respond no matter what the environment. Here, in a one-week period, we might see those emergencies that come through the ER of a private hospital in a year's time, one serving an affluent population of pregnant women with excellent prenatal care.

Fortunately for me, no red blankets were to trouble me this night in the LICU, but my quiet assignment turned sour nonetheless. My first patient, as I found in the report of the nurse going home, was a rather nervous, needy Latina whose middle-aged mother sat beside her, hovering. Mrs. Guadalupe Flores was feverish and had recently been laid on a cooling blanket to bring her temperature down. Her bag of waters, or amniotic sac, had been artificially broken six hours ago. Now she was infected, the normally friendly flora in the vagina having migrated into the fluid surrounding the baby.

The senior resident, Dr. Edmonds, a preppy young man of about thirty, soon appeared to make rounds with the attending staff physician, Dr. Joyce. Dr. Joyce is a member of the faculty associated with this department, an experienced and expert obstetrician. He is responsible for supervision of the "house" staff—interns and residents—and consultation on difficult cases. Several hours had passed with no significant progress for Mrs. Flores, a woman diagnosed with a severe form of pregnancy-induced hypertension. Drs. Edmonds and Joyce made the decision to prepare her for a surgical delivery by cesarean section.

My part in caring for our patient was to get her ready for surgery, a routine job that I can now manage swiftly and comfortably. I needed to prep her lower abdomen in the area of the surgical incision and insert a tube into her bladder to keep it decompressed during the operation. I had to call the blood bank and reserve blood in case of an unexpected hemorrhage. Next, I would go over an extensive checklist with Mrs. Flores to ensure that we had all the information we needed to avoid complications during surgery. I had to make sure that all the paperwork was prepared and that the surgical team was alerted to the impending operation.

As luck would have it, the docs had moved on to my other patient's bed and found more trouble, requiring me to juggle two labor-intensive tasks in the same moment. Dr. Edmonds told me to set this second woman up immediately for a procedure called scalp sampling. This test is designed to assess how well oxygenated the baby is, as there were subtle signs on the electronic fetal heart rate tracing that suggested this baby's status might be deteriorating. The senior resident left it entirely up to me, singular nurse, to figure out how to clone myself for the challenge of meeting the now emergent needs of two mothers and their troubled infants.

Gloria Fuentes, the woman who needed the scalp sampling procedure, was an interesting patient in that she had lost thirteen pounds since the onset of pregnancy, and she was a naturally slight woman. I didn't have time to sleuth out the explanation for this curious weight loss. Her baby appeared to be growth restricted while in utero, even though the little one had spent the appropriate amount of time inside his painfully slender mother. When these babies are born, they have scant baby fat and their skin hangs in wrinkly folds, giving them the appearance of scrawny old men.

As Gloria's labor had progressed, the fetal monitor that tracks the baby's heart rate had picked up a pattern of subtle decelerations, or dips, that were occurring past contractions. These late decelerations correlate with babies who emerge at birth in bad shape. Somehow, this baby's oxygen supply was being compromised. The obstetricians needed to know a little more about the status of this infant before they could decide if they needed to intervene surgically to free the little one from an environment that was possibly no longer healthy.

Once the cervix is sufficiently open, the doctor can obtain a sample of blood from the baby's scalp. The blood is sent to the laboratory, and about fifteen minutes later, the lab calls back with the results. From the pH of the blood, we can tell if the baby is being deprived of sufficient oxygen. Since Mrs. Fuentes's cervix had dilated to four centimeters, it was feasible to do this test and find out if it was possible to temporize in the interest of avoiding a surgical birth.

How could I prepare the first patient for surgery and assist with the scalp-sampling procedure simultaneously? There were two babies in actual or potential trouble, and things needed doing right away. Fortunately, for it was not usually the case, our charge nurse heard of my plight and came to help. How I love Merilee, who so often puts her needs last and looks around for ways to support the nurses under her leadership. She got going swiftly with our patient needing stat surgery, while I set Mrs. Fuentes up for sampling.

Merilee swung past us with her little crew, both mother and daughter frowning as the bed was pushed toward the delivery area. These two women looked understandably nervous and irritable, as things had not progressed happily with this labor. I got the sense that Mrs. Flores and her mother were irked with us, as if somehow this untoward turn of events was our fault. Why was surgery necessary this time when she had delivered her first four children without any drama? Unfortunately, not all births can proceed with equal results, especially with this mom's onset of accompanying pregnancy problems and the recent evidence of an infectious process. Since we care for a largely poor immigrant population with many high-risk factors complicating their pregnancies, we do see a lot of difficult situations.

I was still hoping that when the baby delivered, the outcome would be a happy mother with a good infant. Later, I found out from the nurse assisting in surgery that this was false hope. When the surgeons opened the uterus, Baby Boy Flores was swimming in thick green-brown sludge instead of crystal-clear amniotic fluid.

Meconium is the name of the thick, at times viscous primary stool that a baby sometimes passes before birth, thought to be the result of some stressor. It is a sterile substance but in some instances can be gooey or even tar like. It is dangerous for the baby to suck this stuff into its lungs when first born. The meconium in this patient's case was described as the worst sort—"pea soup" meconium—and is usually an indication that the baby has been profoundly challenged while inside its mother.

Additionally, pus was observed on the newborn's scalp, possibly an indicator of an infection known as beta strep. Sepsis is now also threatening Mrs. Flores's baby if bacteria have spread through his little body via the blood stream. Now in the neonatal intensive care unit, this baby's fate will be touch and go for days.

As for my other patient, an intern completed the scalp-sampling procedure, and tiny tubes of baby's blood were hurried down to the lab. About twenty minutes later, I called for the results. They turned out to be in the low-normal range. We could afford to watch this baby for a while longer. The fetal heart rate tracing now had a rather flat appearance, which is believed to indicate a depressed central nervous system, one not able to respond robustly to the stress of labor. About two hours later, the scalp samples were collected again. This time the results showed a slight deterioration from earlier values, though still in the borderline-normal range.

Fortunately for Mrs. Fuentes, she was on the brink of delivery and would bear her infant without necessitating a hurriedly performed cesarean section. Ten minutes later, I was calling for an intern to take Gloria back to the delivery area to attend her through birth. I let this doctor know she might want to ask the pediatric team from the NICU to be present at the birth. This infant had experienced a problematic gestation inside its mother and had demonstrated a barely normal oxygenation status during labor.

After these two patients had left, I tried to regroup quickly, to clean and restock the room. I was unsurprised when Dr. Schallenberg, the third-year resident assigned to cover the LICU, came to tell me I would be receiving three replacements, back-to-back. They consisted of two toxemia patients, one with a fever of unknown origin, the other with a troubling fetal heart rate tracing. First to arrive would be another patient in premature labor who had broken through the medication given to abate contractions and was now on the verge of delivering a very small infant.

In almost any other obstetrical setting, each of these patients would be cared for on a one-to-one nurse-patient basis. Unfortunately, we are chronically understaffed, this kind of high-stress environment being unpalatable to the typical L & D nurse. We have organized the work as best we can to handle this excessive load. After four years of experience, I am no longer terrorized by the heavy responsibilities inherent in such an assignment. Still, I am anything but blasé about the amount of effort, knowledge, and organizational skills required to meet the needs of these high-risk moms and infants.

My new patients were brought over to me in turn by their nurses and were soon hooked up to all the monitors and pumps. I quickly tried to get to know them and assess their most immediate needs. Amazingly, the second of these women was accompanied by a labor coach who had been one of the original team of nurses to staff the LICU. Some years ago when the first research studies were done using electronic monitoring of labor, it was not the vision that such machinery would be used for all women, rather only for patients with significant problems. A small team of nurses was trained to read the monitor output and care for the selected patients who typically had complex needs. In time, tension developed between the LICU nurses and those who cared for the other laboring patients. I heard some old gossip about a final blowout surrounding this issue, resulting in the disbanding of the group of research nurses. All nurses who worked in this L & D unit completed a course to work with the new technology. Such education was helpful, given the reality that electronic monitoring during labor gradually became the standard of care.

I would have loved to chat with this visiting nurse about all that political stuff from years past. That was impossible, for I was on the run trying to attend to the pressing needs of these sick, compromised mothers and babies. This nurse, who had put aside her professional role to act as friend and coach, was very aware of the demands under which I was working. Meanwhile, she was doing a splendid job of giving attention to her friend, supporting the young woman through a trying labor and making this time much more bearable.

I had my hands full with the patient with the preemie baby. Such small ones slip out much more easily than full-term babies. I think just knowing that a very premature infant is coming lends an added load of anxiety for the mother. As is often the case, young Philomena called to me with each contraction.

"Ay, señorita," she would implore me as she felt her pain beginning. *"Venga!, ayúdame, por favor!"* ("Oh, miss, please come and help me!")

No matter how busy I was in this tense room, these touching words would prompt me to return to her bed to lend her some much-needed reassurance.

Then as her contraction began to subside, I would slip my hand from her thin one and hustle about, trying to complete care for my other two patients.

As dawn arrived, it occurred to me that not many patients had passed by my doorway on their way to delivery. I had had the majority of excitement in this, the complex labor room, for the entire night. At least I knew that when I went home shortly, leaving my undelivered patients in the care of a fellow nurse, I would sleep the sleep of the just. I had done my best by these women, even though some not very happy results had occurred. My perspective on this hectic night's demands is an improvement over earlier days when I used to dream constantly about work, my head in a whirl of screaming mothers, demanding doctors, and hair-raising deliveries.

CHAPTER TWO

". . . it often becomes increasingly chaotic as night turns toward morning."

March 4

HOW CAN I adequately describe a typical night in the high-risk obstetrical unit? The patients, numbering some twenty-five women, are being managed by a medical team of residents, interns, medical students, and a midwife. All but the very seasoned midwife are physicians in training with varying degrees of experience. Registered nurses with a background in the specialty of obstetrical nursing do the hands-on care of patients, with some assistance from a variety of ancillary staff. Licensed vocational nurses, surgical technicians, clerks, and nursing assistants share the workload for some of the less complex unit tasks.

This hospital, one of several separate hospitals on the campus of this medical center, is the clinical experience arm for a university medical school, in collaboration with the city government. Its mission is the care of the city's poor and uninsured women and their infants. This med center is a tertiary care facility, meaning that it provides the most intensive level of care for those with serious health issues, as well as one that covers a wide array of specialty services. In my field, obstetrics, this hospital is a referral center for unusual cases from around this sprawling city. Incidentally, we deliver one in every two hundred infants born in this country. Such volume makes us either the number-one or number-two busiest maternity services nationwide.

Unlike other areas of the hospital where calm and quiet descend over the place when patients go to sleep, our service stays busy. Indeed, it often becomes increasingly chaotic as night turns toward morning. Although research suggests that births are distributed evenly throughout the day and night, it seems that lots of babies want to see their first glimpse of the world as day is dawning. Each of my four children was born between midnight and 5:00 a.m.

As I came out of report on my way to begin my assignment in a labor room for the next eight hours, I passed by the desk that is the hub of the unit. Two clerks staff this battered wooden workstation. These clerks are busier than any secretary I know of, fielding a phenomenal amount of phone, foot, and bed traffic.

One minute the intercom comes on. It's a nurse asking the clerks to send back the obstetricians to get a cesarean section under way. The next minute the emergency room calls to let the clerks know a pregnant patient with a disturbing problem is being transported our way. Then there is the regularly irregular procession of stretchers arriving with new patients in labor to be sorted out and sent to various care areas. The clerks will admit forty to fifty women in an average twenty-four-hour period. Tonight Ruth and Jerome are the clerks on duty.

Ruth is the queen of the desk and delights in terrorizing new and unsuspecting interns and nurses. She barks out announcements and informs us when we are not performing tasks up to the standards she deems acceptable after having worked here for twenty years. She is not impressed in the least by the RN or MD after one's name. She's seen us come and go, and I've heard her giving verbal hell to senior residents. Ruth scared me when I began night duty here; now I know that Ruth's strident voice is mostly bluff.

Jerome is a stylish, intelligent gentleman with an irrepressible sense of humor. He used to be a "difficult" employee when working in an assortment of pokey units around the med center. He was chronically absent from work and was often AWOL from his assignment when he did show up. Someone had the inspired thought to send him here, and this change proved the making of the man. Jerome thrives on the pace here, the excitement that ebbs and flows, the chance to be involved, at least peripherally, in our regularly occurring emergencies.

Jerome has an especially good ear for language and has become roughly conversant in Spanish, the language that most of our clientele speak. As a nurse and intern are hurrying past the desk with a woman on her way to delivery, Jerome can be heard encouraging her to "*Sople, señora, sople!*" (Blow, lady, blow!) He blithely fractures the Spanish language to communicate with interested family members who arrive at the desk to make inquiries. He does so with so much verve and charm that he seldom has trouble communicating with our Hispanic families.

Jerome likes to use his skill for mimicking other voices to play the occasional prank on the staff here. I remember the morning he sauntered off to one of his secret haunts where he called a young, pretty, and rather serious nurse to the phone. Pretending to be the nursing supervisor, he informed Vickie that, due to a staffing crisis, she was required to stay over and work a double shift. In the morning, she was to report up the hill to the infected orthopedic unit, better known as the "pus ward." With his uncanny gift for imitating others, Jerome rendered Vickie hysterical, completely convinced as she was by this crackpot story.

Immediately adjacent to the main desk is a small alcove where the residents congregate to complete charts, check out new arrivals from the emergency room, and consult or lament with each other. Their day starts at 8:00 a.m. when they meet with their team of residents, interns, and medical students to make walking rounds together with their supervising staff physician. As they move along the corridors, the off-going team presents each patient, what has happened so far during her admission, and what their plan of care has been to this point. The medical bigwigs quiz the physicians in training, critique management plans, and offer advice on challenging cases.

Thus begins a tour of duty for the obstetrical team that will only end the following day after they pass on their patients. Even then, these physicians don't leave. After breakfast, they go to the various floors upstairs where they see women who have delivered, either vaginally or surgically. Sometimes these women have new and different problems and need an updated management plan. Some are ready for discharge, and the junior residents and rotating interns are learning how to wrap up the patients' stay and make a plan for their continuing health-care needs. They then hopefully can go home for their one partial day of rest out of each three-day rotation. The next morning they will be in the OB clinic to see patients experiencing complicated pregnancies.

Now at eleven o'clock at night, some fifteen hours into their call, the medical team is beginning their sleep rotation. The senior resident, Dr. Jacobs, has a spacious room to herself, while the junior residents share a much smaller sleep room. The interns and medical students are packed into a room furnished with bunk beds. The senior sleep room is unfortunately located next to the mother-baby assessment room where all newly delivered moms and their infants go after birth. I'm not sure how much good sleep is possible with a bunch of squalling newborns in the next room.

At any rate, it is the privilege of the senior resident to sleep all night if there are no complex admissions, difficult deliveries, or life-threatening emergencies to be addressed. Given the nature of the work here, the senior resident can expect to be awakened at intervals through the night. It would be an unheard-of call during which any of the house staff would get more than a few hours of restless sleep.

This particular senior resident, Dr. Jacobs, will not sleep much due to her personal sense of obligation to our patients. This whip-thin, sandy blonde with a perpetual cleft in the skin folds of her forehead is a quietly forceful, serious-minded leader of her team. She is never completely sure that the rest of the staff can be trusted to keep safe all the high-risk moms and babes who are ultimately her responsibility. Thus, she will keep popping out of bed at almost hourly intervals to check on all her patients and see that care is being provided as she would like.

Besides the three junior residents who make up Dr. Jacobs' team, an extra player is just arriving. Dr. Mooney, an obstetrician in his third year of residency, is taking a turn this month at being the night OB resident. He does not belong to any of the three OB teams who are on the call schedule. Rather, he comes on each night at midnight, Monday through Friday. It is his job to relieve the resident staff so that they can each have a turn at sleeping. He has to try to manage the patients already in beds, as well as those who show up for admission during the night. Operating in this solo manner is thought to be excellent training for his upcoming role as a senior resident starting in July.

Dr. Mooney will monitor the status of all current laboring women and perform workups on all the newly admitted patients. This task is no mean feat should the typical ten to twelve women arrive before morning. It is a matter of his judgment whether he can handle things alone or he should wake up a junior resident, even the senior resident, to help. He must consult with Dr. Jacobs before deciding that any patient needs a cesarean section. If a woman does require surgery, he will wake up the appropriate residents in turn. He does not do any surgery on this night OB rotation.

Dr. Mooney is not the easiest man to work with from the nurses' perspective. He's not well organized and he's not very good at prioritizing. He tends to fall behind on his workups of newly admitted patients and, thus, as the night wears on, he grows increasingly irritable. He will not finish any one job but skips from place to place, taking patient charts along and leaving them behind for the nurse to hunt. He interviews his female patients with a brusque and condescending manner, then instructs them rudely to get onto their back and open their legs for his exams. He appears indifferent to any pain or discomfort he inflicts, willy-nilly. Perhaps Marina Jacobs is aware of all this, and it is one more reason she cannot rest easily.

I am particularly fond of Marina Jacobs. She takes her job so seriously and yet is a good-natured and witty woman. She was a nurse in her first career, and while she rarely alludes to this fact, she treats the nurses here with respect and consideration. I understand that she is married to a wealthy gentleman who finds it very hard to accept the criminally long hours she is required to be here at the hospital as a resident. I sympathize with her. Women still face challenges with the change from days when home was the sole focus for most wives. The demands of a medical residency are immensely stressful.

As I walked down the wing that houses the labor rooms, passing by doors that are left open so as not to be too claustrophobic, I wondered for the umpteenth time why we must crowd so many patients into these small boxlike rooms. There are plenty of unoccupied rooms in the opposite wing, now simply serving as boneyards for the storage of extra beds and equipment. It was not so long ago that I was in labor with my youngest. I remember how very much I needed quiet and privacy to allow me to stay focused, to relax as much as possible during the incredible pain of labor. In my cushy private labor room, with my husband beside me for encouragement and back rubbing, I was in the best of all laboring worlds.

Perhaps the lack of quiet and privacy is the reason I am being accosted with a medley of heartrending cries as I pass by on my approach to my assigned room.

"Ay, ay, Madre de Dios, ayúdame!" ("Mother of God, help me!")

"Por favor, enfermera, make me *una cesarea. Porque, yo no aguanto mas!"* ("Please, nurse, do a cesarean, because I can't stand this anymore!")

Perhaps these women, whom I have found to be lovely, brave, and quite courageous in facing daily lives filled with uncertainty and poverty, could tolerate their pain with a bit more fortitude if there was not so much environmental stress. There are the comings and goings of so many players with whom they must contend—doctors, nurses, housekeepers, and visitors. Then there is the crying and distress of three other women laboring at a distance of no more than two arm's length. There is the incessant beeping of that boon to modern obstetrics, the electronic fetal monitor. The lights are on 24/7. Etcetera.

I, of course, do know the reason for this crowded state of affairs. The workload is very great here. There has been chronic difficulty in attracting and keeping enough nurses willing to brave the demands placed on those who must ride herd on such numbers of complex labor patients. The docs prefer to concentrate the most patients in the smallest area so as to lessen, by a few, the thousands of steps they must take throughout each twenty-four hours of duty here. The patient's emotional needs are the least important factor in this equation.

All the more reason I should scoot down the hall and get to my assigned room. I will relieve the hardworking and typically harassed nurse I am replacing and begin a fresh attempt to do a decent job by these women. It was my choice to work here. In spite of the often unappetizing circumstances, there is also a wealth of knowledge to be gained, an interesting and varied cast of people to meet and work with, and patients who genuinely need our care. There are rewards to be had even in the midst of such a challenging environment. Either that or I am an incredible magnet for abuse. As is my usual habit, I will assess this again in the morning.

CHAPTER THREE

"If amenities such as décor and ambiance were the lure, I'd have left long ago . . ."

March 9

MY ASSIGNMENT TONIGHT is that of the rover nurse. I have a labor room assignment, but it is empty for now. It's always nice to have a spare nurse who can roam around and take the heat off whoever happens to be busy. I think I am a pretty good rover because I'm not too uppity about doing whatever needs to be done–make beds, transport patients, feed babies, or assemble charts in the newborn nursery. Also, I like to tour the labor rooms and help our hardworking nurses who constantly have their hands full trying to keep up with a myriad of tasks. I can start a newly ordered medicine drip, take the hourly vital signs for up to four patients, or coach a laboring woman who needs help in pushing to encourage birth.

Truthfully, it is sometimes refreshing to have a somewhat creative assignment like roving. I might be giving a lunch break to some overworked nurse in a labor room that is nearly impossible to manage due to a "screamer," or too many patients on multiple medications. The rover has the hope of escaping that scene when the nurse returns, refueled with energy and grateful for the respite. Not that a rover doesn't stay busy, but the pressure is just much less. It is an assignment to relish, but most nights there is no extra nurse to spare for the rover role.

A nice event is taking place tonight. We're having a modest party in our rather dismal kitchen for a nurse who is transferring to the day shift. Sue started off valiantly, but the nights are wearing on her. She's told several people that she simply hates being away from her husband at night. Consequently, she calls in sick rather often. This chronic absenteeism of hers breeds resentment on the part of nurses who show up faithfully. Night work is only preferred by a select few, and Sue is not one of them. For her, moving to a daytime schedule will hopefully be a positive change. She'll be a much more effective nurse when her home life and work life are in sync.

I mentioned that the kitchen is dismal. How to describe this wretchedly grim square of a room that is the only space available for the nursing staff to eat their meals while on duty, or sit down and relax for a few minutes? Toward the end of nursing school when I came here for an interview, the nurse manager took me for a tour of the unit. As we passed by the break room, the two or three women in blue scrub dresses who were eating at the worn wooden table looked up at us with mild curiosity. Staring at the utilitarian walls and counters, the smattering of worn coffeemakers and refrigerators, I thought to myself, *God, how depressing. How do they stand it?*

I didn't let this stop me from accepting a position here because this was the only labor and delivery unit in the city that hired new graduates. I had thought I would be sentenced to the customary two to three years in a medical-surgical unit upon graduation. I was expressing my dread of this prospect when a fellow student told me, "You should talk to Julie Fortenese who is going directly to L & D at the city hospital." This tip led me in an unanticipated direction, one that sent me down the path to this unusual and challenging career at a site I would never have thought to explore on my own.

Four years later, the kitchen is just as appallingly grim as the first day I saw it. Now I have learned that this is a minor detail in the tapestry of the work here. If amenities such as décor or ambiance were the lure, I'd have left long ago for one of the elegantly appointed hospitals I could choose from much closer to my home. Nope, it's the people here who are the draw—an intelligent, committed, hardworking, and lively staff, as well as patients who truly need compassionate and knowledgeable nursing care.

Back from our little party, I helped transport a patient to the postsurgical ward. I should perform this task once a night without fail. Doing so would remind me of how infinitely varied and interesting my work is in comparison with those long-suffering, undervalued nurses who care for our postdelivery patients after they leave the more intense atmosphere of Labor and Delivery. Their units seldom have decent staffing, and their work is often tedious and repetitive. But certain of these nurses can also be hilariously allergic to work.

They look on with bleak expressions as you push a new patient on a stretcher toward them.

Whenever I call Miss Arbison in the antepartum unit to tell her that I am transferring a patient to her for care, I listen for the inevitable pause while she digests the bad news. Next, a huge and hapless-sounding sigh can be heard. Sometimes she appeals to me as if it were in my power to send the patient elsewhere:

"I have thirteen IVs . . . I have no help."

I feel a little sorry for Miss Arbison, but not half as much as she does. The other night she tried to work on my tender heart, and I was forced to be blunt as she expressed her customary disbelief that another admission was on the way.

"Well, Miss Arbison, "I said, "it's truly a scene down here. We've got thirty patients in the unit, and babies are popping out wherever you look!" Then I waited for her dispirited reply.

"We-ll, oka-ay, then," she drawled, as if she honestly thought I could somehow make the patient disappear.

After our good-bye party, I started giving a nurse her lunch break, one who'd been working since 7:00 p.m. Then I had to abandon my rover role because the other labor beds were now full. I was admitting the next women to arrive in labor. My first patient turned out to be a cute, shy seventeen-year-old who was braving the IV insertion and the drawing of blood. Her husband and mother were in the room, and since I had just one patient, I was fine with having them both stay with her.

The young mother-to-be, Mariana, was just getting into the active stage of labor with strong and regular contractions. She was handling the intense pain with a great deal of courage. Meanwhile, her scruffy young husband was sleeping, and pretty soon Mama was putting her head down too. I let this continue a bit, unsure of how to handle this situation with diplomacy. I know that it is difficult for those unused to being awake at this strange hour to keep from becoming drowsy.

Finally, after several nurses passed by and found my "slumber party" cause for raised eyebrows, I felt I must intervene. The young girl needed some support from her loved ones. I waited until the young man's eyes fluttered open.

"You seem very sleepy," I commented.

"Yes, I am," he replied somewhat sheepishly.

"I know it's hard to stay awake when you aren't used to being up during the night. I think, though, you should consider going downstairs to the lobby. Mariana is having such severe pain now that I feel it's not fair to have her family sleeping in the same room. If you decide to stay, it would really help for you to hold her hand or rub her back and talk to her."

I left the room to give him and Mama a chance to digest these choices. I had tried to maintain a nonjudgmental tone so that they would not feel that I disapproved of their quite human behavior. When I returned, they were both up, and the husband was standing at the bedside, leaning down to whisper to Mariana. This young couple did fine from that point on, and as her nurse, I was enjoying the novelty of being able to provide personalized care to this sweet girl.

Just before daybreak, Dr. Mooney, the night OB resident, toddled in and decided to move my patient down to a space that had recently been vacated in another labor room. His point was to consolidate the patients. He wasn't impressed in the least with my plea to let the girl remain with me.

"It distresses the oncoming team when they get here at eight and find patients way down here," he told me.

Dr. Mooney had no thought about how distressing it was for the labor nurses to have responsibility for four high-risk labor patients in a room meant for no more than two. Nor could he see how much more desirable it was for Mariana to be in a private spot with plenty of personal attention. I knew even before I asked that Dr. Mooney was unlikely to see things my way.

The floor was quiet except for two other weighty matters. There was a woman in one of our antepartum beds who was estimated to weigh about four hundred pounds. She said 350, but she was utterly massive. She was very embarrassed by her size, a nice woman who kept apologizing at every turn.

Mary Worthington's girth gave rise to the kind of hilarity that only nurses and doctors could engage in at three o'clock in the morning. The kitchen was exploding with laughter as various staff speculated about the events that were involved in the impregnation of this patient. Some surmised that it must have taken at least two extra personnel to prop up her massive thighs. Other gross remarks were offered up about "extenders," pulley systems, etc. Had her prenatal care taken place at Sea World?

If this seems cruel and insensitive, one has to understand that we need our share of humor here to compensate for the pain, the stress that we deal with so constantly. Not one of these nurses and interns would have thought of offending our patient by commenting on her size in her hearing. One additional happening added to the already out-of-control comedy when Mr. Worthington arrived on the scene. He was very tall, thin as a pencil, and was the impetus for much rolling of eyes and giggling. Again, this was out of range of the patient and her solicitous spouse.

We do see a great deal more obesity in this poor population. More than the aesthetics, this added weight can complicate pregnancy. It induces problems with diabetes and hypertension, making care a challenge. There can be such a fat pad over the abdomen that it is nearly impossible to find the baby's heartbeat. The residents must pull the ultrasound machine to the patient's bedside to assess baby's well-being at regular intervals. Surgery on these "chubettes" is daunting. If a C-section becomes necessary, the enormous roll of abdominal fat must be taped away from the incision site so that surgery can proceed. Once the surgery is complete, it is vitally important that the patient is gotten out of bed within a few hours to prevent blood clots, and it can take an army of personnel to execute this event.

The other weighty drama involved a ten-pound, fourteen-ounce baby, a fat little girl whose delivery was the impetus for one of the most terrifying emergencies we face—shoulder dystocia. This calamity results when a large baby tries to deliver and the head manages to come out, but the big shoulders get hung up behind the mother's pelvic bones. Unless the shoulders can be released, there's no way for the baby to deliver, and within minutes, the baby will become asphyxiated. The problem becomes apparent when the baby's head pops out, then retracts back tight against the vaginal outlet and won't budge. We call this turtle sign.

There are measures that are immediately taken, like pushing hard on the place right above those pelvic bones, hoping to release the trapped shoulder. Midwives like to have the mom pull her legs up on her chest as far as possible (the McRoberts maneuver), and I've seen this work well. A huge episiotomy (incision at the base of the vaginal outlet) is made, one that goes through all layers of tissue right down and into the rectum. We're talking about a baby's life now, or impending brain damage with each minute the head stays trapped. No half measures are allowed.

If these tactics don't prove successful, the obstetrician has to try to reach up inside and pull the arm of the baby out to provide some added space. This intervention is no job for an unskilled practitioner. When we are working in delivery, and if there is even a question of a shoulder dystocia, we get on the intercom system and call over to the labor area. The clerks don't mess around, and when the residents hear the announcement of "shoulder," they drop whatever they are doing and *run* back to the delivery area.

Luckily, this baby was delivered by whatever measures were employed this morning. I was not there, but it was felt that the true size of this infant had not been adequately estimated prior to this birth. It also looked as if this baby had one of the common complications of such a traumatic delivery, a fractured collarbone. X-rays were taken in the postpartum nursery to assess for this problem. The baby girl appeared gigantic next to the seven- and eight-pounders alongside her. Huge, but content, she was slurping down her Enfamil with gusto, in no apparent distress.

CHAPTER FOUR

"We're often convinced that there is a special guardian angel hovering over this unit . . ."

March 10

I WAS INVOLVED IN a true emergency tonight, one that shows what we are compelled to deal with here. Events can be going along routinely, with just the effort to help fifteen to twenty women through their labor and delivery. Suddenly something happens to get all of us working at top speed and with all possible skill to prevent a tragedy from occurring. With this in mind, every doctor and nurse who works here goes about his or her duties, unconsciously waiting for the other shoe to drop—the next OB emergency.

I was once again assigned to the special labor room, the LICU. Merilee knows I like to work in this challenging arena, while other nurses are less enthusiastic. I found two patients there as I entered the room at eleven fifteen. One woman, thirty-six-year-old Dorita Clemente, was having her second baby and was not very happy about the way her labor was going. She was looking around with barely suppressed irritation at all the monitors and tubes hooked up to her. She expressed, as best I could understand her complaints, that she had her first baby without all this fuss. Not every woman who comes through our doors is a fan of our high-tech, research-based operation.

Earlier, an intern had twice attempted placement of an internal pressure catheter, a water-filled tube that slides into the opening of the cervix and is compressed between the baby's head and the wall of the uterus. This tube serves to measure the force of uterine contractions rather accurately. It is most important to have this measuring system in place when the mother is receiving the labor-intensifying drug, Pitocin, as this medication can greatly increase the strength of contractions. The insertion of the catheter requires a little time, especially if the physician has recently learned the procedure. Having had an internal pressure catheter inserted during my last labor, I can testify that this procedure can be distinctly trying, even in the hands of an experienced practitioner.

Beverly Amaya, the nurse who had been caring for my patient during the evening, told me that Mrs. Clemente had had an impressive amount of blood oozing from the vagina. Sometime earlier this evening, the third-year resident Justine Ivers had performed a test to determine if this blood was the mother's or the baby's. Sure enough, as I lifted the bedsheet, I saw a circle of old brownish blood about six inches in diameter staining the bedsheet, and also a fair-sized blood clot. There was no fresh bleeding that I could see.

After Beverly had left, I sorted out the needs of Mrs. Clemente and the other patient, and went about attending to them with the near constant drumbeat of complaints from one and wailing from the other. Finally, I did two things in an attempt to pacify Mrs. Clemente. Cynthia, one of our Hispanic nurses, happened to walk through my room on her return from the delivery area. I snagged her to help translate. I wanted to be sure that I understood everything my patient was trying to tell me. My prowess with obstetrical Spanish has grown with time, but when I'm trying to grasp the subtleties, I never hesitate to ask for help. Cynthia talked to the patient and reassured me that I had gotten the gist of what Mrs. Clemente wanted to relate. Emotionally, she expressed her deep dissatisfaction with the treatment she had received from this band of *"doctores."*

Next, I found Justine Ivers, the resident assigned to the LICU, and had her check our unhappy patient. I was hoping that there had been some significant progress in this trying labor during the two hours I had been giving care. Unhappily, she had not gotten anywhere. I would have loved to encourage this disgruntled woman with the news that she was nearing delivery, or at the least, making progress. Reluctantly, I informed her of Justine's findings, to which Mrs. Clemente responded with an exclamation of pure disgust.

About twenty minutes later, the incident happened with lightning swiftness. Dr. Ivers happened to walk through the room, also on her way back from the delivery area. At that moment, I was in the cubicle next to Mrs. Clemente trying to catch up with my other patient who had been somewhat neglected. Justine said, "Oh my, what's that?" I came over and saw the problem right away. In moving from side to side, Mrs. Clemente had dislodged the leg plate that is attached to the mother's body. It is part of the system that picks up and records the baby's heart rate on the fetal monitor strip. When something interrupts physical contact with the mother's body, we can lose the recording. In this case, about four minutes of data had been lost. I simply strapped the leg plate back in place. In the meantime, the resident strolled out.

But to my dismay, the baby's heart rate was down to about seventy beats per minute, not the rate we want to see. I waited another half minute, but when the heart rate did not come back to normal, I called Justine back urgently. She and I initiated all our usual maneuvers to try and alleviate the problem. We turned off her Pitocin, moved Mrs. Clemente from side to side, started some oxygen by mask, and then increased her IV flow. When these measures did not produce results, we had to get our patient up onto her knees with head down in the bed. This position would hopefully take pressure off the umbilical cord and restore a healthy flow of blood and oxygen to the distressed baby.

In our attempt to perform these interventions rapidly, Dorita Clemente proved to be uncharacteristically resistant. Most moms, when told their baby is in trouble, will do their utmost to be cooperative regardless of the personal discomfort they endure. This patient resisted our every effort, even as the baby's heart rate continued at the same slow and dangerous rate. We told her, in Spanish, that this was a life-and-death situation for her infant, to which she responded with a bellow of outrage, shrieking that we were hurting her. Dr. Ivers got so frustrated that she unexpectedly smacked the woman's buttocks smartly, admonishing Dorita to please comply with our requests.

I was shocked momentarily. Justine Ivers is a very decent doc, ordinarily calm and of remarkably sunny disposition. I knew this action to be untypical and, of course, totally unacceptable; seemingly it arose from the young resident's desperation to elicit this woman's cooperation. It was meant, I supposed, to be an attention-getter rather than an act of violence. We knew, as this unsophisticated woman seemed unable to comprehend, that her baby was in terrible jeopardy.

Without even a small recovery, we began to unhook the patient from the heap of paraphernalia connected to her body. We needed to rush Mrs. Clemente to the operating room in anticipation of what we call a "crash" cesarean section. We shouted out the emergency, and the delivery area nursing team and anesthesiologists gathered hastily in the surgical suite. Along with the OB surgeons, this group of skilled practitioners can get a C-section going in a simple matter of minutes. Once the scalpel slices through the skin and each layer of tissue below, the baby is often out in less than ninety seconds. We have all practiced intensely for just such a situation as my patient's when minutes might be crucial to the life and well-being of an infant.

I reluctantly left the operating room after helping other nurses assist Dorita onto the operating table. Plenty of nurses had responded to the emergency, and

I could not leave my other patient in the LICU alone. My thoughts remained with Mrs. Clemente and her distressed infant, even as I became busy attending to my other mother. It was a stroke of luck that brought Steve Barrett, the senior resident who had been called back to the operating room, cruising through my area. He appeared visibly shaken.

"What happened in there?" I asked, afraid his behavior meant that the worst had occurred.

"You know," he replied in a solemn voice after slumping into a chair, "there are not too many times you can say that you saved someone's life. That kid was under a death sentence for sure!"

What he went on to tell me made my night. When the baby came out, it was evident something was very wrong. He was virtually white in color, not the healthy pink of a normal infant, or even the dusky blue of a baby who has not gotten a good breath into its lungs. The pediatric newborn resuscitation team in the room called for a stat delivery of universal donor blood. When this blood was carefully infused, the baby pinked up, opened his eyes, and responded lustily.

What had caused this baby to hemorrhage practically all of its precious, tiny blood supply? In examining the umbilical cord, a defect was found. Instead of the thick white protective cord that encases the infant's tiny blood vessels, forming a lifeline from baby to placenta, this cord had what is called a velamentous insertion. Some inches shy of the placenta, the thick white covering of the cord ended abruptly, and baby's miniature blood vessels were contained only by much thinner membrane.

At some point in the progress of Mrs. Clemente's labor, unknown forces—her movement, a dilating cervix, tension on the cord—had torn the tiny blood vessels, and the baby began to hemorrhage. I observed this when I saw the profound drop in the baby's heart rate. This baby then had only minutes to live. Due to the rapidity with which the surgery was performed and the blood transfused into Dorita's baby, our docs and nurses had saved his life.

There was also this for me to consider. As nurses practicing in this high-risk setting, we try to monitor our patients continuously. I had been with Dorita Clemente constantly and had just stepped over to do something for my second patient when this untoward event took place. If I had been tied up for many more minutes, or if Justine Ivers had not happened to pass through my room at just that moment, there was great likelihood of a tragic outcome for the baby. We're convinced that there is a special guardian angel hovering over this unit. His charge is making sure that the extremely hardworking folks here escape for the most part the inevitable consequences of caring for an enormity of high-risk mothers and their vulnerable babies. Here was a case in point.

CHAPTER FIVE

"They have such sad, pathetic, tormented eyes. Windows, I suppose, on souls in living hell."

March 17

I HAVE BEEN OFF two nights with a nasty head cold. I worked twelve hours late last week feeling perfectly awful. I slept virtually night and day for three days, and now feel human again. I had an attack of guilt about leaving my fellow nurses shorthanded over the weekend, a time of traditional poor staffing. I never call in sick unless it's legitimate–my Catholic schoolgirl conscience won't let me. I have been blessed, in general, with great health, but I don't believe I could have stayed on my feet if I had tried to come to work this past weekend. When I returned, Merilee told me of the absolute deluge of patients admitted while I was gone, and I regretted making life that much more difficult for my friends.

Tonight is cesarean section night, it seems, and I am in the antepartum problems room where we typically care for pregnant women with a variety of issues remote from labor. The room also serves as our recovery room, or PAR (postanesthesia recovery room). The fact that we are doing back-to-back surgeries will mean there will be regular admissions of those patients throughout the night. Two nurses are typically assigned to this room where up to six patients receive treatment, and the workload, the demands of care, are intense.

One interesting patient is a prisoner. Veronica is a twenty-one-year-old woman who was arrested for taking PCP, the animal tranquilizer in vogue as a recreational drug in some tough circles in this city. She is here because she is pregnant, although not in labor. We are keeping her to find out why she has a fever, as there is a chance that her temperature is due to an infection in her amniotic fluid.

It's one of the interesting features of working in this department that we care for all women in custody in this city who require inpatient maternity services. Almost any hour of the day finds us with a uniformed deputy sheriff sitting outside the room of a female prisoner. We seldom know the reason for the woman's incarceration. It's not our business. One deputy told me that 95 percent of women in jail are there because of drugs—either using or selling or both.

Our prisoner patient was initially handcuffed to the bed rail, but the deputy sheriff returned shortly after I came on duty. He replaced the handcuff with a thick chain that coursed between Veronica's ankle and the bed frame. The nurses find this practice rather barbaric. The deputies don't always stay with our custody patients, and the chaining is done to prevent the possibility of a prisoner decampment. Shackled pregnant patients are a worry due to the threat that we will need to move them rapidly to delivery, or even emergency surgery, when the deputy is unavailable to unlock the chains.

Several years ago, there was a lawsuit filed by a prisoner brought to this unit for a scheduled cesarean section. Due to the press of emergencies on the unit, time passed, and her noncritical surgery was bumped several times. She continued to labor away and eventually became completely dilated. She was forced to deliver in the labor bed, as the deputy sheriff did not make it back to the unit in time to unlock the chains. Obstetrics is somewhat unpredictable in this way.

The woman and her baby came to no harm. One could argue that the woman was luckily spared the threat of possible complications from a major abdominal surgical procedure. The court, however, felt that the patient's rights had been violated, and she won her suit. Since then, a key is kept on the charge nurse's set of keys should such an emergency occur. Naturally, we do not advertise this fact.

Getting back to my prisoner patient this night, Veronica proved to be no particular problem for care. She remained quiet and uncomplaining during her stay. We have had a few PCP cases here but have not seen the violent and bizarre behavior that the stereotypical PCP abuser supposedly exhibits.

Some of our nurses have problems taking care of pregnant drug addicts. It offends them so greatly that a woman would become pregnant and continue to take drugs. They have little compassion for these women and give them very short shrift. It is not that they refuse to take care of the drug-abusing pregnant woman. It is more their tone of voice, their unwillingness to try to get to know the individual, that betrays these nurses' lack of sympathy for the chemically dependent mother.

I don't feel such disgust myself and I feel this way despite the fact that addicted patients are not usually very charming characters. They can be hostile, manipulative, incapable of gratitude, and enormously demanding. They tend to absorb great gulps of the nurses' energy, unable as they are to relate to any other's needs but their own.

I know that this situation is a tragedy, not only for the woman but also more surely for their infant. One wonders how these women can even imagine bringing such ruin on the frail shoulders of a helpless baby. But if a woman is doing drugs to get through the ups and downs of everyday living, it makes perfect sense that she isn't necessarily focusing on safe and sensible birth control practices. One measure of how a woman takes care of herself is in the area of sexual responsibility. These women have often abdicated all sense of such responsibility in the pursuit of easing their psychic pain.

Once, as a new nurse going through my hospital orientation in the antepartum service, we admitted a young woman who had confessed her addiction to cocaine to her prenatal doctors. She asked for a referral to rehab to kick her drug problem under medical supervision. She wanted to spare her baby the inevitable effects of her habitual drug use. I was just thinking how admirable this goal was when I saw her rushing down the hallway on her way out, with a sketchy-looking guy trailing after her. "Her pusher . . . maybe her pimp," one of the seasoned nurses commented. "Happens over and over."

Even with the inducement of their baby developing within their body, the feeling of that little one moving around within them, these women are too much in the grip of their addiction. Would that they could adopt a craving for something less destructive, like chocolate bars or romance novels.

Looking back on some of my early experiences as a nurse caring for drug abusers, I was very naïve. I had been taught to look for the classic symptoms of withdrawal–the jitters, shivering, sweating, thirst, urinary frequency, diarrhea, nausea and vomiting, irritability, even seizures. However, the first few addicted women I met were mystifyingly quiet and caused me no trouble. Then I had my first make-a-believer-of–me patient. That woman progressed from mild agitation to being totally distraught, despite larger and larger doses of the calming drug Sparine. She vomited. She felt like peeing every five minutes. She pooped in the bed four or five times, a real treat for the other four patients who were receiving care in this lovely environment. She could not stay still for two seconds, and it was impossible to monitor her baby. At one point, I turned to find her standing straight up in bed.

Try as we might, the other nurse and I could not keep her clean between sweat, urine, feces, vomit, and agitation. Finally, when she had received enough Sparine to fell an elephant, she drifted off into a legal drug-induced paradise, and we were able to swab the decks and pay attention to our other patients. Thank God.

Another woman I cared for when I was training to Labor and Delivery gave me further insight into the character and behavior of the drug abuser. I was assigned to care for a large, older African American woman who admitted to having used heroin for more than ten years. She was experiencing an acute inflammation of her heart valves, typical of one with her drug history. Apparently, her long-suffering family had dragged her to the hospital out of concern for her baby. Though she was well advanced in her pregnancy, this was her first interaction with any health-care providers. We were waiting for the cardiac consult to evaluate her heart problem and work out a plan with the obstetricians for her continuing treatment.

For me, Miss New Nurse, the main challenge in her care was that about every three minutes she yelled out, "I have got to shit, I have got to shit!" The practice here was to keep patients in bed and deny them bathroom privileges, though I think we sort of beat this rule to death. I guess somewhere back in history, a woman was allowed to get out of bed to visit the facilities and ended up delivering in the toilet. With the rule restricting bathroom privileges in mind, I helped this big woman onto the bedpan and closed the curtains to allow her what privacy I could. She kept telling me she couldn't use the bedpan and would call me to remove it. Three minutes later, the same crude announcement: "I have got to shit!"

This bellowing was becoming quite disturbing to the other three patients in the room, not to mention this nurse. Finally, after an hour of such tension, I made an executive decision to get this woman up to the bathroom out of sheer consideration for everyone's nerves. She thanked me, and after five minutes in the bathroom, she returned and got back in bed. Within ten minutes, our patient, who had been lucid and perky, became completely somnolent.

I don't know where she had whatever drug she accessed in the bathroom. It had to have come from a body cavity, since she was barefoot and naked as a jaybird beneath her hospital gown. She probably always walked around with a stash for such emergencies as this. She was gone then, really snoring up a storm.

That's the thing about such patients. They can be rather devious, and I was at the time very, very naïve, but learning. Now I can almost pick out the addicted women because they have such sad, pathetic, tormented eyes. Windows, I suppose, on souls in living hell.

CHAPTER SIX

". . . there was the strained, pressure-filled effort to simply ensure that all of our mothers and their babies were safe."

March 22

I AM TAKING MY turn tonight at being the team leader in the delivery area, which is at the rear of this sprawling department. It would be too much to expect the charge nurse to give leadership to all the staff working in various areas—labor, delivery, nursery, postanesthesia recovery, and antepartum problems. On the basis of geography and the unique procedures that take place there, one nurse is assigned to coordinate the operations taking place in delivery. Each twenty-four-hour period sees an average of thirty births occurring, so there is much responsibility for the person designated to juggle the staff to cover the wealth of deliveries and surgeries.

My main problem as team leader is that I have very few staff to lead. Decent staffing consists of two to three registered nurses and a like number of surgical techs or LVNs. Tonight there are only going to be two scrub techs, Bradley Antonia and Lucy Morales, and me, the one RN. Since there are about twenty-eight patients in the unit at the moment, this night will be chock-full of deliveries.

I feel a bit oppressed getting this heavy assignment. This stingy staffing in delivery is getting to be the norm. I know that Merilee has no choice but to assign a responsible sort of person to be in charge in delivery, knowing that there are so few to handle the inevitable barrage of births. That is some consolation for what I know is going to be a brutal night. We have had some resignations lately, with no nurses for replacements until the current orientation program is completed.

Lucy, Brad, and I stopped at the red line that demarcates the point where the delivery area branches off from the rest of the department. We put on the charming paper booties and green paper shower caps that are necessary attire for anyone entering what is considered a surgical area. We will also put on face masks before entering any delivery room or operating room to give care to patients.

My first goal was to sort out the assignment for my little crew to cover the four deliveries in progress. We needed to send the evening shift staff home. Fortunately, as I found out in my tour through the various delivery rooms, these four deliveries were pretty much in the final stages. The patients, mothers and infants, needed a few simple tasks completed before transporting them to the recovery room.

Whew! There had been twelve deliveries during the evening, and this meant a deep dent had been made in the supplies we keep on hand in each delivery room. I was hoping to get the patients to recovery, then have my team of two hurry back to help me restock the rooms before a new avalanche of women needing to deliver arrived.

I should interject here that we operate in an old model of care for a labor and delivery unit. Many hospitals are reconfiguring their maternity services so that women can labor, deliver, and recover in lovely modern birth rooms. Such a system works well in community hospitals where there are far fewer numbers of births per twenty-four hours. Few hospitals are challenged with the numbers and acuity we see daily, along with the relative paucity of staff to deliver care. As I am writing, the number of women needing our services seems to be increasing, making it harder to think about bringing this department into the modern era in which attention is paid to the niceties. Given our circumstances here, we are continually trucking our patients from labor rooms to delivery or surgery, then back to recovery before eventually sending them off to another floor for their postpartum care.

Brad, Lucy, and I managed to get a start on the restocking, paying particular attention to the preparation of emergency resuscitation equipment we provide in each delivery and operating room in case there is an unresponsive baby born. Soon, however, I heard the cry: "Delivery, multip." This announcement meant that the labor nurse and intern—or midwife or medical student—was at the red line with a patient on the verge of imminent delivery, one who had already had at least one other child, one who we could expect to deliver quite rapidly. Brad and I went to meet the labor crew and went about helping the intern get his patient into the delivery room and set up. Not too many minutes later, Jaime Bautista, one of the junior residents, called me on the intercom to apprise me of the fact that he was bringing another patient back for a twin delivery. Boom! We were in business.

One thing disturbed me about that first delivery. As Brad and I were helping to get the patient Mrs. Quiñones onto the delivery table, Brad did not display much consideration. In fact, he was commanding her, quite brusquely, to move on over.

"Come on, come on, señora," he berated her in an impatient voice.

I saw a look of massive frustration and anxiety on the face of this heavy, late-thirtyish Latina as she fought to keep from pushing her baby out into the world while trying to comply with Brad's rude commands. She made it onto the delivery table with only seconds to spare. I had to warn the intern, fussing with setting out his instruments, to turn in time to catch the little projectile of a newborn baby as it came torpedoing into his hands.

Brad is a very experienced scrub tech, one to whose expertise in surgery I must many times defer. He is currently a student in nursing school, planning to pursue a career in surgical nursing. Hardly a day passes in nursing school without students being counseled to pay attention to the totality of the person, to try to meet emotional needs as well as physical ones. I'm not sure you can teach that to people. They have to have bought into that philosophy long before they arrive in nursing school, and I don't believe Brad has.

As a young man, as a man, period, Brad will never feel that moment of acute agitation, of supreme dependence on the kindness of others that a woman experiences in the moments just before giving birth. There is never a rationale for harassing a woman at that moment. I plan to talk to Brad about this when time permits, even with the understanding that he will likely think I am speaking in Zulu. Too many nurses have let his overt insensitivity pass by. I only hope I can conduct such a discussion in a way that doesn't make me out to be Miss Goody Two-Shoes.

The twin delivery went very well, though such deliveries are always a bit harried. Two sets of everything must be provided–two baby warmers, two delivery records, two sets of identification bracelets, two sets of tubes to obtain blood samples from the umbilical cords, two sets of pediatricians to care for the newborns, two setups for oxygen and suction. This delivery proceeded without a hitch, and in no time there were two identical, adorable little boys lying side by side, squinting myopically at the strange light world. How different this world was from the one they had just exited where they were packed tightly, one against another, in their mom's womb. In this case, their sex had been known and they already had names–Emmanuel and Noe.

The night continued with a just barely manageable stream of deliveries. Brad, Lucy, and I repeatedly returned to the red line to pick up patients ready to give birth. I put a woman on the table in one room and began to set up equipment and open packs. A moment later, I heard the agitated voice of an intern in the next room. I went in to find him struggling alone with a woman who wanted mightily to deliver her baby right in the labor bed. I sent the young physician to put on some gloves. In the meantime, the little dark head was beginning to emerge. I grasped a bit of the bedsheet and merely guided the wet, glossy head as it continued to come.

The intern Dr. Crosswaite returned with clamps, scissors, and a bulb syringe to complete the delivery. While we were helping his patient over to the delivery table, the doc next door called me to return to her so that I could get her suture needed for the episiotomy repair. I got the suture for her, then checked on the wiggling baby who had been deposited in the infant warmer, still covered with blood and amniotic fluid. I cleaned the newborn, weighed it, and wrapped it for the mother to hold. By then, Dr. Crosswaite needed me again. At times, I also had to exit to other delivery rooms where Brad and Lucy were assisting with deliveries, as they cannot administer any medications.

So did our night fly by, hour by hour. Physically, such a night is grueling. The countless steps, the ebb and flow of adrenaline as the intense moments before each birth take place, the anxieties and irritation of interns and medical students who are relatively inexperienced, and also now desperately tired from inhumanly long hours on call—all these factors take their toll. I did not allow myself to think about even a minute's respite, for that would have been a cruel cheat. There was, instead, the certainty that even such a night as this was surely, inexorably, coming to an end.

One last drama occurred about five thirty in the morning. From my post in one of the routine deliveries with which I was assisting, I heard the call in the corridor of "crash coming back!" This was the signal that an emergency was coming to the operating room. Brad, Lucy, and I had to leave our cases hastily to assemble in the OR. The scene there was chaotic as a team of nine obstetricians, nurses, anesthesiologists, and pediatricians prepared for surgery that needed to take place as fast as possible.

Dr. Mooney, who had checked this woman subsequent to a deep drop in the baby's heart rate, had found that the umbilical cord had prolapsed ahead of the baby and was being crushed by the little head. He still had his gloved hand in the patient's vaginal vault, trying to push up that little head. He had crawled into the labor bed to prevent downward pressure on the umbilical cord during the hurried tour of the hallways back to the OR. Now he was crouched below the operating table and was soon engulfed by the green surgical sheets that were placed hurriedly over the patient's abdomen following a "splash" prep. He would stay in this most awkward and uncomfortable position until the surgeons got into the abdomen and delivered the baby from above.

We all went about our various jobs with a vengeance. Brad opened up all the surgical packs for Lucy, who was scrubbing this case. She hurried in from a hasty hand wash and assembled the crucial equipment necessary to get the case going. She fitted wicked, sharp blades onto the knife handles and passed a dry sponge to catch the first splash of blood from the incision. The two OB surgeons got themselves into their sterile gowns and gloves and rapidly draped the patient, whom I had already prepped in the rudimentary way we employ for emergency surgery. Lucy and I conducted a quick count of one pack of surgical sponges so we could start our careful watch over those being used inside the patient's body during the case. While all this was happening, the anesthesiologist had paralyzed the patient with a curare-like drug, then inserted a tube into her trachea so that he could breathe for her while she was asleep.

The result of this furious yet well-orchestrated and combined effort was that a weakly squalling infant girl was handed minutes later into the waiting and competent hands of the pediatric resuscitation team. Dr. Mooney could finally emerge from his contorted position at the foot of the operating table, and the team could relax a bit. What had been a life-threatening emergency was now transformed into routine surgery. Dr. Mooney went back to the labor area, and the two OB residents continued to stitch and tie knots as they put the belly of the patient back together, layer by layer. As the nurse in the case performing the circulating nurse role, there was a host of minor taskwork things I had to do.

The moments I sat to fill in information on the operative report and delivery record were the only few minutes I had of rest for this whole intensely demanding night. At least the case was proceeding quickly with two such experienced docs doing the sewing. There is almost nothing worse in life for a night nurse than being stuck in the operating room for hours while an intern is taught to cut and sew. I realized that I had expended my last reserves of energy hours ago and was functioning purely by rote to complete my duties and then make my escape when the day nurse assigned to be team leader popped in to relieve me.

So the night drew to an end. What I regret most is that such nights, with so few nurses to assist in delivery, preclude any chance that the patients will have an optimum experience in childbirth. I usually love working in delivery. I love the chance to participate in what is a stressful but ultimately rewarding event in a woman's life. I ooh and aah over each newborn, whether it is the cutest kid I've ever seen. I congratulate the mother, letting her know that she is admired for her tremendous effort in bearing her child. I like assisting young doctors who, having successfully delivered a new life, seem more open and eager to chat and share their thoughts while they slowly sew up their patients' bottoms.

Tonight there was not one scrap of this. Instead, there was the strained, pressure-filled effort to simply ensure that all of our mothers and their babies were safe. The physicians don't seem to understand or care that Brad, Lucy, and I are doing the work of six or seven people and deserve some credit for a great effort. They are irked and annoyed that they have to perform their procedures with the minimum of nursing assistance. Understandably, I will hope for a different type of assignment when I return tonight.

Addendum: I did seek out and talk to Brad Antonia on another night. He was taken aback by my comments regarding his inconsiderate treatment of Mrs. Quiñones, the mother he had chastised for her lack of cooperation in moving onto the delivery table. He excused his behavior by telling me that he was looking out for the patient's welfare, hoping to avoid a bad tear for her if she delivered in an uncontrolled way. I pointed out to him that Mrs. Quiñones had delivered eight children in her life to that point and that her baby could have practically *walked* out, so relaxed must her vaginal musculature have been. In any case, no mother deserves to be berated, no matter what the cause, in those last overwhelming moments before birth. He just looked at me, so very skeptical. Yep. Surgical nursing is definitely the field for Brad. That way, most of his patients will be asleep and covered up by sheets while he is caring for them.

CHAPTER SEVEN

". . . she smoothed the dark cap of thick curls on his tiny head, and crooned adoring words in Spanish . . ."

March 24

LAST NIGHT WAS my turn to work in a labor room. Some of my fellow nurses handle this assignment much better than I do. In fact, it's their preferred assignment.

For me, it is a constant reminder that the reality of caring for the laboring woman in this place is far from my vision of such work. I had never considered a career in nursing until I had my own childbearing experiences, and it was the skillful and compassionate care of my nurses that inspired me to enter this profession. In making the decision to go back to college, to switch career paths in my late twenties, I never imagined myself giving support to laboring women in such surroundings as these. Because I have found other reasons to love this work, I put up with the less-than-ideal circumstances I find here.

This hospital dates, from its inception, to mid-twentieth century, and our unit was once the orthopedic department. These small labor rooms into which we crowd four beds were originally intended for two patients. With four patients in these rooms, it becomes a challenge to extricate a woman's bed to transport her to delivery. There have been occasions when the fit was so tight that the bed wheels locked, and an intern had to crawl onto a bed wedged in the doorway to assist with a birth.

Laboring women need quiet and privacy, two commodities in desperately short supply in this place. Given that most of our clientele are immigrant, poor, or uninsured means that they cannot protest the lack of amenities here. For most of our patients, this is the hospital of only resort. Not for them the lavishly decorated, private birthing rooms now in vogue in the typical community hospital. Here, the emphasis is on the medical management of their high-risk obstetrical issues. Medicine and the hospital administration don't seem to give a hoot whether the patients are content with the ambiance.

Contributing to the already overcrowded scene in our labor rooms is our desire to accommodate each patient with a support person. In the past, families left the laboring woman at the emergency room door and were not to be reunited until after delivery. We try nowadays to let our patients have a visitor with them whenever desired. The only reason for prohibiting a visitor is the need to ensure another woman's privacy during some procedure. I am adamant about finding out at the earliest possible opportunity if my patients have family or friends with them, and arranging for their visit. Unfortunately, this results in further crowding of already tight quarters. Other nurses can find a variety of reasons to chase visitors out of their labor rooms. I have to catch myself when I begin to succumb to the lure of eliminating this one factor in the environmental stress here.

These rooms are claustrophobic for other reasons. When we have four laboring patients at the same time, in actuality, we are caring for four more patients–their unborn babies. These tiny, enormously vulnerable passengers bear every bit as much careful watching as their high-risk mothers. Thus, at the side of each labor bed is a cabinet containing the fetal monitor.

I think of this machinery as a translation device that converts the passive voice of the baby into a digital readout. The data revealed on the monitor tracing tells us how baby is tolerating the stress of labor. There isn't a nurse here who hasn't left the labor room to take a patient on the short trip to the delivery area, then returned to find that one of the other babies has taken a dive. This decompensation is exhibited by a dramatic drop in the fetal heart rate. Thus, nurses here tend to be paranoid about leaving their labor rooms, even briefly to draw up medications or retrieve a chart from the desk.

Eight hours can be most confining, particularly if it is one of those times when almost constant turmoil prevails, patients crying or screaming with every contraction, multiples of medications ordered, procedures carried out. There is a hellacious amount of stuff to do, even if one does the minimum of following physician orders and attending to the pressing medical considerations of these high-risk moms. But obstetrical nursing is so much more than just the technical part of care. I try always to remember that these women are no different than

I was, straining to cope with the terrible stress that is labor, and doing it in circumstances so much less pleasant than I enjoyed.

However, I am not superwoman. How to juggle all the high-tech demands of modern obstetrical care with the very human needs of my mothers? Should I be attending to all the tubes and lines hooked up to my sixteen-year-old labor patient, or should I spend my time rubbing her back or holding her hand? This is my constant dilemma.

Sometimes I have three women receiving Pitocin (contraction-stimulating drug) via pumps, and several receiving a drip for management of their blood pressure problems. Each of my patients is in a differing stage of labor, and almost all will need some intervention for their increasingly painful contractions. I will administer a narcotic ordered by the resident or assist with epidural anesthesia placement by an anesthesiologist. For women experiencing birth for the first time, they will inevitably need some coaching when they become fully dilated to encourage them to push effectively.

With such a plethora of demands, it kills me when my teenager begs me for the hand-holding aspect of my care, and I am unable to respond. I cannot ignore the many immediate orders or treatments. At such times, I can feel quite inadequate, knowing that my care falls quite short of what I would do for my laboring moms if only I could clone myself. Over time, I have made peace with the inequities of life for me as a nurse working here. I do my best to perform a balancing act between the medical interventions dictated by our patients' complex pregnancies and the compassionate side of attending to the women in my care.

Tonight I had three to four patients all night. The one saving grace was that Susan McLoud, a midwife, was managing several of these moms. Susan is in her midthirties, an attractive woman with a mop of curly black hair just beginning to be peppered with silver. Susan is so everlastingly kind to her patients and takes such obvious pleasure in handing babies into their mothers' arms. I can't help wishing she had a few babies of her own. She's still single, however.

I have nothing but admiration for our midwifery team. They are a select group of intelligent, caring, enormously skilled practitioners. They staff a family birthing center upstairs where patients with normal pregnancies go to receive maternity care. They give their patients their expertise in obstetrics, support them and their families during labor, and do lovely, calm, controlled deliveries. They treat their patients with a maximum of consideration for their dignity, and they aren't afraid to show empathy and interest. It's what every woman should have in her childbearing experience. It's not difficult to see how much I like and respect these women. As expert and caring clinicians, they give nursing a good name.

Based on the demands of care for so many laboring women, it was decided that it would be beneficial to have a midwife added to the provider staff here, along with the team of residents. They could share with the visiting interns their expertise in birth, learn more about the identification and management of problem pregnancies, and simply provide another set of hands in this labor-intensive setting. Now we have a midwife with us around the clock. Lucky us.

The midwives participate fully in the work here. Supposedly, they try to assume care for our least complicated patients. We do have a number of women without risky pregnancies who come here when the Family Birth Center is full. In reality, the midwives get busy and help out wherever needed. They work up patients, do exams and physicals, draw blood, start IVs, and monitor fetal heart rate patterns. They function much more like the more experienced junior resident, with the added advantage of their more personalized treatment of patients. As one admiring resident expressed it, "Our midwives are the goddesses of birth."

Tonight Susan was giving her usual brand of tender loving care, and was working quite hard. It got busy in the delivery area, and she and I had two women getting closer and closer to their time to deliver. She sent one woman back to the delivery area with an intern, and she and I ended up having to let the other woman deliver in our labor room. This was a quick, clean, and very controlled delivery. We simply wedged some padding under the woman's buttocks to provide space for suctioning the baby's mouth on delivery of the little head. I am not sure that the patient thought there was the least thing out of the ordinary, so skillfully was this bed delivery accomplished.

Later, the intern brought back that other patient and said to me that she had not been able to get the baby delivered after forty-five minutes. At this very instant, the patient's quiet Latino husband showed up, and the couple was visiting a bit when Susan returned, aghast to find that this woman's baby was still inside. By now, notwithstanding the forty-five-minute delay, this baby was set to come out. Of course, now all the delivery rooms were occupied, and another labor room delivery was our reality.

Automatically, I asked the husband to step out for the birth. Susan asked me why he could not remain. I had been reacting without thinking, for family members are not usually present at delivery in this department. It was a stroke of luck having someone present to promote the idea of the spouse's involvement in the birth. I went out into the hallway, made sure Mr. Najera was comfortable with this plan, and brought him back into our labor room.

So he remained, both he and I standing opposite to Susan at the bedside. This very sweet older gentleman whispered words of shy encouragement and love in Spanish to his most hardworking wife. They related that they had one child, a six-year-old girl, at home. In the Latino culture, as with many others, sons are so important. I know that a baby of either sex would be equally welcomed by this lovely couple, but secretly I was hoping this baby, now minutes away from birth, would be a little *hombre.*

For a woman with one delivery in the past, Mrs. Najera did not have a very intense urge to push. Susan continued to coach her patient calmly. Though the patient's efforts seemed somewhat sluggish, or maybe reflected her anxiety about the impending birth, Susan gave encouragement and a sense of confidence to both parents. It was her tone of voice that gave us all the sense that everything was proceeding normally toward a beautiful outcome.

Soon the head was bulging, and a feeling of intense excitement was with us, gathered as we were in this intimate grouping. Susan invited the mother to touch the now-visible hair of her baby's head, but this was clearly too much of an unconventional idea. Just then, the whole head slipped out and then the shoulders. Susan lifted the half-delivered body so mom and dad could see their darling, pink-skinned baby, already squalling with its first breath. Then the whole body delivered–a boy! There almost isn't any moment as special as this, as the mother and father who began this journey with their unseen infant so many months ago meet their newborn for the first time. I had probably witnessed many hundred deliveries by this time, but tears leaked out and ran unashamedly down my cheeks. The new parents were laughing and crying too.

Participating in this joyful birth was a rewarding way to end what had been a sometimes frustrating and problem-packed night in this labor room. It is this reoccurring experience of the most intense pleasure for my patients and their loved ones, even in an environment so lacking in niceties and involving women with very worrisome problems, that restores me to a sense of what I am about here. Thank you, Susan, for this reminder.

Now Mrs. Najera was cuddling her beautiful infant son. I watched with intense gratification as she smoothed the dark cap of thick curls on his tiny head and crooned adoring phrases in Spanish . . . "*Mi amor, mi corazon, mi vida.*"

CHAPTER EIGHT

"She existed for years on minuscule amounts of sleep and an addiction to Pepsi."

March 26

ANITA EWALD IS in charge tonight and having a bad time of it. She is the relief charge nurse, a voluntary position that means she will usually be team leader if Merilee is off. Anita has worked here longer than any nurse on staff. She is a marvel of experience, calm, and knowledge. The one thing she is not is a magician, and even one so unflappable as she is hard-pressed with the staffing situation this night.

Two of the nine nurses scheduled called in sick. Then one hour into the shift, a heavy glass cabinet door in a delivery room slid off its track and landed on the toes of one of the nurses. In great pain, she had to be escorted to the emergency room for treatment. Anita simply could not stretch herself to cover for all these missing personnel. Mrs. Arnaught, the night supervisor in the nursing office, said she was calling Merilee to come in.

I regret the way we all prey upon Merilee. She has such a sense of responsibility about work and almost never turns down a request to come in to help, even tonight when she hasn't had a night off in almost two weeks. We all cherish our time away from work. As the hardworking single mother of five, Merilee has as many compelling reasons to keep her at home as any of us. Of course, she can always use the extra money she earns for these overtime hours, but she needs a personal life too.

Well, here she is, having come in to help with another staffing donnybrook. Anita gladly handed over the keys to Merilee and continued with the care of patients in a busy labor room. All of us were breathing easier, still working very intensely, but inexplicably feeling that added sense of security that we have when Merilee is taking charge.

When I was first assigned to the night shift some four years ago, Merilee was a staff nurse with only slightly more experience than I. A young, dynamic nurse who was heading up the night staff was preparing to move to Chicago to enter a midwifery program. She recruited Merilee quite ruthlessly to succeed her. I think she had taken Merilee's measure quite accurately, noting her intelligence, sense of responsibility, and generous nature. I remember how very reluctantly Merilee agreed to give the role a try. I know she felt quite hesitant about assuming the extra stress of the charge position, given that she was still getting her feet on the ground as a relatively new nurse.

As I came to know Merilee over the next few years and learned something of her background, I truly marveled at the strengths I found in this woman whose life had rarely been an easy one. Even her struggle to become a nurse was more than what most people would think of attempting.

I sometimes like to pat myself on the back because I attended nursing school while pregnant with my youngest. I delivered over Christmas vacation between first and second semester, missing only one day of class. It was quite a struggle for me, trying to fulfill the incessant demands placed on nursing students while continuing to juggle my parenting tasks with a new baby and three other young children. I will never forget the evening my overburdened husband tossed my medical-surgical nursing text in the trash can and told me in no uncertain terms that I was to drop out tomorrow. And how my eight-year-old sweetheart of a daughter later went outside and retrieved my book.

In spite of his meltdown, my husband was largely supportive and never begrudged the financial umbrella he provided for my endeavor or the extra help he extended in the care of our little brood. I had special assistance from a wonderful nanny who cared lovingly for our baby, Patrick, and kept my household in better order than I was want to as a housewife. I did not have to work to bring in money to help keep the family finances afloat during nursing school.

Merilee had none of this assistance. She had been working for a utility company, the main support for herself and her five kids. Meanwhile, her marriage had foundered around the erratic working habits and growing drug dependency of her husband. Looking to the future for herself and her family, Merilee decided to enroll in college and prepare to enter nursing school.

A most intelligent woman, she achieved good grades and made the dean's list. Her hectic days involved leaving the classroom to rush to the phone company to answer calls for directory assistance. She then headed home to change diapers, read her anatomy text, make school lunches, and kiss her kids good night. She existed for years on minuscule hours of sleep and an addiction to Pepsi.

She once related to me how much it distressed her to leave her eldest daughter, Monica, with so much responsibility for the younger children. Monica used to ride her bike from school to the day care center where she picked up her younger sister, a two-year-old. A little mother in bobby socks. When you are a caring parent like Merilee, seeing your child forced to grow up so soon like that takes bites out of your heart.

Today this honey-blond, slender wraith of a woman has put her stamp on this unit during the night shift. Merilee has an unassuming manner as she reads report to us at eleven fifteen. Sometimes she has to deliver bad news—the staffing is pitiful, and those here will have to assume the work of the regulars who didn't see fit to show up. Somehow, though we can feel pressure rising at the prospect of what we are facing, we don't complain. Merilee will work harder than ever to ameliorate the difficult circumstances. Sometimes she has to deliver bad news in the form of the latest vagaries of the hospital administration or the most recent directives from the chief nurse who seems completely divorced from the reality that her nurses face daily. Merilee has a way of removing the irritation from such seeming idiocies as she delivers the bad news with humor and grace.

In spite of growing up in a somewhat dysfunctional family and experiencing a very troubled marriage, Merilee has emerged as a lovely, strong, and decent woman. In an age in which obscenities and crudities pepper everyday conversation, Merilee is notable for her restrained and ladylike speech and decorum. She's no plaster of paris saint, mind you. She has a frank, open-minded attitude about a wide range of social and sexual behaviors. I've had my more straitlaced, judgmental eyes opened in conversation with Merilee. That's been good for me, a person who needed to loosen up a bit.

She's a nut about music too. Her greatest fantasy in life is that one day she'll wake up and find herself transformed into a late-hours radio disc jockey, free to play her own peculiar favorites: a blend of rock, soul, rhythm and blues, romantic Spanish ballads, even some rap. She's one of those folks who has a bear-trap recall for even the most obscure hits from some '50s garage band. We once had a hilarious fallout in the dressing room as we came off of a hard night. I happened to mention that Bill and I had tickets to see a Linda Ronstadt concert during the upcoming weekend. Merilee began to shake and shudder. How dared that woman even presume to think she could sing Merilee's favorite Smokey Robinson hits? The two didn't even belong on the same planet.

I know something else about Merilee. She's quite a romantic. She tends to be attracted to men a bit off the beaten track. Take Craig Murphy. He's what I think of as the *homme sauvage* type. A tall, lanky African American resident, he has a battered sort of face that isn't in the least conventionally handsome. His one outstanding feature is a pair of intelligent, brilliant dark eyes. Dr. Murphy's looks do not detract in any way from his appeal as a brainy, dedicated, and skillful physician. He is well liked by his fellow docs as well as the nursing staff. Merilee likes him a bit more than most. She confessed to me that she has had a crush on him for several years, though she knows the man is happily married and very proud of his beautiful wife.

And Dr. Murphy is aware. He likes and respects Merilee too. You can observe this dynamic when in their presence together. It's not a sexual thing, I don't think. It's just the way men and women connect, even though their lives are progressing along different tracks. That's why Dr. Murphy stunned Merilee as she was coming out of her office last New Year's Eve around midnight and planted a fully realized kiss on her astonished lips. Merilee needed that kiss. How clever of Dr. Murphy to notice that, and see that it got done.

CHAPTER NINE

"A sense of humor is the indispensable requirement for working in this place."

March 27

I AM FINDING THAT I have to finish these entries the next day or a few days later, since there has been zero potential for even a minute of break time except on the rare slow shift. Last night I was in the PAR/antepartum problems room, and the other nurse and I needed our track shoes because we ran incessantly. I was doing my once-weekly stint of four hours overtime, and twelve hours straight left me with a splitting headache from overtiredness. I had hummed all night–kept tabs on all my patients' problems, struggled to keep up with the routine tasks, made a stab at doing halfway decent charting, and collaborated with the docs so that each patient's needs were met. Yet there's rarely a morning when I can turn my patients over to the newly arriving nurses like packages tied up with a bow, as others seem to do quite handily.

The patients mainly consisted of a stream of postoperative cases, all cesarean sections. These women have about a two-hour stay in recovery until they are judged stable. Their blood pressure, pulse, breathing, and temperature have to remain in the normal range. They have to recover from the anesthetic and be able to move their bodies freely. They can't be bleeding or spiking a fever or seizing, or have respiratory difficulties or cardiac irregularities. While we have them in recovery, we see them through the initial few hours beyond surgery. We make sure they are in the kind of condition that will allow them to be transferred safely to the postsurgical unit one floor above us. During their stay in the new ward, they will not be receiving such intensive evaluation as we are providing here.

Last night, every patient we received had one or another of the problems I mentioned and required close monitoring. This was especially true for one diabetic mother who had both high blood pressures and high blood sugars. She required a stat dose of insulin. Mrs. Gladwin had also sustained a rather large blood loss during surgery, requiring us to give her two separate blood transfusions.

Our patient Jolene Gladwin was being covered by a dedicated resident and intern from the antepartum service who manage our diabetic moms before, during, and after delivery. Dr. Adelman, the third-year resident, had gone home when she felt that her patient was stable enough to have any problems handled by her intern. In reality, Ben, the intern, went off to the call room on another floor to sleep. It was left up to Julie and me to keep close watch on this rather sick woman whose condition was proving to be so labile.

Years ago, diabetes was an almost unmanageable problem in pregnancy. Babies died before birth because sugars in their mother were not in good control. At some point approaching term, the functioning capacity of the placenta would begin to deteriorate. It is likely that, in past eras, some previously unexplained deaths of large babies near term were due to undetected cases of maternal diabetes. There were also greater instances of birth defects in babies who were conceived during times when mom's blood glucose was in an abnormal range.

Today the picture is quite optimistic. We have an excellent clinic for expectant diabetic mothers. These patients learn about diet and exercise, and they learn how to check their blood sugars at home and have frequent clinic visits. If their blood glucose is not in good control, they are admitted to the hospital and treated. Sometimes incredibly high doses of insulin are required to control blood sugar levels in these diabetic mothers, doses that would kill an ordinary person. Such high doses are needed because the placenta is producing substances that make the mother's system highly resistant to utilizing insulin.

The babies of our pregnant diabetic moms are scanned at intervals to see if they are becoming too large under the influence of higher blood glucose levels. During their third trimester, such patients undergo twice-weekly testing in a special clinic to see if their baby shows any signs of decompensation. These newborns always go to the NICU because they can have problems regulating their own blood sugar in the immediate days following birth.

Including our diabetic, a number of our patients in recovery had very fast pulse rates, and the trick was to figure out the cause. Was this due to an infection? Had their blood loss been the cause? Was the heart trying to hurry the red oxygen-bearing cells around the body because they had to make up for the work formerly done by lost blood cells? Was there too little urine output, indicating impaired kidney function or problems with fluid balance that particularly cause problems for toxemia patients?

My partner, Julie Fortenese, and I dealt with all these issues in the midst of emptying pee, medicating for incisional pain, turning and positioning for comfort, cleaning up and trying to chart, keeping medications up to date, and most importantly, doing frequent assessments of each patient. Julie and I went to nursing school together, then completed orientation to Labor and Delivery together, and are friends by temperament as well. When we work together, as we were fortunate to be doing last night, we complement each other's efforts so that nothing is left undone. If I am concentrating on getting a new patient admitted, Julie will get busy and get all the hourly assessments done on the stable patients.

The best thing about our relationship is that no matter how pressed we are, we will find something to laugh about. A sense of humor is the indispensable requirement for successfully working in this place. Last night, Julie had me shaking with laughter as she related some of the tragic-comic details of the adjustments she and her new spouse are making now that the bloom is off the honeymoon.

"You know things have changed when, first thing on awakening, you notice not so much his gorgeous, hair-covered chest but rather those gunky little crystals in the corners of his eyelids."

Early on this particular morning, demand for our nursing care reached its most intense state, struggling as we were to get our patients spiffed up for the oncoming team of nurses. Suddenly, we had a last-minute admission, a patient who had been transferred from an outside private hospital. Carla Montes, one of our typical Spanish-speaking immigrant clients, had gone to the emergency room in that affluent community hospital because she was bleeding. Her pregnancy was complicated by placenta previa, in which case the placenta had implanted over the cervix instead of along the sidewall of her uterus. Something had occurred to start an uncontrollable hemorrhage, and she required emergency surgery to prevent a tragic loss of mother and baby.

You can bet the staff at that private hospital was most indignant, having to use their operating room and surgical team for this disaster, a nonpaying patient. Even though they are supposed to be in business for the good of mankind, affluent community hospitals can be so very territorial about their place, resenting a poor person for somehow sneaking past the doors and invading their sacrosanct facility instead of having the sense to go where they belong, the city hospital.

I questioned whether feelings of hostility about being imposed on in this fashion had led that hospital staff to transfer Mrs. Montes and her baby in a clearly unstable condition. The young mother still could not move her legs from the spinal anesthesia, and she was shaking severely, her skin sweaty and clammy. They had no business tossing her into an ambulance and sending her to us in this uncertain condition. Her baby, too, was very cold by the time we got it, wrapped in a thin blanket and not even diapered or clothed.

The residents here wrote up the incident, a classic case of "dumping," something prohibited by federal regulations. Then they called the physicians at the sending hospital to convey their feelings about the irresponsible manner in which they handled this woman's care. I am so grateful that I work in an environment in which we take care of the patient's needs first and worry about the money later.

Mrs. Montes seemed to be a sweet, rather shy, and bemused young woman. Her baby had to sit with us, unable to go to the nursery while the rigmarole of getting ID bands was accomplished. When the baby has not been born on-site, the process for the identification of the baby is much more complicated. We are so careful not to separate mother and baby until accurate name bands are attached to each. Our patients worry about their babies getting lost or mismatched in the sheer volumes we care for here. We have the same concern. I went to get a warm crib to hold the baby and warm blankets to wrap the little tyke in, as well as his shivering mother.

There was a kicker to this fiercely busy night. When I returned to work, I heard that the senior resident Jonathan Byreski had complained to the brass about a nurse in the PAR (this room) who was sitting, doing needlepoint. The nurse irritated a tired, overworked intern by calling him to come and obtain a blood specimen from a patient to check her hematocrit. This is a very routine job, part of the "scut" work expected of the interns and medical students who rotate through the obstetrics unit. Often nurses will go ahead and do this very simple bit of work to help facilitate the care of patients. I routinely take care of this issue rather than bother waiting around to find one of our exceptionally busy docs to come complete this task.

If the story was true, the nurse in question could be faulted for inconsideration, possibly laziness. I know I would have been irked if I had been that intern. Still, this was a minor complaint, ignoring the reality that the entire unit was in the throes of intense demand with babies being born continuously. Every nurse I observed was busier than ten beavers. Could this senior resident not find one word of praise for the many hardworking people on duty instead of focusing on the shortcomings of one?

I suppose I'll consider the source. I worked with Dr. Byreski last year in this very room. He had gotten up at 6:00 a.m. to do some discharges before morning pass-on rounds. He wanted to send one woman downstairs to the antepartum service, as we had successfully stopped her premature labor.

"Say," he asked, looking up at me from his desk as he scribbled in the chart, "did we ever send a urine specimen for culture on this patient?"

I came over and paged through the chart and had to let him know that this routine part of the admission of a patient with this diagnosis had been overlooked when she was admitted two days ago. I asked if he still needed the specimen sent, which would have required me to catheterize our patient. He shook his head in the negative.

It was later when I was writing my discharge note that I found this creative remark from Dr. Needlepoint about that never-had-been-sent urine specimen.

"Lab states specimen tube broken after being dropped on the floor."

CHAPTER TEN

"...protecting himself by wrapping himself in an insulating layer of silence, while he ponders all that has taken place . . ."

March 30

I BELIEVE THAT CERTAIN experiences I have had in nursing will remain with me for life, embedded in my consciousness with bold quotation marks. One such event occurred this night.

I had been assigned to be in charge of the nursing staff in the delivery area. This team leading role is not so much a power position as it is a means of organization and communication between the labor and delivery areas. If a woman needs to go to surgery or some special kind of delivery is anticipated, the docs or nurses in the labor area notify the team leader in delivery. She or he must try to assemble the proper staff, the necessary equipment, etc.

Tonight I had a wealth of staff: three RNs, three scrub techs, and an LVN. We are experiencing a momentary upsurge in staffing, and these generous numbers made my role as team leader much more palatable. With so many hands to share the work, the night proceeded routinely in a stream of deliveries and a few cesarean sections.

In a quiet moment, I decided to go over to the labor rooms and try to get a sense of what business might be coming our way in delivery. I wasn't looking for trouble but found that there were two patients with problem pregnancies that we in the delivery area could expect to deal with shortly.

They had moved these two patients to an overflow labor room. One woman, Paula Sarmiento, had ruptured her amniotic membrane, and fluid had gushed out at this very early point in her pregnancy. Her baby was estimated to weigh about five hundred grams, or a little more than one pound. Now she was infected and in labor. Some babies have actually survived at this weight, but the chances are pretty much nil, and this situation is more of a miscarriage than a premature birth.

However, if the infant delivers and has signs of life–a heartbeat, breathing–the baby is given immediate support by the pediatric resuscitation team, then taken to the NICU for continuing care. There the dilemma begins. Should all aggressive measures be taken as if the pediatricians mean to realistically try to salvage the terribly fragile infant? Most would agree that this is a pretty fruitless venture.

Even if, improbably, such heroic interventions saw the little mite through the life-and-death crisis of its entrance into this world, there is the question of the quality of life that would follow. Almost inevitably, there would be handicaps and developmental problems. Medical technology and new treatments have made this a true dilemma for both the parents of such small infants and the practitioners who deal with such decisions for care. I have been present in the room when the pediatric specialists have discussed these issues with parents needing to ponder the choices of "comfort care" versus aggressive management designed to do everything possible to salvage such tiny tykes. I do not know what I would do in such a case. I only know from my experience that, many times, the parents want heroic measures taken even in the face of a potential lifetime of disabilities for their very premature infants.

The other patient I was concerned with had one of the most heartrending tragedies a young woman can be called upon to face. Carmen Benevides was in labor with a grossly malformed infant. The fetus had been detected earlier in its gestation to have an encephalocele. This is a horrible situation in which the scalp bones do not grow normally, and the brain tissue extrudes through the opening in the head. There are differing degrees of this condition, some of which can be repaired after birth and allow for a normal life. This was not going to be one of those cases. It was not expected that, once this infant exited the safety of the womb, it would be able to survive.

In either of these two cases, the resulting delivery could not be officially judged a stillbirth until the baby was born without signs of life. Mentally, I had to think what should be done if either of these women came to delivery before I went home. As it turned out, the very tiny Sarmiento baby delivered precipitously in the labor bed. The pediatricians took the little one downstairs, as he did have a heartbeat and some limited respiratory effort. I heard that the staff pediatrician was coming in from home to help evaluate whether heroic measures should be initiated.

I went to see how Mrs. Benavides was doing. What an ironic surname this poor woman had, for she could hardly be said to have a "blest life" at this moment. She had been pushing for nearly two hours, her face red and expression exhausted. Just as I arrived at the labor room, she was judged to be ready to come back to delivery. There was a wonderfully kind intern, Dr. Mordecai, who would be with her for this tortuous birth. Dr. Mordecai was going into family practice and wanted to care for his female patients who were experiencing normal pregnancies. This would be the most challenging delivery he would undertake in his two-month rotation with us. He had stayed with Mrs. Benevides continuously through the last hour as she was being supported to bring her baby into the world.

It was almost dawn now, and he had been up continuously for what was to be his last twenty-four hours of call in Labor and Delivery. He would soon be returning to his residency program somewhere in the South. What a trying delivery for him to attend. Still, I was grateful that this birth was in the hands of a sensitive person.

Carmen's young husband, too, had been tremendously supportive, and he wanted to be present in the delivery room. This situation was touchy, and staff would have typically discouraged him, thinking that the distressing time might prove just too traumatic. He might faint or otherwise become ill. This had certainly happened, even in normal deliveries.

I discussed this issue with Dr. Mordecai. He said he felt that, based on the very considerate behavior displayed so far by the young man, his presence in the delivery room was desirable and would only prove helpful. On this we were in complete agreement. Why should this poor woman go through such a tragic experience surrounded only by virtual strangers?

I went to find the person who was up for the next delivery, thinking to give advance warning so that we could anticipate some of the needs of both patient and staff. The scrub tech whose turn it was to assist with the birth heard me out and then responded to the news by making a face. Believe me, it is the most human thing in the world for medical personnel to want to avoid these deliveries. Not only are they emotionally crumpling, but also the paperwork and extra responsibilities involved in supporting the family and then doing the postmortem care make these cases a daunting prospect. However, on another night with skimpy staffing, if I had to be in the OR circulating a C-section, Joyce would be faced with this kind of situation by herself.

After the labor nurse and Dr. Mordecai brought Mrs. Benevides into the delivery room, I became busy with the logistics of helping move our patient onto the delivery table, setting up the instruments, and getting Mr. Benevides situated at his wife's side. It occurred to me at that point to wonder what Joyce was doing. Looking around, I saw that she had disappeared. Even though Joyce was not my personal pick to support a patient during the coming ordeal, she could have helped with a variety of tasks, and we could have supported each other and our grieving parents.

I didn't have time to go on the hunt for the missing scrub tech. It's not the first time one of them has made themselves scarce during the delivery of a dead or damaged infant. I don't know if it's lack of proper training, fright, or just distaste for these particular circumstances. When one goes to school to become a surgical technician, it's all about memorizing instruments, learning the flow of different surgical procedures, and practicing handing the proper tools to the surgeon at the proper moment. It would astonish me to find that surgical tech students go through special course work to prepare them to deal with dead babies and their grieving families.

This content in my own orientation to L & D was handled in a pretty perfunctory way by my preceptor nurses. They concentrated on the unique paperwork involved and the process of wrapping the infant corpse for transfer to the morgue. Not one word was expressed about the demand for the exquisite sensitivity and support we needed to extend to the distressed parents in such devastating times. When confronted with my first real experience of the birth of a dead baby, I was devastated and realized that I was most ill prepared for that moment. Moreover, none of us in that room had been there for the sobbing mom, choosing just to get through the technical features and avoid dealing with the tragic reality for the parents. Ever since that horrendous experience, I determined to concentrate on the needs of the family rather than my own distress.

Now with this impending birth, a feeling of deep sadness prevailed for all of us in the room. There could not be one shred of happiness from this ordeal, only relief that the physical pain was nearing its end. An emotional disaster of immense proportion was commencing.

As the head delivered, I quietly asked Dr. Mordecai to place the baby in a towel I was holding so that Mr. and Mrs. Benevides could have a moment to adjust to the fact of the birth. As I turned with my sad burden to lay the infant on the warming table, I realized that this child had the worst abnormalities I had encountered in my attendance at hundreds of births. In truth, I was having difficulty managing my reaction, and I kept my back to the others in the room until I could control myself better. Besides the extruding brain matter, there appeared to be a great cleft lip and palate, and, worse, no discernible eyes. Otherwise, the body was that of a perfectly formed girl. Nature can be so phenomenally cruel.

The pediatric nurse clinician who had come to assist with the care of the newborn found no heart rate, no breathing, and she pronounced the baby. She left. Now would be the time that I would generally spend some minutes with the mother or couple, gently introducing them to their little one, allowing them to look, touch, and hold their dead baby. If the parents wished, a lay baptism or blessing would be given, and a name chosen. Most importantly, I would let them see that I felt their loss of a special child and that they could have all the time they needed to say good-bye. When the parents signified that they were ready to let go, I would prepare mementos for them—a lock of hair, footprints, handprints, identification bracelets, crib cards, and photos of their baby, both undressed and then dressed in a tiny infant gown, cap, and wrapped in a baby blanket.

In this case, I began to try to wrap the infant girl in such a way as to minimize the worst disfigurement. A moment later I stopped. I wasn't sure if this was the time to do this care, especially as Mrs. Benevides was undergoing a rather painful episiotomy repair.

I decided that I would put off the usual interventions until she was not in the midst of physical pain, that I would see if I could take her to a private recovery room, and we would delay the parents' meeting with their baby until we could prepare them for what would be a devastating experience for anyone. But it should not be put off too long. Those who have long experience in helping parents through this kind of loss say that it is better to assist the parents to deal with what has happened and allow them to say their good-byes to their baby, rather than carry the regret of not having done so to the grave.

Since no words had yet been spoken since the birth, and since a very discouraged and tired Dr. Mordecai was sewing away at a painfully torn bottom, I went over to the apprehensive couple and said, as best I could in Spanish:

"I want to let you know what has happened. I'm very sorry to have to tell you that your little one was born dead."

"Nació muerto, mi bebé?"

"Sí, una niña."

After they cried and embraced, having a few minutes to digest this crushing news, I went back again to ask if they wished their baby baptized. When they replied yes, I asked what name they wished given. They watched me pour the water and say the words of baptism in Spanish.

I had learned, in a strictly technical way, that dead babies are not baptized. Most of our patients, though, are Catholics with a very limited education. This is not the moment to intrude with a discussion of the theological merits of the baptism issue. The main thing is that the parents feel they are making a loving gesture to their little one in commending their baby to God's care. The baptism, the naming of the child, help to create memories of their infant whom they will never know as a whole person. Later, it will be a Margarita or Jose, a Jennifer or Matthew, a real child that they will remember rather than a vague nonperson.

I noticed a phenomenon in this distressing delivery that occurs pretty often. Dr. Mordecai, whom I had come to respect as an intelligent and sensitive young man over the course of his two-month stay with us, seemed so terribly abashed by what had transpired in this room. He had extended himself so generously as this grief-stricken and suffering mother had neared the hour of birth. He had sat on the bed and personally helped and encouraged her to push.

Now seated at the foot of the delivery table, he was completely silent through all of my work with this young couple. What I could see of his expression, obscured as it was by his face mask, led me to think that he had suffered a profound shock. He seemed incapable of entering into any conversation with the bereaved parents or me.

I believe that if we were able to step away and talk, I might find that this was the first stillborn baby he had delivered. It has to be the most devastating experience, after someone has become accustomed to having live, vigorous babies deliver into one's hands, to instead grasp and pull a lifeless, often somewhat-decomposing infant from a woman's body. In this desperately sad birth, he was confronted with a wretchedly disfigured infant as well. I do not think that these young physicians in training are in any sense prepared and taught what to expect in such an emotion-fraught procedure. Even some prior explanation could not really convey the distressing reality of delivering such a terribly malformed and lifeless infant such as this one.

I think nurses are more inclined to get involved in trying to meet some of the emotional and spiritual needs of parents undergoing such a traumatic event. Knowing what a thoroughly kind person Dr. Mordecai is, I believe it is not a lack of willingness to be involved but rather a sudden onslaught of feelings of inadequacy, of not knowing quite what to do, or say, in such a case. I cannot fault him in any way for this quite understandable withdrawal from his patient, for I myself had responded with avoidance in my own first experience of such a birth. He is probably protecting himself by wrapping himself in an insulating layer of silence while he ponders all that had taken place in this room.

After the baptism, Mr. Benevides felt he needed to go to his family, all of whom were waiting downstairs, to inform them of the birth and death of their baby. Mrs. Benevides had to be heavily medicated at this point to relieve the pain of a very tortuous episiotomy repair. Mr. Benevides walked past the baby's body, in no way anxious to see his child. I did not press the issue. Maybe later, we would all do better.

Just then, a disturbing note intruded on what was an already painful situation. I felt the presence of someone behind me, and I turned to find another nurse, Jeanette Moran, putting on a face mask as she entered the delivery room. Jeanette had been working at the opposite end of the department in the recovery room. I stared at her somewhat stupidly. She didn't say a word, seemed actually to be avoiding making eye contact with me. She went directly over to the warmer to look at the baby. After staring at the body for a minute, she turned and walked out without a word to me.

Finally, it registered. Jeanette had come all the way back here just to get a look at this poor creature. How totally, cruelly insensitive. It was fortunate that the mother was quite drowsy from her medication and that the father had gone out so that the indecency of this act was lost to them. This was an unconscionable invasion of these grieving parents' privacy. If I had not been so slow on the uptake, so completely unprepared for this behavior, I hope I would have had the courage to deny this nurse entrance to the delivery room.

Addendum: The next night we were together on duty, and I happened to relieve Jeanette in the LICU. I told her that I felt the need to discuss the incident of the previous night. I asked her for her reason in coming into the delivery room. She said that she had heard that a grossly malformed baby had been born and she wanted to take a look.

I told her that I had been very distressed because of the possible implications for the bereaved parents. If she had a curiosity, medical or otherwise, to view the infant, she could have waited until the body was out of sight of the family. To intrude on their tragedy in such a way was not right.

She had the grace to admit that her behavior was not very wise, though she had meant no harm. She took this criticism pretty well and exhibited no obvious hard feelings. Maybe this will help me to be more direct with other staff in the future and in turn learn to accept criticism myself in a healthier way.

Having been a shy person well into my adult life, I have had difficulty learning to express my feelings in an upfront way. One cannot succeed in this profession unless assertion, at least on behalf of the patient's welfare, is a personal strength. Somehow, I've got to learn this elusive trick of stating my strongly felt views without being paralyzed by nerves, yet managing to allow the other person to keep their ego intact. Sorry as I was to have to tackle this uncomfortable exchange with another nurse, I hope we both learned something in the midst of it.

CHAPTER ELEVEN

"Her language varied between the deeply profane and the deeply religious."

April 19

ALREADY IT IS the middle of April. There has not been a minute at work to write even a line. I was sacrificing my lunch break at the start of this venture because I cannot seem to get motivated at home to catch up. When I have my personal life going on away from this place, I don't like to dwell on all that takes place here. To have a prayer of returning night after night to the pace at which we operate, I have to keep my life with my family separate from my work. Such division helps me maintain a store of energy and emotional peace on which I can draw to give decent care to our patients, as well as to my husband and kids. I try instead to sit down on my break and scribble my thoughts. As it happens tonight, for the first time in immediate memory, all my patients are quiet or asleep in the postanesthesia recovery room and I have a moment to sit and think.

We have been jammed with patients incessantly. I know that the current turmoil in Central America is bringing more immigrants, both legal and illegal, into this area. The great majority of our patients remain Mexican women, but each night we admit a share of Nicaraguans, El Salvadoreans, Guatemalans, Costa Ricans. Some Asians. Some Middle Easterners or Eastern Europeans.

Muslim women are interesting. They most often arrive accompanied by a friend or relation who speaks some English so that we are informed from the outset of the patient's requirements. She must only receive care from females. We do all we can to accommodate these foreign-born women, but there is a smattering of feeling among the staff that those who come here unwilling or unable to pay for this service ought not to start out by specifying whom they will accept as caregivers. For myself, I try to understand that these women are operating under a cultural imperative much stronger than any desire to "fit in."

My most memorable nights lately have taken place in the labor rooms. The fact that I can face the prospect of an eight-hour assignment in one of our labor rooms is testimony to how much I have progressed since I emerged from my orientation to this unit. Taking care of four high-risk obstetrical patients in labor was initially more than I could handle, and I kept waiting for someone to catch on to my lack of prowess. I marvel now that no actual harm came to the women and their babies while I struggled to master the work.

Most of my difficulty derived from an abysmal inability to organize the work to be accomplished. I would get caught up in trying to give emotional support to some scared teenager when I needed to be setting up medications or getting a new patient admitted. I would get terribly behind. Then I would become panicky at the prospect of having to admit to the nurse taking over my room how shockingly inept I was at the job that everyone else seemed to manage with aplomb.

It was a mystery to me in the beginning, trying to guess when a woman was about to deliver. Once, while still an orientee, I was learning the role of the rover nurse. I was giving a labor room nurse her lunch break. Before she returned in a half hour, two of her patients had delivered in their labor beds because I wasn't alive to the signs of impending birth.

One of these women, a heavyset older mom, was placidly chatting with her neighbors in the next beds when a puzzled look appeared on her face. She made one muted grunt, and in the next moment, there was a vigorously squalling infant in the sheets. For the next year, I was paranoid that my labor patients were going to repeat this disconcerting behavior. I drove the interns nuts, calling them to come check my patients if they displayed the least behavior reminiscent of that early experience.

I could not tolerate that out-of-control feeling I had when it was my role to manage my labor room far more so than the intern or resident. There was enormous responsibility taking care of these women who came with a variety of health and obstetrical problems, as well as their oh-so-vulnerable babies. Many times I was the only person watching the four fetal monitor tracings, hour after hour. It was my job to judge when someone was getting into trouble and summon the appropriate help. For the first time in my life, I had a most compelling reason to get organized. Both lives, and my chance to feel personally successful in my work, depended on it.

Mostly by getting into trouble and learning what not to do next time, I began to get a grip on the work. I needed to be continually prioritizing the endless tasks to be done, making sure lives were safe first. If it was impossible to get everyone's vital signs taken hourly on the dot, then I would at least stick a thermometer in the mouth of the woman with the flushed face whose baby was beginning to display a very fast heart rate. Chances were that an infection was evolving. I had to make judicious decisions about increasing the drug Pitocin, which the medicine folks prize as a way to hurry along the labor process and effect timely deliveries. I sometimes had to weigh the wisdom of advancing this medication on four separate laboring patients, or otherwise be faulted for "not riding the Pit pony" by the residents.

I also started, very nervously, doing vaginal exams instead of chickening out and calling the obstetrician. It is impossible to become a proficient obstetrical nurse without developing competency in this skill. I have always been a very private person. I had to get over the feeling that I was intruding excessively by putting on a glove and feeling inside a woman's vaginal vault. Having seen the unbelievable insensitivity on the part of various practitioners here, both physicians and nurses, I was resolved always to perform such examinations in a gentle way with an eye to preserving the patient's dignity.

One of the greatest feelings of personal accomplishment in that first year was solving the mystery about when the baby was going to come out. I learned to put together different bits of information, such as the changing behavior of the mother, the indications on the fetal heart tracing, plus the growing prowess in performing internal exams. These assessment skills enabled me to stop calling the doctor to evaluate my patients' readiness for transfer to delivery. Very seldom, if ever, did my patients give birth unexpectedly. None of this came easily to me, for I was far more anxious than the average nurse. It was in this year that I first began to pull silver strands from my brunette head of hair, though I was only in my early thirties.

Though I can much more comfortably face the prospect of working in our labor rooms, the job is by no means a piece of cake. In the average community hospital, the high-risk patients we pack four to a room would be cared for in private birth rooms. They would enjoy the attention of a nurse with responsibility for no more than one, or two at the maximum. The high-risk nature of these problem-laden pregnancies—diabetes, hypertension, epilepsy, autoimmune disorders, cardiac disease, cancer, chemical dependency, etc.—means that labor cannot be viewed as a largely natural process. We must be constantly vigilant to catch emerging problems. We could spend all our time watching the fetal monitors, administering medications, playing with the pumps and tubes hooked up to these patients, and assisting with various procedures. At the root of all this high-tech activity is still a woman in pain and feeling anxious, struggling with questions, cultural variances, communication difficulties. We would not be able to say we were meeting these women's needs if we did not remain cognizant of these personal and many times emotional issues.

In the midst of the furious business of working in these labor rooms, there can still be some very special moments. I remember the sweet Latina mother who watched silently from her labor bed as I rushed about the room, trying to meet a variety of needs and also trying to get the disheveled room straightened up for the oncoming nurse. Those day shift nurses, primarily the veterans, could be merciless in taking report if one tried to pass on any unfinished tasks. On that morning, after watching me big-eyed as I strained to catch up, she beckoned me over. Between a stiff set of contractions, she reached out to take my hand.

"*Seño* (Miss)," she said earnestly, "you working too much. *No es bueno.*"

How touching it was to me that, in the midst of her struggle to cope with her own pain, she was concerned about me.

I had one of the funniest women come into my room early Sunday morning. Josie Williams had a small baby, and her labor was progressing swiftly. Rebecca Stanley, the midwife, was helping admit this patient. I appreciated her calm and supportive attitude because Mrs. Williams was enormously sensitive to pain. She rapidly went from mild uterine cramps to overwhelming killer contractions the moment her bag of waters broke.

When the pain got strong, Josie was inconsolable. She refused to try and breathe with her contractions, looking at us, her coaches, as if we were insane to think that such torture could be ameliorated by puffing briskly. Instead, she screamed like a banshee with the onset of each pain.

Her language varied between the deeply profane and the deeply religious. One contraction produced "Goddammit to hell!" The next elicited "Oh, sweet Jesus, spare me!"

In addition to her expressions, Josie behaved wildly. She wanted to get out of bed and walk, but this we had to deny her because her baby was showing some interesting dips of its heart rate. She was devastated to hear about her incarceration, and with each subsequent pain, she behaved more bizarrely. She turned completely upside down in the bed, threatening to pitch off the end. Next, we turned around to find her standing straight up on her feet, stark naked, her hospital gown dangling from her IV tubing.

I have learned that when a patient acts like this, it is a sign of two possible things. Either she came over to us from the psychiatric hospital across the campus, or she is a perfectly normal woman whose labor is streaking along lickety-split. Since Josie Williams had been pleasant and chatty when we admitted her, I was looking for an imminent delivery.

Dr. Meed, whose sense of humor is very dry, was enjoying Josie's dramatic exhortations to heaven as he was seeing a new patient on the opposite side of my room. Since our wild one kept taking off her gown, and there were visitors in the room, we had the curtains closed. In a moment, Josie screamed out, "Dear God in heaven, help me!" Rebecca and I heard the disembodied pronouncement of Dr. Meed, in a deep voice several octaves lower than his usual: "Yes, my child, I hear you."

Saturday evening I had come in early to work four hours of overtime. I ended up with a rare assignment, being the special one-on-one nurse for a cardiac patient who was just beginning her labor. This was a very pleasant African American woman of about forty-three years who had some pretty big heart problems, with high blood pressure as well. Claudette Lofton had never delivered a baby and had believed herself to be beyond the childbearing age. She had a history of a fibroid tumor in her uterus, and when her stomach began to expand slowly over the past months, she assumed this to be a reoccurrence of the benign growth. At five months' gestation, when her baby began to move about inside her, she discovered her pregnancy. Despite warnings that this pregnancy might be life threatening, she committed to carrying her child to term.

Now Mrs. Lofton was in the complex labor room, the LICU, experiencing increasingly intense contractions. She was terrified that she was not going to make it through labor, that the stress would precipitate a heart attack. We shared her concern, of course, and she was about to have epidural anesthesia placed so that she would not experience pain that was increasingly distressing.

It's tricky, though, this business of putting epidurals in heart patients. The usual practice of loading the patient with IV fluids as part of the procedure is pretty much not recommended. Just being pregnant is a problem for a cardiac patient due to the extra fluid the body accumulates as a natural response to the growing fetus. More fluids make more work for the heart, as would the IV loading we typically do prior to placing an epidural block. The docs, both obstetricians and anesthesiologists, collaborated on the decision of how much IV fluid should be infused. Within minutes of the successful placement of the epidural, Mrs. Lofton told me anxiously that she was feeling chest pain. Believe me, her doctors and I paid attention.

While I had Claudette as a patient, there were endless tasks that needed doing by her doctors and me: special lab work, then the epidural, then the placement of an arterial line. Shortly after all this, I noticed that her infant's heart rate was very flat, a concerning finding. Accordingly, our team had to subject Mrs. Lofton to the uncomfortable scalp sampling procedure. Thank goodness, the results came back showing baby to be OK. I began to worry that we would simply bother this nice, cooperative woman to death.

Finally, when all the busy work was accomplished and Claudette was comfortably settling into labor, it was change of shift and I was being moved to the PAR. I was regretting the need to leave this assignment because I was now quite fond of our amiable and unassuming patient. Fortunately, our charge nurse, Merilee, who was also working overtime, was taking over her care. Merilee seldom gets the chance to do this kind of primary nursing. She is too busy overseeing the needs of a very complex unit. She is a tremendously warm and caring person, and as the night progressed, she developed a terrific rapport with my former patient.

Mercifully, Claudette Lofton's labor progressed swiftly, and some hours later, she delivered the most adorable little boy. I had come over in a quiet moment to see this special family and had the joy and privilege of calling in the husband from the waiting area. Mr. Lofton looked terribly anxious, unsure if my news was good or bad. I smiled to reassure him. "Have we got a surprise for you!"

When I put that little blanket-wrapped package in his arms and he saw the bright, dark-eyed face of his infant son, this gray-haired gentleman broke down. "Thank the Lord Jesus!" he exclaimed in a reverent voice. Neither father nor mother could take their eyes off the little five-pounder, as if he was a miracle too precious to be real. The nurses in the room took great satisfaction in seeing such genuine joy involving this birth, which surely would have been viewed by some as a disastrous undertaking.

Merilee took plenty of photos of the little guy so that Claudette could look at them when she had to separate from her baby to go to the intensive care unit for her recovery. She was not out of the woods yet. Even though she had delivered without any of the calamities we had contemplated, she was about to enter another tricky phase. After delivery, the body calls all the extra fluid it collected in the pregnancy, plus additional fluids we had infused during labor, and dumps it back into the circulation to excrete it through the kidneys. Here would be another big load on a damaged heart. This special patient would need to have her fluctuating fluid balance and her cardiac status watched most carefully.

Addendum: Merilee returned to visit Claudette in the ICU on the following night and found her just as pleasant, most grateful to be still present in this life, and looking forward to taking her baby home.

CHAPTER TWELVE

"What a woman!" he complimented her . . . "Are there more like you at home?"

April 25

WE ARE HAVING a beastly night. There are not enough nurses. There is not enough helper staff, like those who wash and make beds and clean the rooms after deliveries or surgeries. There are too many glaring problems that dilute the doctors' ability to cope. What would be a nerve-wracking issue in a normal labor and delivery setting is relegated to the mundane here. There are too many worrisome situations that demand immediate attention.

We started off the night with one major headache, a woman in labor who was acting acutely bizarre. She had a history of heroin abuse but swore she'd had none today. Right. She was in active labor and becoming increasingly obstreperous. She hit and kicked several of the nurses. It was impossible to monitor the well-being of her baby. It might have been the case that she was beginning to withdraw from her drugs and that she was suffering labor with the additive of those horrible symptoms.

One could hear her bloodcurdling screams all through the halls, and we were running out of ideas about how to handle her. Her unkempt boyfriend was trying his best to calm her, but to no avail. Finally, we decided that this was too much for her fellow roommates in the labor room. Who could tolerate the stress of labor with such proceedings going on just a few feet away? We moved her down the hall to a room that is usually reserved for infectious cases.

That solved one problem, but produced another. There was no extra nurse to render care to this woman. She was placed in restraints so that she would not be able to harm herself, her baby, or those who were trying to care for her. Merilee had to give this strange wild woman what care she could in the midst of being in charge on this sinfully busy night.

One of the nurses most overworked tonight was the one assigned to the normal recovery room. This two-room suite with a small office in between that is used to assemble baby charts and feed newborns is always busy. Every woman and her infant come here for a brief period of observation, for what passes in this place for bonding, and to be cleaned up a little and have some nourishment. Baby and mother have their vital signs monitored for at least an hour, and the little one gets a shot of vitamin K. Babies do not start to produce this blood-clotting substance until they have begun to take nourishment, so we give this injection to prevent the possibility of a hemorrhage.

Mother-baby assessment is the only area in this unit for which there is no natural limit. No matter how jammed things are, we have to line the mother-baby couplets up in the hallway to wait for their admission. Also, when the surgical recovery room is full, postoperative patients are overflowed to this room. At certain times, the RN working in this room is unfairly expected to take care of more patients than anyone else, and sometimes rather unstable ones at that.

Tonight we could only spare one nurse to work in this assignment. As Merilee outlined the dilemma in report, Anita volunteered to staff this room, understanding that an overwhelming situation could develop if the anticipated numbers of deliveries and cesarean sections began to pile up. Anita would have three nursing assistants to help, two gentlemen who mainly assemble charts and transport moms and babies to their rooms on the postpartum floors, and one nurse's aide to help clean and feed patients. Anita would be doing the lion's share of the skilled nursing care, checking to see that both mother and baby were recovering satisfactorily from the birth experience. She would give all medications. She would have full responsibility for postsurgical cases.

A total of seven women delivered by cesarean section this night. To my dismay, all seven had to go to Anita's mother-baby recovery room because the PAR was full. These seven postop cases were intermingled with all the routine postdelivery couplets. I was directly across the hall from Anita in a labor room and I began to feel almost panicky when I realized how overburdened was the nurse who had this unlucky assignment. I went over every spare moment I could, took vital signs, gave baby shots, and made baby charts.

It was a blessing that Anita had volunteered for this burdensome role tonight. She is our most diligent, most mature nurse. She goes about her work with an almost preternatural calm. She is the generous type who never seems to resent the extra minutes she spends sharing her enormous knowledge and skill as an obstetrical nurse with those much younger and inexperienced. When I first came to the night shift out of orientation, with a million questions each time I came on duty, she was endlessly patient. She never once gave me the impression that she considered me a pest.

There are simply no words to express how hard Anita worked during this eight-hour period. I was in absolute awe of the calm way she accepted her excruciatingly difficult assignment. Knowing what a watering pot I can be, I believe I would have been in tears at some point if I had been the unfortunate recipient of such responsibility, such an impossible workload. I remember once having worked in this area during a similar onslaught, and in moving one mom and baby out into the corridor to make room for another admission, I happened to see a problem with one of the discharged couplets. The mother was sound asleep and was not clutching her newborn very securely. I went over to reposition the baby and was horrified to see that he had turned a vivid shade of blue. I called for NICU help, and we found that the little guy was OK, just cold. Thereafter, I could never be blasé about an assignment to this area.

For myself, I had two teenage girls in labor with their first babies, a fifteen-year-old and a nineteen-year-old. Neither had any family members with them for support. As it happens so often, the fifteen-year-old behaved more composedly than the older girl. Pain is such an individual thing.

The fifteen-year-old was a funny little person, with glasses the thickness of Coke bottles. She had a giggle for everything but contractions. Willy Bremer, the night OB resident for this month, came in to work her up and happened to notice her age.

"Fifteen," he mused in an undertone as he scanned her chart.

"*Fifteen!*" he exclaimed in a louder, astonished voice as he turned to her and caught her attention. "What are you *doing* here? You should be at Disneyland!"

There was a pause while Dr. Bremer and his puzzled patient sized each other up.

"Why didn't you write me?" he quizzed her in a solemn voice. "I would have sent you a ticket."

Giggle.

Then she informed us, in a tone meant to impress, that her sister had married at age twelve. I wondered about a familial IQ deficit.

Willy moved on then, and a new patient was admitted to my labor room. I had been subliminally aware that two "crash" C-sections were in progress at that moment, as I had heard them being called out as doctors and nurses had rushed women back to the operating room. These two emergencies, plus the bizarre patient in isolation who was getting close to time to deliver, had effectively absorbed most of the resident physician staff. Yet as soon as I got my new patient hooked up to the fetal monitor, it was apparent that I would have to find some help.

Every time this woman had a contraction, her baby's heart rate took the ominous dip that is known as a "late" deceleration. It's usually OK if the heart rate dips in coordination with the contraction, like a mirror effect. Late decelerations, however, have been implicated in bad outcomes for the baby, being a sign of an oxygen-hungry, compromised infant. When I am watching one of these decels in progress, I seem to hear baby's voice saying, "Help me, I don't feel so well."

I found the best-overworked intern I could, and he was impressed with the few minutes of monitor strip we had so far. He ruptured the woman's bag of waters. Thick, green-brown viscous muck poured out over his gloved hand instead of normal amniotic fluid with its crystal-clear appearance. We knew this babe was in trouble.

Mom was naturally alarmed and wanted to know if everything was all right. I would have liked to reassure her, but could not. Dr. Bremer came to see about this latest drama and told us to hustle this woman over to the LICU for scalp sampling. We needed to find out immediately how this baby was doing.

No one expected the results of the blood gas sampling to be good, and the values confirmed this belief. They were just awful: 7.19 and 6.9. So this meant yet another crash C-section. I wondered if our worst nightmare was about to commence—no rooms or folks to perform the surgery, with a baby's life and well-being on the line.

God bless this staff. Somehow they found a room, two OB surgeons, and some delivery nurses to assist, and they got the distressed baby out in minutes. The Apgar score, a rapid assessment of newborn well-being, started off poorly but picked up at five minutes. The baby was taken down to the NICU. A chest x-ray would attest to whether any of the yucky, thick meconium had been sucked into the lungs before the pediatricians present for the surgery had been able to evacuate it.

I was back to two patients and running over to assist Anita whenever I could, when Merilee came to see if I could help her with the woman in isolation. She had delivered, totally freaked out and combative. After that, she had flopped over on her stomach and refused to let anyone touch her. Merilee had let her sleep for a bit, too strained to fight with her anymore. But newly delivered patients must be assessed at intervals, especially to check for more-than-average bleeding. Merilee thought that the two of us might be able to do it together.

We got her onto her back, but not without a struggle. She kicked and fought us, calling for her boyfriend, "Spider! Spider!" to come and save her from her tormentors. After pressing on her uterus just a bit, more than a half liter of collected clots and free blood plopped out of her body. She had long ago ripped out her IV, the first line of attack for a person with heavy bleeding. I knew the one person to deal with this situation was Dr. Bremer, and went to find him.

Willy has a rather interesting sense of humor, wickedly funny and cynical. He does particularly well with patients who are a little whacky because he never makes the mistake of coming straight at them with commonsensical, rational talk like I foolishly tend to try. One night we had a mildly schizophrenic patient, again in the midst of a hemorrhage, who kept threatening to leave the hospital, stating repeatedly and vociferously, "I know my rights. I know my rights."

Willy was her resident, and when he heard her protest loudly that she knew her rights, he came to the bedside and blew her away by complimenting her on her prowess as a constitutional scholar. While our intermittently psychotic patient stared at him, suspicious and baffled by this odd conversational gambit, he commenced reciting the Preamble to the Constitution, as in "We the people, in order to form a more perfect union . . ." He soon had this girl mesmerized. She turned to me as he continued his recitation. "I'll take the blood," she said in a shaky voice.

Knowing how Willy loved this kind of stuff, I could not wait to see how he would deal with our wild woman. And she was quite a sight. As we entered her private birthing room, she looked up at us with a sneer, seated in a puddle of amniotic fluid, blood, and feces. She had given blows to those who had attempted to get her cleaned up, unable to understand in her strange state of mind that we were trying to help her. Her hair was a bird's nest, and she looked as if she could definitely benefit from a good hosing down. What would Willy make of this scene? He did not disappoint.

"What a woman!" he complimented her after taking in the spectacle. "*Are there more like you at home?*"

Our new mother glared at Willy menacingly. He got rather tough with her—verbally, that is—because he had to reestablish an IV line to get some much-needed fluids into her. She proceeded to jerk every which way, trying to thwart him. He got the line in, by God, handling her firmly but not abusively. While he was accomplishing this mission, Merilee and I unobtrusively arranged clean sheets around her. Almost before she knew what was happening, we had stripped away the major pile of mess. I distracted her by asking if she knew if Spider was waiting nearby, while Merilee did some added cleansing and assessment of her bleeding.

I guess nights like this are what compel me to stay here—the mixture of humor and pathos, the sweat and strain that go into giving safe care to this colorful group of patients. I love to laugh, and that I could laugh in the midst of this brutal work situation told me volumes about myself, that I was where I was meant to be. Then there were my wonderful friends. It was a toss-up between Anita and Merilee as to who deserved a medal more this night, the one with her mega numbers of newly delivered moms and babies, and the other with her "Spiderwoman."

CHAPTER THIRTEEN

"There is nothing so immediate in this whole world as a baby coming . . ."

April 30

I'M KNEE-DEEP IN burnout and pondering what to do about it. Most nurses experience this malaise at some point in their careers, so I know that I need to come up with a remedy to get myself back on track, emotionally and physically. I feel fortunate in having found work I love, and for which my personal skills seem well suited. Yet the workload has become brutal, seemingly increasing as I write. There are changed circumstances bringing more women to our doors, dictated by unfortunate events in their countries. We were already intensely busy when we inherited this new group of immigrants who were directed our way as the only portal for the birth of their infants. Dealing with this barrage of patients, doctors and nurses here are crushed with the responsibility for the care of so many.

Additionally, there is night duty. Being up at night when one's personal body chemistry rebels takes its toll, and I am not feeling so healthy. I recently returned from two lovely nights off, during which I lazed around and attended purely family-type activities–a Little League game, a dance recital, and my daughter's Confirmation. Such enjoyable diversions, coupled with decent sleep, should have returned me to work feeling refreshed. Instead, I was unbelievably keyed up.

We've had two pretty mellow nights, although my labor room was a little on the wild side last night. It was the beginning of daylight savings time, and we only had to work seven hours instead of the usual eight. I was ridiculously relieved by this one-hour respite.

I know I don't conceal much with my facial expressions. Whatever I'm feeling must be written broadly across my features. At least a few times each night someone asks me if I am either tired or sick. Yes, I'm tired, but it's as much a mental letdown as a physical one.

This burnout syndrome is definitely affected by our growing patient census. When I first started working here, we usually had seven to nine RNs scheduled per shift. Now that number would be woefully inadequate. We try to staff fifteen to sixteen RNs, as well as other ancillary helpers. Because we fail to achieve this goal on a regular basis, we often see nurses getting fed up and making their departure to hospitals with a much less crazy pace. Therein lies the distressing reality that we will likely be experiencing a chronic deficit of nurses, even as the patient census continues to grow.

Some nights are predictably busy, such as those following the Tuesday and Thursday high-risk OB clinics. On those days, the physicians tend to pick up various problems and send large numbers of women to us to have their labor induced. On these occasions, we could easily use twenty nurses. We typically have twenty-four women in labor rooms, six or more antepartum patients with problems, all the delivery rooms going, twelve or thirteen cesarean sections per twenty-four hours, and mothers and babies on stretchers lined up in the hall to go to the recovery room.

We always took pride in being one of the busiest labor and delivery units in the United States. Recently, we heard that we have competition from some other medical facility that is exceeding our record for most deliveries per year. Whatever the statistics, the truth is that the volume of patients here has outdistanced the capacity of this unit to house and care for them. But this is still the hospital of last resort, where all those who do not fit into the traditional health-care system must come.

And we are obligated to provide them entry, regardless of whether we are in any sense comfortable to do so. Most times, there is simply no other hospital that will take them. If these women present at a local community hospital's ER, unless they are threatening to deliver on the spot, they will transport them here posthaste, even if they have no patients in their maternity unit. There is nothing so immediate in this whole world as a baby coming, so we struggle, in spite of our woefully inadequate resources, to do the job.

For myself, in addition to the increase in the census, I realize that working when the rest of the world is asleep is another factor in my burnout syndrome. Research has revealed that people who routinely work hours that disturb their normal sleep and activity cycle take years off their lives. Intellectually, I know that I should be considering a move to a day schedule. Yet there is a lure in working on this unit at night, and I find myself reluctant to give up night duty just yet.

During the day, starting at 8:00 a.m., the new team of residents, interns, and medical students starts its twenty-four-hour cycle. They are all fresh and they tend to swarm over the patients. Plus, there can be mobs of other people here throughout the day due to our being a university teaching hospital. Nursing students from various colleges, our own nurse orientees, research fellows, social workers, attending physicians can all play a part in adding to the environmental stress in the unit. Added to this coterie of professionals are other extraneous types–family and visitors, deputy sheriffs, electricians and painters, housekeepers and chaplains.

At night, we are blessedly free of this swarm of folks. The hardworking physicians try to grab a few hours of much-needed sleep, although there is no guarantee that they will not be called out of bed to work when things heat up. Night nurses try to disturb these tired men and women only for something of moment, and we thus learn to function rather autonomously. There is a feeling that one of the benefits of night work for the nursing staff is that we have an enhanced impact on patient management. Mostly what I like is the smidgen of peace and tranquility that descends over the place when all nonessential staff lights out for home and hearth.

While I was in my orientation to this unit, which took place during daytime hours, I learned that inevitably I would be sent to the night shift to begin my practice. I was told as some consolation that I would be working with a group of nurses who were notable for their support of each other. I have found such comfort in this reality. My relationships with most of the night nurses have been richly satisfying. Two in particular–Merilee, the charge nurse, and Anita, the assistant charge–I consider to be modern-day saints. These strong and compassionate women are two of the finest persons I have met in this life. It means a lot to me working with such a decent group of people, adding incentive to stay where I am on the night shift. Yet I can see a natural limit coming because my body is beginning to protest mightily the lack of normal sleep.

I have chosen for family reasons as well to stay with this schedule. I want to be home when the kids come in the door from school. I want to help with homework and be there for the many activities in which they are involved. I have never missed a football or softball game, a doctor's appointment, or school function. Some Saturdays have me at the city park, standing on the median between two soccer fields, watching simultaneous games in progress. I'll sleep in the car for an hour, bribing my daughter or my older boys with some snack bar money to watch their little brother while we wait for a later game to commence.

Once the kids are in bed, I'll try to catch a little nap before leaving for the hospital. My husband is a night owl and struggles with getting up early, though he is in charge of sending our crew of four off to school or day care. We have orchestrated this system to accommodate two working parents, which is a novelty from times past when the little woman was charged with home and kid care, while dad went off to the career world.

When I think about all this, there are many more inducements to settle in and make peace with this work, this schedule, imperfect as the situation is. I will try to rebalance my attitude and appreciate the benefits I accrue for both job and home life. God willing.

CHAPTER FOURTEEN

". . . remarking on his size fifteen shoes and their relationship to other unmentionable parts of the big man's body."

May 13

BRUNO IS IN my labor room tonight, stocking the various items needed for the care of laboring women. Bruno is a hospital aide, and what I think of as one of the certified characters who people this unit. Hospital aides and nursing assistants perform a variety of extremely task-oriented jobs here, freeing up the nurses to do the actual hands-on care of patients. Their work is unglamorous in the extreme, and they get paid a few dollars above minimum wage for their efforts. One wonders how some of these folks stick around for thirty years or more of endless cleaning, trucking patients to their rooms, running errands, and stocking supplies. But for some, this seems to be the extent of their ambitions.

Bruno is a tall, muscular African American of middle years. He has the open, guileless expression of a young boy. I would guess his IQ to be somewhere in the seventy to eighty range. He may not have been born with this lower degree of intelligence, but some who have worked here for longer than I say that he suffers from the effects of "gin brain." He has been totally sober for as long as I have known him.

Bruno was promoted to his current position from a previous job cleaning in the hospital cafeteria. One thing we nurses all admire about Bruno is the great pride he takes in his work, the energy he puts into the simple tasks he performs.

When Bruno is assigned to stocking rooms, as he is tonight, he will come and get me and take me to the storage room where he has unboxed bags and bags of IV fluids until the shelves are bursting with them.

"See, Natalie, I's the only one that puts out all this Staphene," he brags to me. He has confused the word "saline" with "Staphene," a strong cleaning agent. If you hooked up Staphene to a patient's IV line and ran it in, I'm sure the victim would be dead in minutes. But Bruno is inordinately proud of having this word in his vocabulary, and I do not have the heart to correct him. Thank goodness the saline comes in clear plastic bags, and Staphene is delivered in opaque, clearly marked containers.

Bruno takes equal pride in his car, an impressive brown lowrider with tons of chrome. Every morning before leaving for home, he polishes his car to a sparkling shine. I've watched him standing in the parking lot near the emergency room entrance, showing off his beautiful, faultlessly clean engine to one of the residents coming on duty. He is a generous man who doesn't mind going far out of his way to drive someone home who is not feeling well or who has transportation difficulties.

On the unit, Bruno has one passion: food. He is a big man but doesn't have an extra ounce of fat on his large frame. He has the appetite of a growing teenager, and yet he seldom brings any substantial amount of food to work. Instead, he lingers around the kitchen during break hours, looking interestedly at whatever has been brought for meals by other staff. He invariably succeeds in getting a handout, no matter that some find this behavior irritating.

He looks forward to our informal potluck dinners with the anticipation of a child promised a trip to Disney World. He has even been known to come in from home on his night off to be here for such events. If Bruno can't be present, he begs the nurses to set aside a portion of everything for him to savor on his return.

One Christmas season, someone with an unkind sense of humor played a trick on Bruno. He, by his lights, was unlucky enough to have been scheduled off on Christmas night. He would miss the annual midnight feast that the nursing staff plans for those who have to be here for the holiday. A signup list of festive foods was posted on the refrigerator door to ensure that a variety of dishes would be forthcoming. A prankster penciled Bruno's name in, and beside it wrote "a turkey and a ham." When he saw this forgery, it had the intended effect of throwing Bruno into an almost apoplectic state.

"I's off on Christmas," Bruno told each of us worriedly. "I cain't bring no turkey and no ham."

No matter how many times we reassured him that no one was expecting either of these donations, that it was all a joke, Bruno remained consumed with apprehension that he was on the hook for the bird and the ham.

After having led a harrowing life in his drinking years as a virtual street person, Bruno is inordinately proud of his paycheck and the proper life he leads these days. A few months back, he wanted me to tell him about the employee credit union that to some of our coworkers figures as a veritable life source since their paychecks go there automatically. I explained how to sign up and how he could have a savings plan to set aside a small bit of his earnings each month. Now he stops me regularly to exclaim about the wonder of having "mos' fi' hunnert dollars saved up!"

Rumor has it that Bruno is married to a professional woman who keeps him very much in line. I asked him once how he keeps himself occupied when not at work. He told me he drives the wife around to her appointments. Sounds like he doesn't get a whole lot of sleep. It is pretty hard, in fact, to picture the childlike Bruno and his insurance agent wife *in flagrante delicto*, but they say the happy couple is expecting a child.

Jerome, the clerk, takes every opportunity to tease Bruno as he did this night, remarking on his size fifteen shoes and their relationship to other unmentionable parts of the big man's body and his impending role as an expectant father. Bruno accepts the kidding with a shy smile.

Though it's a fact that Bruno hasn't much in the think tank, he is kind, hardworking, and ever willing to lend a hand when called upon. He never misses a night's work; in fact, he earns a perfect attendance award year after year. For him, work is not something from which to escape but rather an endless source of self-esteem and social contact. That's not a bad attitude. Not bad at all.

CHAPTER FIFTEEN

"What had been a very well-managed delivery had turned into one of the rare and life-threatening obstetrical emergencies."

May 17

I WAS INVOLVED IN an interesting case last week when I was working in the delivery area. It was not such a wild night for a change, and there was the luxury of two nurses assisting with some of the births. Caroline, a tall, slender woman with the satiny black skin and soft, sibilant tones of the Bahamian people, was partnering with me whenever there was a chance. We had become good friends since I was given the job of orienting Caroline to this department. In training her, I found out that she had come to us with a background in midwifery, having studied in Scotland as part of her British nursing education. How on earth did she end up here?

"I never wanted to be that cold again in my life," she told me, grinning hugely.

Something unusual occurred when we received a patient who was accompanied by two midwives from upstairs in the Family Birth Center. It was shortly after midnight, and the midwives explained to us that they were transferring their patient due to a prolonged second stage. The significance of this obstetrical term was that an inordinately long period had ensued since complete dilatation, without the baby arriving. Mrs. Coronel had been pushing for all she was worth and was still unable to deliver. When Caroline and I had helped push the labor bed into the delivery room, the midwives explained that they intended to deliver the patient in bed as opposed to the delivery table. They wanted us to help Mrs. Coronel into a squatting position. This position is often helpful when a baby is turned in a way that makes it difficult to effect delivery. The sturdy side rails of the labor bed would help support our patient, giving her something to grasp while squatting.

Mariana and Estelle, the midwives, prepared their sterile field. Caroline and I explained to Mrs. Coronel what we wanted her to do, why it was important, and then assisted her to squat in the bed. This is surely one of the most earthy, homey sights imaginable: a largely naked, Indian-looking woman squatting, trying to bear down and expel her baby. It made me think of Pearl S. Buck's description of the Chinese peasant wife who delivered in a field and then got up minutes later and resumed her work. I believe this squatting position is the favored choice in many places around the world where childbirth is still managed pretty much at home with other kinswomen or with lay midwives in attendance.

There is real purpose to getting women into this position because somehow it helps provide that little bit of extra room that allows the head to deliver. Yet at the very moment we decide to employ this stratagem, a woman is typically exhausted from her previous efforts to push in a supine position. We have to give much support and encouragement to convince these tired women of the efficacy of squatting. On rare occasions, we end up with the baby spitting out in the bed once it has propelled itself beyond the barrier that had it hung up. Oh, well. That was the idea.

Mrs. Coronel was a very cooperative, very motivated woman. After just two or three pushes while squatting, she was ready to deliver. We helped her to lie back down, and Mariana began to facilitate the delivery. Midwives are expert at preventing tears as baby emerges, and they rarely perform an episiotomy, the prophylactic cutting of tissue meant to give the baby's head some extra room to exit. I have seen them employ this measure in a few cases when it seemed indicated, so they are not rigidly opposed to episiotomy. Nor are they slavishly wed to cutting female bottoms, as most of our residents have been trained to do.

The baby delivered, healthy and beautiful, like so many of our infants with a full head of curly black hair. All four of us, Mrs. Coronel's caregivers, were feeling that special sense of satisfaction when we have helped to achieve a much-longed-for birth after a difficult labor. I noticed a pretty large spurt of blood from the vagina, almost like blood spouting under pressure, but in a few seconds the bleeding appeared more consistent with normal postdelivery flow.

A gush of blood typically precedes the delivery of the placenta, a gross-looking but remarkable organ that sustains the nutrition and oxygenation of the baby while inside its mother. Mariana had coiled the umbilical cord extending from our mother around a clamp and was tugging gently to see if the placenta had separated from the wall of the uterus. It had not, and she settled back to await this routine event.

Then there was a second spurt of blood, and the big, homely-looking placenta plopped out into a basin, aided by the gentle pressure of the midwife on the cord. I started the IV infusion of Pitocin, a medication routinely given post-placental delivery. Its mission is to aid the uterus to contract to a smaller size, thus closing off the gaping bleeding sites left when the placenta shears off the lining of the uterus. Mrs. Coronel, however, continued to bleed briskly. Mariana swept the vaginal vault with her gloved hand, and what she felt had her prompt me to get the resident back to the room immediately.

The uterus, instead of clamping down into a tight ball, had virtually turned inside out like a sock rolled on itself. It had partially prolapsed beyond the cervix into the vagina. The immediate problem was that the uterus was going to bleed mightily until it could be inserted back into its proper place. What had been a very well-managed delivery had turned into one of the rare and life-threatening obstetrical emergencies.

Dr. Medavoy, the junior resident, responded to our call. Sizing up the situation, she asked me to get the senior resident quickly. While we waited for Dr. Chew, I gave the medication the junior resident requested to relax the uterus, reversing the effect of the Pitocin. Caroline called for the anesthesia resident to join us and put Mrs. Coronel to sleep for the coming procedure. How terrifying for this lovely, newly delivered, and euphoric woman to have all these manipulations so abruptly implemented. Unfortunately, there was no time to delay if this bleeding was not to cause her serious harm.

With no small effort, Dr. Chew managed to maneuver the uterus back into its normal place above the cervix. Mrs. Coronel lost two pints of blood in the process, and Dr. Chew was bathed in red from head to toe from his efforts. What had happened in this delivery room was an unusual obstetrical complication, and he said that, in four years of residency, it was only the second time he was involved in such an emergency.

Mariana and Estelle were going through the natural and understandable second-guessing of themselves, rethinking the delivery to see if there was any forewarning of this rare complication or if any of their interventions had contributed to the problem. An unskilled practitioner can unsuspectingly cause an inverted uterus by pulling too aggressively on the umbilical cord without keeping another hand on the belly to stabilize the uterus. These were two very experienced practitioners, and, moreover, I could visualize with certainty Mariana's gloved hand on Mrs. Coronel's abdomen. The midwives could not be faulted for their technique. Still, Dr. Chew grilled them about what had transpired minute by minute.

It was understandable that he would want to review the sequence of events closely. He is responsible for all that happens on this unit during his call. This coming Friday morning, Dr. Chew and his team will stand before an auditorium filled with perhaps two hundred assorted doctors, nurses, and OB physicians in private practice who gather weekly to review and critique interesting cases. This rare uterine inversion will certainly come up for discussion, and I have seen little mercy meted out to those who blunder in their management.

CHAPTER SIXTEEN

". . . the usual Friday night deluge of staff calling in sick."

June 14

FRIDAY NIGHT. THIS date is the beginning of a new shift for me in which I work from 11:00 p.m. to 11:00 a.m. Most nurses prefer these twelve-hour shifts, as they allow more time off for family, school, and other activities. The work life so intense, it seems to help to have little runs of working, then time off.

One challenge is this weekend requirement, such that every other Friday I will begin a three-night stretch, or thirty-six hours. The one compensation is that, on the alternating Fridays, I will begin a three-night weekend off. Since this schedule is a regular repetition of a set pattern, one can map out one's work schedule for five years or more in advance. A nurse is able to see with certainty which holidays and weekends he or she will be on duty, or off. It makes planning for personal and family activities much easier.

I am still uncertain if my body will tolerate being up all night, then made to stay up the extra four hours. This new shift also has me straddling two different groups of nursing staff. I will have to test my belief that the wonderful camaraderie that exists among my friends on the night team is missing from the day group.

Besides the predictability and the added days off, I have another inducement to try and make this schedule work. In the fall, my youngest will no longer be in day care and will start kindergarten. This particular twelve-hour shift will allow me to end my day at 11:00 a.m. and zoom down the highway to pick Patrick up. It will continue to permit my being there when the older kids get home from school and be present for meals, homework, after-school activities, etc. There is no perfect schedule for the working mother.

Tonight we have the usual Friday night deluge of staff calling in sick, which translates for some into having something more interesting to do. It's the weekend. Ergo, Martha Quinones, LVN, and Dana Desmond, RN, will need to take off at least one of their scheduled shifts to accommodate their social engagements. It is almost always the same folks who are missing in action. They seem to have no conscience about leaving their coworkers in the position of straining to cover for these no-shows.

I confronted Dana quietly one time about her blithe disregard for the rest of us when she called the unit at ten minutes to eleven. We were notified that she was still on the ski slopes and probably wouldn't be able to make it to work that night. Since these ski slopes were on a mountain 250 miles away, she could safely pronounce her inability to be present in the next half hour. Several nights later, back at work together, I let her know that, as the team leader that night, she'd left me and everyone else in the lurch. She went on the offensive with me by responding sarcastically, "Well, Nattie, some of us actually *have* a social life." Wow. Great cut. I'd almost be willing to overlook this snotty remark if I could carve several inches off her beautiful long legs and add them to my short little pegs.

The physicians have a very different means of ensuring that no one among them leaves their peers to do their work. There are no acceptable reasons for failing to show up for a call, short of death or maiming. If they are physically under the weather, no matter. They show up. I'm not sure how they enforce this mandate so successfully. I just know that their system of peer pressure works impressively. I'm somewhat jealous that we can't, as employees of a government agency with civil service and union protections, enforce similar compliance.

The physician system is somewhat inhumane in that there is no distinction between degrees of illness. I have seen female residents, sick as dogs with pregnancy-related morning sickness, tottering around the department trying to do patient care while hanging onto an IV pole, fluids and electrolytes infusing to keep them upright. But they show up.

I asked one of my friends among the residents why they would think to begin a pregnancy during an intensely demanding medical residency. She replied that they were already behind most women, having spent an extra four years in medical school. Involved in four more years of residency and sometimes approaching their thirties, they felt the need to get cracking or risk missing out on childbearing entirely. Made sense.

I simply have to relax about our chronic missing-in-action nurses. It does no good to dwell on the inequities here. For me, this is still the only game in town. Because certain people I associate with here have a different work ethic than mine doesn't mean that I'm entirely right and their attitude stinks. Dana, the gorgeous socialite I mentioned earlier, has gifts that make her a fascinating person to work with. She's a "valley girl" and just a bit less used to delayed gratification than I am. She makes us laugh with her offbeat quips and her unserious outlook on life.

She once charmed a very stern nurse manager out of enforcing the sacred one-year commitment to full-time duty that each nurse must agree to before being hired. Dana asked her if she could work four nights a week instead of five. Mrs. Boschen responded that she was surprised Dana would ask for such a privilege, as she had just completed her orientation. "Yes, but I just got married, and my husband would like me to get oriented to *him*" was Dana's smiling rejoinder. By God, it worked.

Dana is so unbelievably gorgeous, tall and slender, with an impressive bust line. Coupled with a mane of blond, flowing curls and big, dark eyes, Dana's uncomplicated attitude toward life makes her an attraction to the many comers and goers who pass through this unit. I once watched a little vignette occur at the labor desk as two young medical students were getting a tour for their upcoming rotation with us. As an intern and Dana swung by the desk and made the turn on their way back to delivery with a patient, I saw the two young guys perk up. They stared at the spectacle of Dana passing by with wide eyes and dropped jaws. They exchanged a look with each other, as if to say, "Do you feel lucky?"

So back to this night's events. Or actually, back to some nights ago. I had another novel experience working in delivery. Mrs. Anita Hernandez, a good-sized Hispanic woman with a good-sized belly, was brought back to the delivery area to have her baby. She already had one little boy at home, she told me, as we worked with her through her last few contractions. The slight, very vivacious intern Dr. Patel, an East Indian by birth, was eager to assist, this being one of the first deliveries she was attending solo. I had rapidly come to like her enthusiasm. There were no special problems anticipated with this birth for either mother or baby.

When the infant made its entrance and delivered, Dr. Patel cried quickly, "Call pediatrics. This baby is pretty small!"

I went over to look. Sure enough, the little infant girl seemed a bit premature, but she was squalling vigorously and had great color. I felt a little silly calling the newborn resuscitation team for a perfectly healthy though somewhat small baby, so I suggested, "Let's put her in the warmer and watch for a bit."

I went over to the warmer where Dr. Patel had laid the newborn infant and dried off the little squirt, and was trying to assess how premature, if at all, she was when Dr. Patel shrieked, "Don't push! Don't push!"

With my back turned to Manek, my reaction to this agitated exclamation was to try to imagine why this young doctor was getting so frantic about the impending birth of the placenta. Usually, the physician very much anticipates the appearance of the afterbirth, as they are standing by on tired feet. I went back and peered over Mrs. Hernandez's stirruped leg and was met by the sight of two tiny pink feet protruding through the vaginal outlet.

"Undiagnosed twins!"

I ran to the intercom and called for a resident to come. This presentation of the infant is somewhat of an emergency situation, the tiny footling breech set to deliver and no certainty that there is ample room for the head to come down. Chances were, in this case, that there was plenty of room, since one little body had just exited. However, there have been times when a crash cesarean section has been done for the second malpositioned twin.

Luckily, Dr. Hirsh, a second-year resident, was in the delivery room adjacent to ours. Hearing my panicked voice, she ran in to help the excited intern and nurse. Within a minute, a little identical-looking sister joined the first newborn in the warmer. I hastily placed a piece of tape on the blankets to identify number one and number two. The pediatric resident decided that these two cuties needed to go to the preemie nursery, as one remained a slightly dusky-blue color and the other was somewhat limp in muscle tone.

Mrs. Hernandez was so ecstatic, laughing and crying simultaneously. As I brought her out of the room on our way to recovery, her husband and mother-in-law appeared. The three of them went to town in rapid-fire Spanish, and the reaction of joy to the unexpected birth of two babies was heartwarming to watch. These folks were seemingly unsophisticated and of very modest means, yet they saw this multiple birth as an unusual blessing. I was fortunate in having the chance to take Mr. Hernandez and Grandma Hernandez down to the special care nursery. I watched as their eyes lit up at the endearing sight of two tiny mites lying side by side on the examining table.

For myself, I will remember for the future: "Big belly, tiny baby; look for the instant replay."

CHAPTER SEVENTEEN

"... I knew that my words were like pouring gasoline on an open flame for this man.

July 31

A HUMAN DILEMMA OCCURRED tonight, and as usual, I wanted so much to jump in and solve the problem for my patient.

I met a father in the mother-baby assessment room, a handsome Latino with red eyes and obvious alcohol on his breath. Once in a while, a prospective dad will spend the period of his wife's labor by conducting a prebirth celebration, and this man was a bit tipsy. He was behaving himself, just, and was encouraging every passerby to admire his infant.

Later, I was making a bed in the hallway while this couple was visiting, waiting for the nursing assistant to take the new mom and baby up to her room on the postpartum floor. The husband called me over and in fairly good English asked me to help.

"Excuse me, but does my *esposa* sign the papers for the operation for *no mas* babies?"

With sinking heart, I accepted this woman's chart as he handed it to me. He had likely pulled it from its resting place, tucked under the foot of the stretcher's mattress. He was not entitled to go into her medical record, but I could imagine he felt every right to do so. I started paging through her chart, giving me a moment to try and think how to handle this touchy situation.

Indeed, she had signed the consent for permanent sterilization and would be set up for this minor surgical procedure later this day or sometime before her discharge. This document verified the mother's having attended the mandatory class we provide to inform women about all the ins and outs of the procedure to prevent future pregnancies.

As I continued my look into the new mother's personal information, I learned that this patient was a twenty-nine-year-old woman who had just delivered her sixth child. Amazing. She looked to be no more than nineteen.

I hadn't answered the new father's question because, truly, he was not entitled to this confidential information. I suppose the conflict in my expression gave him the answer he was seeking.

"Well, I'm telling you that I no give my *permiso* for the *operación!*" he shouted belligerently at me.

Maintaining a neutral tone and calm expression, I explained that only the patient can consent to or refuse treatment. We would have to be guided by his wife's wishes. Oh god. As quiet and noninflammatory as they were spoken, I knew that my words were like pouring gasoline on an open flame for this man. In the Latino culture, the male is the absolute king of the castle, even if the castle is a modest one-room apartment in the barrio.

Next, the belligerent husband pointed his finger at me and announced angrily, "*Entonces*, she will tell you right now, she no want the *operación!*"

I looked at the slender, pretty woman in the bed staring at us with a wooden expression. Who knew what exactly she made of all this, for she purported not to speak any English. Many times, while they are too shy to use their broken English in front of a strange group of medical gringos, I have found that my Spanish-speaking patients understand quite a bit of our language. This woman seemed to have decided to remain studiously passive, as if she was indifferent to what was transpiring between her husband and me. I guessed that this conflict, playing out in our hallway, was an echo of a difficult conversation that had taken place between this man and wife sometime in the recent past. And yet she had signed up for the sterilization class despite her spouse's objection.

Our conversation continued with our new father prodding his wife to tell me she didn't want the tubal. In the end, she nodded her head and said the words he was demanding. I appealed to his sense of compassion.

"Can't you try to see this from her viewpoint?" I asked gently. "Six babies before age thirty are so many for you and your wife to care for."

He was unmoved by my words and reiterated with arms crossed on his chest that "*Sí*, but she no gonna have the *operación.*"

I knew there was virtually nothing to be done. I asked the senior resident, one of the most decent men I have ever met, to intercede. Jaime Bautista confirmed what in my heart I already knew: that we simply could not interfere in what was strictly a family decision.

I suggested we write for a social worker visit. Once she was upstairs, someone could come and expend what effort was possible to lend support to this gutsy young woman who was trying to limit her expanding family. Part of this support would be to explain the various ways she could prevent future pregnancies with an array of contraceptive choices at her disposal. I was realistic enough to believe that there was every chance we would be seeing her in this unit within the next few years.

Jaime wrote for the social worker consult and at the same time canceled her preop orders for the tubal ligation. The patient would have to reassert her desire for sterilization at a later time if she made that decision, and we would respect her wishes no matter what she decided. I am thinking that she won't opt for the surgery now in the face of her husband's fury. What would such fury portend for her were she to go ahead with her desires?

All this made me nearly sick. I constantly have to remind myself that we can only scratch the surface when it comes to meeting the many needs of this population we serve. Who knows what the day-to-day trials of these poor immigrant women are? I could appreciate a smidgen of this woman's ordeal, being myself one of nine siblings in a big Catholic family. My parents loved all of us, but their ability to meet the emotional and physical needs of myself and my younger brothers and sisters was diluted with each new mouth to feed. This Mexican wife, in the face of a culture and religion that denies her the right to realistically contain the size of her family, had made a brave decision. Would that events had proceeded differently. For myself, I strained once more to let go of those things over which I have no control.

CHAPTER EIGHTEEN

"There was just a little of the comic element to relieve my abject horror . . ."

August 1

I MADE A BIG blooper today. It was a case of simple human error, but at the time I was filled with an inordinate amount of remorse, considering that no life was lost and no one was physically harmed. There is great potential for damage to be done here due to the vulnerability of our patients, along with all the good we accomplish. I am one to be hyperaware of the emotional trauma we can inflict on a somewhat defenseless population, and so my faux pas of this morning hit me hard.

The story began sometime in the middle of the night as I was taking my rare turn at being in charge of the unit. I don't assume this role too often because Merilee, the night charge nurse, or Anita, the relief charge nurse, perform this job so admirably. Tonight, I arrived on duty to see my name down on the assignment sheet to team lead.

There's a running joke here that they should put me in charge more often because it's almost always slow when I am the team leader. It's true. We never seem to be jammed when I'm in charge as we are nine nights out of ten. I respond to this by saying that God never asks more of one than one can handle, and he knows how limited my talents are at coping with frantic situations.

I was mostly busy giving breaks to everyone. Our labor room nurses do not have the luxury of being able to leave their assignment to get some coffee or eat their meal without a nurse coming to stand in their place. So having six labor rooms going meant that I had to rove between them, taking over for half-hour or forty-five-minute stints depending on whether the nurse was working eight or twelve hours.

In the course of relieving Donna Cassiday in her labor room, I worked with a patient who had a history of two previous cesarean sections. This woman was very skeptical about Dr. Anna Gertmenian's glowing pep talk on the merits of having her baby vaginally after her two surgical deliveries. There has been a lot of research done recently to identify the safe situations in which a vaginal birth can be attempted following a previous delivery by C-section. Donna's patient repeatedly protested, always after a contraction, that she didn't want to harm her baby. As time wore on, I think she was beyond ready to accept the bliss of anesthesia and get this labor over with, even given the prospect of the painful postsurgical recovery. Who could blame her?

Only being her nurse for one hour, plus caring for three other patients simultaneously, I could not get to know this woman well. Still, I thought she seemed to be a rather immature person. Or a drug abuser. Drug abusers have enormously low pain thresholds, and this woman's behavior was somewhat reminiscent of those many women I had cared for with addiction histories. I felt sorry for Donna, now returning from her break to deal with this woman's incessant demands for attention.

Then I moved on, and later that morning I had the pleasure of admitting a prisoner patient in another labor room. She was a heroin addict now experiencing stiff contractions and, at the same time, in full-blown withdrawal. She was absolutely miserable. I commented to the pretty sheriff's deputy that "this is a horrible situation for this girl, going through labor and withdrawal at the same time." The deputy gave me a cynical look to say that she was not moved.

Ms. Canliss, an attractive twenty-three-year-old with troubled eyes, was already begging for something–anything–to cut the pain. She let me know how soon and how much methadone she thought she would require to get comfortable. She was too agitated to cooperate so that we could monitor her baby consistently. She apologized for being so antsy and making my job harder, but she was incapable of tolerating her labor and could not benefit from any of the advice I offered. Once again, the nurse who was to assume Jennifer Canliss's care returned from break, and I left the room with a guilty sense of relief.

At seven, my team-leading duties were thankfully over, and I was assigned to the LICU for the last four hours of the shift. It was hectic there, very hectic. Already in residence were two primiparas, women in labor with their first babies. Both were completely dilated. The rather obnoxious third-year resident Harry Forsythe, who was just coming on for the start of his call, informed me in a sarcastic tone of voice that I should render some good coaching and get these two women delivered. As if it was somehow the fault of nursing that these women still had babies inside. In between these two first-time mothers, there was a quite large woman who had multiple IV lines with medications infusing in both arms. She needed careful watching for her very labile blood pressures.

The women who were completely dilated and pushing were having alternating contractions every two minutes. I would coach one patient, then move to the other end of the room for the other's turn. Coaching is an art, a sort of cheerleading action, coaxing and encouraging the mother toward moving her baby down through the birth canal. Women are often exhausted from many long hours of labor just when nature demands an almost superhuman effort on their part to help expel their baby. This challenging time is especially true for those at the point of delivering their first child, as the tissue, the musculature of the birth canal, has never been asked to stretch this much.

I don't badger women who are pushing, as some do. I get just as much response from positive, supportive encouragement. In difficult cases such as these two, when coaching proceeds to the goal of delivery, the nurse or other caregiver is exhausted as well. I was elated to have gotten one woman ready to go back to delivery.

At that point, one of my favorite residents, Jennie Moya, all four feet eight inches of her, came into the LICU, looking to see if I still had a full house. "Oh, good," she remarked, spotting my vacancy. "I need that space to send you our heroin addict. She's having problems with her baby's heart tracing and needs to be scalp sampled."

Oh good, my foot, I thought, because I had just discovered two problems with the other girl who was pushing. She was very warm and needed a special workup to try and find a reason for her rising temperature. Also, her baby's head was turned in such a position that no matter how hard she pushed, she wasn't getting anywhere (asynclitism). I was helping the medical student do the fever workup when my new patient was brought in, trailed by Dr. Moya and a group of curious nursing students.

Since there were all these extra people available to help, I gratefully let them assist the resident in getting the patient into the tortuous position required to obtain the scalp sample. Picture this. You are in hard labor and hooked up to about six different lines and tubes. Your medical team tells you that you have to scoot your pain-wracked body down to the end of the bed and dangle your bottom off the end with your legs up in stirrups. Then they stick a hard plastic cone into your vagina, up against your baby's head, and tell you they are going to pierce your baby's scalp to get a blood sample. No wonder some of these foreign-born women who have come here from the most feudal backgrounds in Third World countries act as if they have strayed into a medieval torture chamber. Trying to explain that this test is necessary to assess their baby's well-being doesn't really seem to penetrate their obvious feeling that we have abandoned them to a cruel fate. As the nurse under demand to set up and assist with this procedure, I can relate.

Since I was currently consumed with multiple tasks in this busy room, I let the nursing students do most of the work with my newly admitted patient. I could hear her complaining agitatedly, expressing great dismay at everything that was being done to her. I had a vision of myself dealing with her earlier that morning and thought: heroin user—prisoner patient—withdrawal behavior—totally consistent with. So absorbed was I with my other two patients, I could only manage to trot over and retrieve the tiny glass tubes containing the scalp samples from Dr. Moya and prepare them to be sent off to the blood gas lab.

Then the phone on the wall rang. It was the boyfriend of my new admission, wanting to speak to her. Prisoner patients aren't allowed visitors or phone calls. We also aren't allowed to give out any information about our patients, prisoners or not, over the phone. The conversation proceeded like this:

"Hello, this is Joe Jones. I want to speak to–"

"I'm sorry, she isn't allowed to have phone calls."

"Well, why not?"

"I'm sorry, she's unable to speak on the phone to callers."

"Well, I'm coming down there soon, so I can see her, right? I'm the baby's father."

"Regrettably, she isn't allowed to have visitors either."

"But why?"

We went on this way, with the young man increasingly upset and with me trying hard not to give more than the minimum of information. Finally, when he got even more insistent about coming down here and I began to picture some big security showdown on the unit, I said,

"Look, if you're going to persist in coming here, I can only refer you to the sheriff's office. They will tell you the same thing, that she is not allowed any visitors."

"The sheriff's office! Hey, now, wait a minute!"

"Yes. You see, patients in custody are not allowed to receive visitors or phone calls."

"Custody? What are you talking about? My girlfriend isn't in custody. There must be some mistake."

So sure was I that the woman we were talking about was the heroin user I had admitted earlier in that other labor room, I solemnly assured him again that he would not be able to visit and he should refer any questions to the sheriff's department. He was quite decent, continuing to assert that there must be some mistake. I said, finally, never thinking that there was even a remote chance of my being in error,

"Well, I will surely check to make sure. It's always possible I could be mistaken." This last I said merely to placate him, as he seemed to be such a decent person.

Julie Fortenese, my good friend, had arrived to relieve me at the end of my shift and was listening to my conversation with this man. There was a stricken look on her face. I set down the phone and went to look at the patient and check her chart. I was incredulous when I discovered that this was not the prisoner patient after all but the fussy woman in the other labor room, the one who'd had the previous C-sections and didn't like her labor. Jennie Moya had either confused the patients herself or had decided to transfer this patient at the last moment without conveying the news to me. Because the women bore a striking resemblance to each other, both physically and behaviorally, I had made a glaring assumption.

With a sickening sense of guilt, I went over to the woman who had just heard herself described as a jail inmate to her baby's father. I found her sobbing. As if the indignity and discomfort of the scalp sampling were not enough, now she was the victim of my slanderous misapprehension. Never had I committed such folly. Ouch!

I got back on the phone and admitted that I had confused this man's girlfriend with another patient. I apologized for any distress I had caused him and assured him that he was welcome to come and visit. He accepted my words with no apparent hostility and said he would set out for the hospital. Then I commenced the delicate job of trying to repair the damage I had done to this poor woman's psyche. As much as I wanted to help restore her equilibrium, I was also conscious of a very human desire to cover my backside a bit. All I could envision was myself sitting in a courtroom trying to excuse my behavior, like the surgeon trying to explain how he had come to remove the healthy kidney.

Well, it was time to go home. Julie tried to help me regain a sense of perspective about my little imbroglio. Izzy Holguin, the day charge nurse, reassured me that my faux pas was hardly a case for Crime TV. There was just a little of the comic element to relieve my disgust with myself for having so blithely misidentified my patient based on some very superficial judgments. I could see the humor, sort of, even as I cringed at the thought of my carelessness. I went home and poured a glass of wine at noon, something I have never done. Still, I had a hard time getting to sleep.

CHAPTER NINETEEN

"They cease to be individuals and figure more as numbers, or a workload, encumbrances to be avoided if at all possible."

August 4

TONIGHT I HAD the experience of taking care of what was for me a complete oddity—a white middle-class yuppie. Gina Anderson's adventures with us were so illustrative of the disparity between health-care services for poor or uninsured individuals, and those available to Americans fortunate enough to have medical insurance. This patient also gave us a kick in the pants where we sometimes need it most, in the area of consideration and good manners.

I was working a few hours overtime on this relatively quiet Saturday evening, so staff and patients were still perky. The nurses displayed none of the pallor or sometimes drooping eyelids of those of us who toil through the night. My assignment was to a moderately busy labor room housing three women in various stages of labor. Two of the patients were my familiar brown-skinned, black-haired, and dark-eyed Latinas. The remaining patient was a complete outlier, a blonde, slender, blue-eyed woman in her early thirties, well kept, makeup flawlessly applied, and sporting a short, stylish haircut. She was listening with concentration as Petra, the nurse manning this room since 7:00 a.m., gave me the history of each woman for whom I was assuming care.

My pretty gringo patient had had quite a difficult day. In fact, life had delivered Gina Anderson some surprising curves lately. She had recently left a successful career in real estate to open an antique store. She had been in the process of obtaining a private health insurance policy when she, a single woman, had unexpectedly found herself pregnant. Now still early in her pregnancy, she had gone to her upscale gynecologist for treatment of a urinary tract infection and, incidentally, some premature uterine contractions.

The private MD had tried to have Ms. Anderson admitted to the high-risk obstetrical unit of an ultramodern, expensive regional hospital that had a great reputation for obstetrical and NICU care. When she got there and it was discovered that she was uninsured, she was put in an ambulance and sent twenty miles to us at the city hospital.

"I have money," she assured me in a dispirited voice, "but that wasn't good enough. I felt like an infectious disease, the way they acted there." She continued her explanation: "I'm so naïve. I thought I was brave, striking out on my own after saving for my business for years. Now I feel like I've strayed into an alternate universe."

What she did not realize was that there was a bottom line for the sending hospital. If her premature labor could not be stopped and she ended up delivering a tiny, severely compromised infant, that facility might end up with costs for neonatal intensive care that could easily run into the hundreds of thousands. Ms. Anderson's savings, however enviable to most, would be a stick in the wind. Thus, she and we were experiencing the phenomenon known in the medical community as "dumping." In such cases, troublesome patients with the potential for financial liability to the institution are shuffled off as quickly as possible to places like this, ones that do not ever refuse to treat anyone based on financial considerations.

I chatted with Gina, intent on showing her that even though she was in a place where the physical amenities were few, the care and skill of the nursing staff and the physicians were first rate. Soon Dr. Jurgensen, the senior resident, and one of his junior residents, John Tulley, came into my room on walking rounds. When they got to the bed of the chic blonde, they continued their typical practice of reviewing and discussing the status of the patient. The two carried on their conversation as if totally ignorant of the fact that an intelligent, well-educated person who spoke their language was listening intently to their every word.

"You know, Bruce," pointed out Dr. Tulley, "it's questionable if she even belongs here. She's twenty-one weeks by fair dates, but she's only 480 grams. I think they bagged us in the ER. She should have gone to gynecology admitting."

"No way does she belong here," agreed Bruce Jurgensen heatedly. "Who's working in the ER? I'm going to call Jessie Morales in GYN and tell him I'm sending this one over to him."

"What are they talking about?" asked Ms. Anderson. "What's happening?"

She was having trouble translating the medical lingo that revolved around the appropriateness of her admission to Labor and Delivery instead of the gynecology service. In general, we only treat pregnant women in this unit whose babies have reached the age of viability–the ability to realistically survive if they have to begin life on the outside as a little preemie. Gina Anderson was in a window of time in her pregnancy when she might be judged as having a minimally viable infant. Or not.

The main problem I saw was that neither of these young male residents was acknowledging their patient's ability to understand events nor considerate enough to spend a few minutes explaining their plans for her treatment. As I very often do for my patients, and sometimes in less-than-perfect Spanish, I had to fill in the blanks for Ms. Anderson, which left her somewhat but not wholly mollified.

About fifteen minutes later, Dr. Jurgensen returned alone. "Start getting her unhooked from all this stuff," he directed me, pointing to all the paraphernalia surrounding her–the fetal monitor leads, the IV tubing, and bag of fluids. "We're going to transfer her up to GYN admitting. I called, and they already know she's coming."

There was just a hint of breathlessness in his voice that told me something was up. He started to assist me in getting her ready for transport. Senior residents are not in the habit of performing these nursing activities. He even helped me detach all the belts and leads from our patient's belly, while I found a pole on which to hang her IV bag. Then he and I threaded Ms. Anderson's bed out from among the others in the small and very congested labor room. We soon reached the labor desk where I began to check her out from the patient log.

As we pointed her bed down the corridor and had pushed it about twenty feet toward the exit doors, Dr. Morales from the GYN service literally burst through those same doors and strode purposefully in our direction.

"Bruce, I told you, she's not ours!" he informed Dr. Jurgensen bluntly.

"Horseshit, she's not" was the usually quiet, well-mannered Dr. Jurgensen's uncharacteristic response to his colleague. "The kid's not five hundred grams, and she's coming to you."

"No way," returned Jessie Morales in his most adamant voice. Their ripostes were traded back and forth directly over Gina Anderson's head. I was watching her and could see her bright, now increasingly angry eyes traveling from one resident to another.

"*That's it!*" she broke in, startling the two exasperated physicians into shocked silence. For the first time, seemingly, they turned to our patient to see what her strange outburst could mean.

"You know, you are two of the rudest men I've ever met in my life," she chastised them in a voice livid with anger. "Stop arguing over my head like I'm a sack of smelly fish. If you can't be civil, I'm going to get out of this bed and go home on the bus–that is, if I can figure out exactly where I am!"

You go, girl!

Dr. Jurgensen is the son of a wealthy and popular obstetrician in private practice. He plans to join his father in caring for women in the very neighborhood from which Gina Andersen springs. He looked very much taken aback by the young woman's words. His handsome Nordic features were suffused with bright red color as he noticed for the first time the gaggle of nurses, visitors, and housekeepers who had stopped on their way down the corridor, transfixed by this scene.

He quietly instructed me to push Ms. Anderson's bed back into the spot from which it had just minutes ago been vacated.

"It's OK, Jess," I heard him tell the GYN resident. "She'll stay with us."

Thereafter, events proceeded calmly. Dr. Jurgensen followed me back into my labor room. He explained to our patient the details of her situation and apologized for squabbling with the GYN resident over territorial imperatives. Her care proceeded routinely and successfully from that point, and some hours later, she was transferred to the antepartum service where she would continue to be observed and treated for a possible mild kidney infection. Her preemie labor had subsided as fluids and antibiotics had kicked in.

Oh my. I have to acquit Dr. Jurgensen of being a total jerk. At least he had responded decently when confronted with a teachable moment due to our patient's assertion of her right to be treated in a professionally correct manner. He's simply worked too many hours in this place, seen too many patients so that they cease to be individuals. They figure more as numbers, or a workload–encumbrances to be avoided if at all possible–because there's always another busload arriving. Gina Anderson had stopped Bruce Jurgensen in his tracks and forced him to deal with her humanity in a respectful manner. Would that more of our patients had the gumption to demand similar attention, because they deserve no less. For my part, I must remember that it is my place, my duty, to be a voice for those of our patients who do not feel able to speak for themselves.

CHAPTER TWENTY

"When am I going to develop some spine?"

September 8

D ID I JUST say that it's always slow when I am in charge of the unit? Two nights ago, it was my turn to preside over hell night.

Started off OK on a moderately busy night. The absolute minimum of staff was on duty. Every labor room was crammed with women having babies, and there was no rover nurse to assist with any unusual circumstances. However, the first few hours passed uneventfully. I made out the assignment sheet for the upcoming week and delivered narcotics to labor patients or those in the delivery area.

The first hint that I was in trouble came when one young nurse, Tracy, came out of her labor room and said, "Oh no, Nattie, I forgot to tell you there's someone in the isolation room!"

We have one room reserved for pregnant women who come here with various problems that require our isolating them from the rest of our mothers. Reasons for such sequestration might be suspected or diagnosed infectious diseases such as tuberculosis, hepatitis, parasitical infestations, measles, chicken pox, etc. Because so many of our patients come from Third World countries with less-than-robust vaccination programs, this room gets frequent use. It has a special air exchange system, and our nurses are trained to deal with various protocols for differing types of isolation precautions.

I opened the door, and, sure enough, there was a young woman lying placidly in a bed. Her fetal heart monitor was industriously churning out data, useless unless observed by a knowing caregiver. This patient had been on her own for more than an hour and a half. Fortunately, she was not in labor and had been with us merely for observation while her TB status was verified. My guardian angel at work, I guess.

I found Jennie Moya, one of the residents, and explained the situation. She looked at the woman's chart, then examined the fetal monitor output and decided we were not offering this woman much that was meaningful. What relief. She could be transferred to the isolation room on the antepartum service one floor below us where they could continue to work her up. I was satisfied with this disposition, since it was coming up on time to relieve the labor room nurses for their well-deserved dinner breaks. It would have been tricky if I got stuck taking care of a patient in the isolation room.

But that's exactly what happened. The emergency room called to let us know they would be bringing us a woman, ready to deliver and sporting a diagnosis of hepatitis B. I was still involved in finishing the discharge of the rule-out TB patient. Part of the care of such patients is the special "terminal" cleaning that must be done once they have delivered or vacated the room. Good luck on my finding a housekeeper at this hour to swiftly turn the room around so it could be used for another such infectious case, as I speculated was to be my theme for this night.

Many of the delivery rooms were in use, excluding the one we use for isolation patients. Ideally, I would elect to send the ER patient directly there upon her arrival to our unit. Brad Antonia and Jack Strauss, two scrub techs from the delivery area, arrived to advise me that "the woman coming up from the ER ought to be delivered in the isolation labor room. It's too hard to clean a delivery room after a 'dirty' case when we are busy. It ties up a delivery room that we might need for another birth."

I became instantly irked because I sensed that I was being sandbagged, ganged up on. True, it's a pain to assist with the delivery of an infectious patient in one of the birth rooms in the back. There's extra work for everyone involved. But at that moment, I still had my possible TB patient in the isolation room. I'd have to put her in the hallway with a face mask in place and try to assemble quickly the equipment for the delivery of the woman who was likely en route from the ER. The two scrub techs were very assertive, and in a very passive-aggressive manner, I rapped out my assent.

When am I going to develop some spine? I was in charge. It was my decision to make, but I had let myself be manipulated into agreeing with someone else's plan that wasn't the best for overall unit needs. I knew that it was more important that I be available to help with the various problems occurring all over the unit. It was also important that I be able to give breaks to the labor room nurses. Our labor rooms are so intense, packed as they typically are with a multitude of problems and heavy workload for the caregiver. The nurse rarely leaves his or her room. After confinement in such rooms for many hours, it is essential for the nurse to leave for a respite. I have worked so many nights when the person in charge was not able to get to my coworkers and me because there were simply too many priority issues demanding attention. I regretted that the next few hours would prevent me from relieving my team for a much-needed recess.

In my admittedly sparse history of team leading, I had made the break issue a high priority, as much for the patients' sake as for the nurses. The demands upon a nurse confined to these labor rooms with so many medical/obstetric problems requiring constant multitasking, plus the environmental stress involving crying, sometimes screaming patients, can lead to decompensation, less-than-optimum attention to patients' needs. It is the human condition. The half hour away from the scene in these hectic labor rooms can refresh the nurses and bring them back ready to tackle the challenges anew, with some store of energy to serve the patients' needs.

At this juncture, stuck with the one discharged patient in the hallway and leaning on the housekeeper to get the isolation room rapidly cleaned for the ER patient, I fumed at my lack of assertiveness. I needed to understand that the role of team leader dictated that I make the best decisions possible and not let myself be prevailed upon due to a lifelong problem with people-pleasing. In the moment, I had failed to grasp the role of the true leader. But, baby, I was learning.

I ended up spending five hours in total in the isolation room with the delivery of our patient with hepatitis. Fortunately, seeing that I could not get to them for their breaks, the other nurses got together and found some creative ways to deal with their absent team leader. They watched each other's patients, taking on a double load at times so that their friends could at least get an abbreviated break. I was very proud of the generous spirit that prevailed among the RNs. Meanwhile, I trudged through my delivery and recovery of the isolation patient.

Mrs. Gregory turned out to be a terrific mother, as I got to see after the delivery was accomplished right on the transport stretcher. It was a pleasure seeing her, and later her husband, exclaim over their lovely newborn daughter. I had to keep exiting the room to deliver medications to the delivery area, so I pushed the baby warmer close to the mother's bed and let them continue with this emerging love affair while I pursued my errands.

Two helper-type personnel gave me a hard time about not getting their breaks until late in the shift. These nursing assistants were busy transporting the endless stream of our mother-infant duos up to the postpartum unit. It's a good thing I'm not bucking for a leadership position because I'm not a bit good at dealing with malingerers. One of these two, Delia, a portly black woman, told me, "Well, yes, the mother and baby had been lying on a stretcher in the hallway for several hours." But her feet were swollen, and she felt it imperative that she sit down and eat right now.

After I had tried patiently to appeal to her sense of duty, fairness, compassion, whatever, Delia let me know that she was unmoved by my exhortation. Here, again, I got passive-aggressive. Rather than giving her the order to take up the next patient, which was my prerogative, I instead threw up my arms in exasperation. I told her there was no point in trying to appeal to her sense of decency. It was up to her, I continued, adding that I thought she needed an attitude adjustment.

I hear that Delia wrote a long, impassioned, and not-too-coherent letter about this incident to the head nurse. Well, tough. No one else was complaining at that point about the tardiness or even lack of breaks. Everyone had been working many long hours at a cruel pace. Delia had a reason to resent me based on previous encounters. Twice before I'd awakened her to tell her she needed to be up doing her job. I'm not a barracuda about these nursing assistants or housekeepers whom I find nodding off in slow moments, although it is technically a firing offense. I had come across this woman snoring under a mountain of warm sheets when the place was exploding with activity.

Why do these people come here if they don't like hard work? That's what is served up here, night after night. It's ten times as intense as in a private hospital. We sure manage to attract an inordinate number of people who spend the majority of their limited portion of energy trying to avoid work or shifting it to some other dedicated person. My mission, should I choose to accept it in the interest of not bursting a blood vessel and to become a passable team leader, is to learn to simply and directly tell such slackers to be about their business when it is my role to do so. I am now on a mission to actualize some of the lessons I've learned throughout this night's adventures while being the nurse in charge.

Addendum: Early in my first months working in this unit, I had been assigned to mother-baby assessment. We had two male nursing assistants in the role of transporting our endless production of patients needing to be taken upstairs to one of the three postpartum wards. It was vexing to me to see the line of discharged mother-infant couplets moving very slowly. Finally, I elected to take the next patient up myself. As I pushed mom and baby on their stretcher down the corridor toward the postpartum unit desk, I passed two individuals lounging in the area, seated in visitor chairs. A nurse's aide and our staff transporter looked up at me sheepishly. I said nothing until Gary and I were back in L&D, where I asked him to please get cracking and help get the long-suffering patients up to their rooms. The next night on duty, the charge nurse told me that Gary had resigned on taking his leave the previous morning. He informed the staff that his reason for exiting was that he couldn't stomach having to work with a bitchy nurse like that Natalie. Oh, well.

CHAPTER TWENTY-ONE

". . . we found that the appreciative and sympathetic laughter of friends took all the sting out of these incidents."

September 15

S O DULL TONIGHT. There are only two women in labor, and all of us are sitting around enjoying this amazing oddity. Gathered around the dented wooden table in the break room is a collection of five of my fellow nurses, an amazingly attractive group of young women. Somehow, you wouldn't expect to find this sort of individual caring for the poorest, neediest population in our city in an aging, unattractive hospital surrounded by the barrio. I find a great deal of fineness of character, generosity, and intelligence behind the very lovely exteriors of these young nurses.

We got to telling stories, and as the minutes passed, a theme evolved: "my most embarrassing moment." The self-deprecating, colorful humor was so raucous that we had the interns and medical students, packed into bunk beds next door for a miserly few hours of sleep, thumping on the wall. God, it felt so good to laugh like this for a change.

This wildly funny exercise in self-expiation turned out to be rather therapeutic. Once we told our story, some never having revealed their folly to another person, we found that the appreciative and sympathetic laughter of friends took all of the sting out of such incidents.

My story revolved around an occasion in my teenage years when I was babysitting for a young doctor and his wife as they were preparing for a weekend trip. I was only staying to bridge their leave-taking and the arrival of the grandparents. After they had left, I discovered two jumbo-sized Hershey bars in the fridge. I helped myself to one, puberty having caught me in the grip of almost insatiable hunger, and eight brothers and sisters rarely leaving so much as a flake of chocolate on our premises.

About forty minutes later, Dr. Valentine let himself back in the door while I was in the bedroom changing some little tot's diaper. "Guess what, Natalie?" his voice announced, reaching me mid-diaper change. "We got thirty miles away before we remembered our Hershey bars!" I heard the refrigerator door open, then silence. He beat a hasty and face-saving (for me) retreat, leaving me to flay myself, as I have done ever since, with the humiliating memory of this petty crime.

One of this night's stories stood out, though, for its ability to evoke that sense of exquisite embarrassment that only females can appreciate concerning our pursuit of women's health.

Dana's aunt was driving across town to have her gynecologist perform her annual exam and Pap smear. She was a tad nervous, as some of us are when en route to this annual invasion (albeit for a worthy cause) of our privacy. She was stricken with an irritable bladder and stopped at a gas station to pee. As luck would have it, the restroom was devoid of toilet paper. She rummaged through her purse until she found a wadded-up scrap of Kleenex. Then she was on her way.

Minutes later, naked, paper-draped, with her legs up in stirrups, she awaited her doctor. He came in the exam room, greeted her, and seated himself in preparation for the gynecologic exam. He lifted the drape. Dana's aunt heard only silence, followed seconds later by an eruption of choked laughter.

When he managed to recover himself, the doctor raised his gloved hand so that this mortified woman could see the object of his mirth: a sodden wisp of Kleenex with a postage stamp clinging to it.

"I'm always hunting for these," he informed her. "This is the damnedest place I've ever found one."

CHAPTER TWENTY-TWO

"Imelda's back resembled a roadmap . . ."

November 12

I HAD AN EXPERIENCE in my labor room last night that shows up my continuing lack of rapport with the anesthesia department. We are fortunate in that we have twenty-four-hour coverage on this unit by anesthesia staff. At night, there are two residents, as well as a certified nurse anesthetist. CNAs are advanced practice nurses who can administer anesthesia and assist the residents. We need these folks and could use more around the clock due to the emergency nature of some situations in obstetrics. There are times when surgery must commence within minutes in the interest of preventing harm to either mother or baby.

When they are not providing anesthesia for surgery, the anesthesia residents are involved in placing epidural blocks. An epidural is a nice form of anesthesia that works very well for the laboring woman, providing total or near-total relief of pain without mother and baby receiving opioid narcotics. Epidural anesthesia works especially well for women having their first baby when labor frequently lasts many long hours. For these patients, the repeated doses of narcotics needed to achieve good pain control would not be in their best interest or that of their infant.

I had epidural anesthesia placed about two-thirds of the way into my first labor and can testify to its blissful effect. Pain relief was total. When the anesthesia wore off after several hours, more medicine was injected through a small tube that was inserted into a space near my spinal column. I was pretty well wrung out after eight hours of stiff contractions occurring every two to three minutes. With the epidural in place, I chatted with my husband for the next four hours and felt enormously positive about the impending birth of my first child. I became an instant proponent of epidural anesthesia.

A very experienced army physician who had specialized in obstetrics and had also mastered the techniques for various blocks effective in controlling his patients' pain had placed my epidural. He inserted the tubing and administered the magic medication in mere minutes. I remember how minimally uncomfortable the procedure was and how total was the absence of pain. Here, our anesthesia residents are still in the process of learning the procedure for placing epidurals and do case after case to improve their skills.

One of my young patients experiencing her first pregnancy was having her epidural placed as I came into the labor room at eleven. She was a hyper, very tense little teenager who was all over the bed with each contraction. Moreover, her mother was at her side whispering in her daughter's ear to push with her pains, thereby helping her obtain a swollen cervix. The epidural she received was a good one, and soon she was snoozing peacefully while her uterus continued to contract rhythmically.

When I got to know my patients a bit, I found another young first-time laborer, Imelda Arrellano, who was now four centimeters dilated. She needed to get opened up to ten centimeters to accommodate delivery. Seeing how she was beginning to lose control more and more with the onset of each pain, and knowing that these were not even the worst to come, I started advocating for an epidural for her.

She looked frightened when I explained what was involved. A fair number of our patients have been warned against the use of this type of anesthesia in the belief that it may cause paralysis. After our talk, and with each subsequent pain, having seen how dramatic had been the amelioration of her roommate's agony, Imelda said she was ready to go for the epidural. Dr. Clemons, the OB resident, readily agreed to order the procedure.

When the anesthesiologist arrived, he set things up. I helped the dark-haired, muscular young man get Imelda into the desired position. In this tight fetal curl, most patients are somewhat uncomfortable due to the impedance of their pregnant belly, and also due to the intermittent occurrence of painful uterine contractions. Imelda, my teenage patient, was no exception in having difficulty curling up satisfactorily and in maintaining this awkward position when her pain commenced.

After preparing her back with an antiseptic solution, the youngish anesthesiologist checked for the anatomical landmarks that would show him where to punch in the large-bore needle through which fine tubing is threaded. Once the tubing was in place, he would be able to infuse the pain-relieving medication. He found his spot, injected a little local painkiller to numb her back against the sting of the bigger needle, and punched through the skin. And punched again. And dug around, trying various angles. Sometimes there's only minimal discomfort through all of this, but in this instance, Imelda screamed and cried out.

"What are you doing? That hurts terribly!"

Ignoring her exclamation, Dr. Phelps persisted. All in all, he went up and down her back making six or seven punches. Sweating, I was a wreck, trying to help Imelda maintain the correct position and encouraging her relaxation. She continued to scream, and I couldn't help but become anxious myself. This procedure was causing our patient more pain than anyone could have expected.

The more he tried, the less willing Dr. Phelps was to concede defeat. Finally, though, there simply wasn't any other place to go on this tortured girl's back. He had to desist. He told her, in a very irritated voice, "You have very poor anatomy for this procedure." Somehow, his not-too-subtle judgment seemed to say, the blame for this mess had to be shifted to the patient. I waited long enough to see his back out the door before summoning Dr. Clemons, who wrote an order for Imelda to have some Demerol. This drug allowed her a few hours of restless sleep and somewhat diminished pain.

Meanwhile, I tried to catch up with all the work I had delayed while helping with the attempted epidural. I know that the obstinate young physician had meant well. I felt that he might have considered, with the unusual amount of pain the girl was having as he poked around in her back, that there was some valid reason why, for her, this wouldn't work. I couldn't say if it was his ego that was under fire or stubbornness or some other facet of his personality that made it so hard to admit defeat.

Three hours passed, and Imelda had only managed to dilate to five centimeters. She was about to enter the active phase of labor, and with the Demerol worn off, she was again in apparent agony. Here came the second anesthesia resident, Dr. Storich, on a remarkably generous search for business. I am much more accustomed to getting cussed at when I call one of these guys in their sleep room to tell them an epidural has been ordered for someone at four in the morning. Dr. Storich was apparently feeling very enthusiastic about his newly acquired prowess in placing epidurals. He noticed how antsy my teenager was with her contractions and asked me if she was a candidate for an epidural. I explained emphatically that Imelda's back resembled a roadmap from all the previous pokes and that his partner had finally given up.

Dr. Storich rolled his eyes at me and gave me a knowing smirk as if to say, "That wouldn't have happened if I had been on the job."

"I guarantee you I can get it in, slick as a whistle," he bragged. So he proceeded to persuade Imelda, now hugely skeptical but impressed by his confident assurance that things would go better. Being left pretty ragged by the many hours of contractions, the lingering woozy effects of Demerol without its pain relief, she was lured by his pep talk about the prospect of total pain abatement.

Back she went into the fetal tuck. Again, Dr. Storich injected the local painkiller and started to dig around in her back. Again, she screamed and wiggled frantically. He began going up and down her back, just as the other resident had done. By this time, my nerves were positively shot. My husband informs me that when I am frustrated, as I surely was at this moment, I have a habit of heaving an enormous sigh. I am completely unaware of this unless someone points it out to me. Either I was in the midst of one of these unconscious sighs or something in my expression upset him, because Dr. Storich stopped his relentless probing of the young girl's back and complained sarcastically to me.

"You seem to be having a problem. It isn't helping a bit when you can't at least be supportive."

I was shocked to realize that I was betraying my reaction to this painful scene. In general, I'm one of the nurses most supportive of the anesthesiologist. Unlike some of the other nurses who are younger, single, and without children, I know up close and personal how labor pain feels. I went through one labor with the benefit of an epidural, and three without. If my patients want and need the pain relief possible from an epidural, and they are lucky enough to have an anesthesiologist available to put one in, I will do my utmost to assist the physician in performing the procedure. But Dr. Storich was so very irked with me, and I had to examine my conscience.

"I guess I can't help empathizing with Imelda," I explained in a quiet undertone. "She is having such great discomfort."

"Well, you could better expend your efforts in helping her stay in the correct position!" he lambasted me in a disgusted voice. Again, it wasn't his lack of skill or some anatomical impediment. The poor outcome here was either the patient's fault or mine.

I was thoroughly disgusted by now. These residents rarely have the luxury of a labor nurse free to pay attention to their needs for the entirety of the procedure when placing epidurals. She or he is exceedingly busy taking care of the pressing needs of multiples of women with obstetric and medical problems, as well as their vulnerable infants.

I have heard the director of OB anesthesia caution the new residents training with him to face the reality that they will often have to place their epidurals without the assistance of the labor nurse for just such reasons. I am one of the few who consider it somewhat of a priority to assist with the anesthesia placement. The more help I can give, the better the chance that it will be effected quickly and successfully.

Dr. Storich finally gave up. Imelda was exhausted, her long, black hair tangled and matted from her twisting and writhing in pain. She was surely wondering by now about the knowledge and skill of her caregivers. I felt a certain degree of guilt in all this because I had been the initial person to sell her on the idea of the epidural.

It was nearing dawn by this time, and my relief from the team of day shift nurses would soon be arriving. I had asked for another assignment for the remaining four hours of my shift. Situations like this one remind me that it is almost imperative to get out of the labor room after eight hours. I often feel like I have undergone labor myself. This morning I was hugely grateful to be sprung free of this exasperating scene, and I went away feeling sick about ever thinking "epidural."

Ironically, the very next night I was working in the LICU and had to call another anesthesia resident to place an epidural. Dr. Eisenstadt was very hostile when he answered me on the phone. The attitude he conveyed was a livid sort of fury that he was being awakened at 3:00 a.m. to come and relieve someone's pain. I wonder if he will change his tune when he graduates into private practice and receives a summons like this, one that will put a tidy sum in his wallet.

This husky, dishwater-blond fellow with a baby face and brilliant blue eyes walked into the LICU and sullenly looked over the woman's chart. Not even addressing one word to the patient, Dr. Eisenstadt directed me in a very brusque voice to "get the woman into position." I struggled to stuff down my resentment at this kind of treatment. In theory, these folks are on their own. Apparently, Dr. Eisenstadt had forgotten his mentor's speech about his need to learn to place epidurals without consistent nursing assistance. Here in the early hours of the morning, I could sense the powder keg state of the young man's emotions, and I determined to take the high road. Ignoring his abysmal rudeness, I explained in Spanish to my patient what the doctor wanted her to do and went about moving her into the curlicue position.

Dr. Eisenstadt draped her and prepped her back with iodine solution, then tried to find his anatomical landmarks. He didn't like the set of the woman's shoulders. Instead of directing the patient to change to a more favorable position, he stood up abruptly, stripped off his gloves, and lit into me in a furious voice.

"You've seen this procedure before! Can't you get this woman into the correct position?"

This last was rapped out in a raised tone of voice that betrayed how close to the edge of total exasperation this man was. But he was also massively out of line with me. Motioning him away from the bed, I let him have it right back.

"You *listen* to me! You have only to tell me what you want this woman to do, and I will translate to the best of my imperfect ability. But, by god, don't get into an argument with me over the patient's head. I'm trying my best to help you, and neglecting my other patients to do so!"

Dr. Eisenstadt faltered, his handsome, surfer-babe features now appearing far older than those of a man in his late twenties, and so defeated.

"Look," he responded remorsefully, "I'm so very tired. I've been up now over twenty hours. This is serious business, poking around someone's spinal column."

"I do sympathize," I countered. And I meant this, however little I intended to be abused by him. "I know that you are tired, but I cannot change the situation here. The obstetrical resident ordered this epidural, and it's my role to be the messenger. I will help you however I can. Just don't make me the enemy."

After this little exchange, which allowed us both to vent our feelings and establish a bit of a personal relationship, things went much better. I kept translating and nudging this chubby Latina into position so that she was a bit more compliant. He thanked me repeatedly for my efforts, although never apologizing directly. Fortunately for our patient, the epidural was successfully placed and worked to make her comfortable.

It is certainly not my place to do so, but I want so much sometimes to remind these anesthesia residents that it is not their prerogative to sleep. The incredible pain of labor does not change its intensity when the sun goes down. When it is busy on this unit, the obstetric residents, interns, and medical students often go twenty-eight or more hours with not a wink of sleep.

Having young physicians in training stay up these god-awful hours is not good for either the docs or the patients (and, incidentally, the nurses). It is the traditional training of American physicians, thought to prepare them well for the rigorous challenges and stress they will face in future practice. This is not a humane system of education in which they are participating. It is the uncomfortable and sometimes cruel price they pay for a very prestigious training in the practice of medicine.

CHAPTER
TWENTY-THREE

"God hold that child in an everlasting embrace, and someday ease her grieving mother's heart."

December 24

CHRISTMAS EVE. NONE of us, no matter how much we love our work, want to be here on a holiday like this. I have been rather fortunate in being home on Christmas morning, which is our family's traditional celebration. Merilee, in making out the schedule for the night staff, is always as generous as can be. She particularly tries to ensure that nurses with families of young children have at least part of the day off. I have been with Bill and the kids for the opening of gifts more often than not. This year I am here on Christmas Eve and consider it fortunate that I will be leaving early in the morning to be with my family.

Of course, all of us want to be at home with our families, and the absolute minimum of nurses and other personnel are scheduled on these major holidays. The unfortunate result is that, if we are stuffed with patients, the unlucky few on duty have an extremely difficult ordeal. This night we are getting by with the most skeleton of crews, and I understand that the day shift has even fewer numbers coming on to relieve us.

As day was breaking, all the labor rooms were gradually occupied. As quickly as a nurse took a woman back to the delivery area, another patient would be moved into the empty spot. Knowing how few of us there were to cope with the persistent onslaught of patients, knowing that there were paltry numbers of nurses coming on to face the enormity of this stressful load on Christmas morning, I watched the clock uneasily. Small bits of holiday cheer were evident. The Christmas tree by the desk twinkled with multicolored lights. Some of the nurses wore red Christmas elves' caps. We were spurred on in our efforts by thoughts of home and hearth.

Just as the small team of day shift nurses was gathering in the break room to begin morning report, a red blanket was brought up. "Resident RB," called out the transporter as she pushed a stretcher into the spot in the LICU where emergency cases are evaluated. I had been the LICU nurse this night, but the room was emptied of three laboring patients sequentially just before dawn. I was in the street clothes that I had donned in preparation for a quick exit to home. I stepped over to join the team of residents and interns who had assembled to see what this last-minute problem would portend for them.

And what a disaster awaited us. This young Latina turned out to be the victim of a tragic misunderstanding, an unfortunate set of circumstances that resulted in her baby having perished inside its mother. Blanca Ordones had been downstairs for weeks under the care of the antepartum service, being kept on bed rest for symptoms of pregnancy-induced hypertension (toxemia). Her blood pressures were slightly elevated, and there was excessive protein in her urine. The question for the medical team was whether her toxemia would remain in the moderate range or progress to the severe degree.

She also had an unusual infection in the bones of her jaw. With her blood pressures remaining stable, she was transferred up the hill to the main hospital to have a tooth extracted. Each day she had been visited by an OB resident to ensure her pregnancy status was evaluated during her stay in the "pus ward." Dr. Kazinski, our senior resident, had consulted with her counterpart on the infected ortho service, and the game plan in place was for them to notify us if Blanca had any worsening symptoms with her toxemia.

That physician in charge of the ortho unit was not there on Christmas Eve. When Blanca began to exhibit new and extremely high blood pressures, the nurses resorted to calling the officer of the day. The physician who is in that role has to respond to problems called to him or her from all over the hospital. Without coming to see Blanca, possibly with little understanding of the ravages of pregnancy-induced hypertension, and also unaware of the game plan to notify the OB service of any worsening symptoms, that doctor told the nurses to simply give our patient repetitive doses of a blood-pressure-lowering medication. Well meaning though this physician's intentions were, this was not the standard of care for toxemia patients, not by a long shot. Not only did Blanca's pressure continue to record at alarming levels, but when the nurse went to check for the baby's heartbeat at the next interval, she was unable to detect anything.

Now with us here in the LICU, the intern who accompanied Blanca from the main hospital was subdued and a little shaky. I think he was in awe of the fact that a blood pressure problem could have such a devastating effect in a young woman, resulting in the demise of her infant. Dr. Kazinski came into the room and quietly began to roam over Blanca's gel-smeared belly with the transducer of the ultrasound scanner. What she saw was confirmation of the worst. She put down the equipment. No one had yet told Blanca why she was here with us. Dr. Kazinski turned to the young mother with a solemn expression.

"I'm so sorry, Blanca. Your baby has died."

The resident put her arms around our young patient as she sobbed in shocked disbelief. A few tears slid down Jessica Kazinski's cheeks as Blanca rocked against her.

"*Ay, no-o-o,*" she wailed. "*Mi bebé!*"

I was witness to this horrendous tragedy. After a few minutes, it was decided between Jessica and me that we would move Blanca over to the isolation room to lend her some privacy while she got through the initial shock of her baby's death. Blanca would need to have her labor induced as rapidly as possible, as we suspected that she had now developed the most serious degree of toxemia, one severe enough to be the probable cause of her baby's demise, severe enough to be putting her own life at risk. I began to push the bed out of the LICU, Blanca now looking subdued and deeply distressed.

My problem was that there was no one to take care of Blanca. Ordinarily, I would hand her over to the oncoming staff of nurses. My shift was over now, yet I had known even before Blanca had come to us that there were not enough nurses to go around for all the patients currently here, and those who assuredly were on the way. How could I, knowing how sick this young woman was, take the chance that she would receive adequate care from the few overwhelmed nurses on duty?

On the other hand, my husband and children were at home waiting for me. Knowing how eager the four kids had been last evening, how they made me promise to be home as soon as possible, I felt massively torn. Bill has never been quite able to picture the demands placed on me as a nurse here, and I dreaded what I knew would be his reaction to my staying. For I'd quickly arrived at the inevitability of having to remain to care for Blanca. I do not ever remember this degree of conflict between my life with my family and my chosen work.

By the time I got Blanca to her new room and put on a blood pressure cuff for her first set of vital signs, things had already begun to deteriorate for the grieving mother. Her pressure was an astounding 220/105, and she had begun to bleed sluggishly from the vagina. Placental abruption, a classic case. Her placenta had sloughed off partly, or totally, from the wall of her uterus, leaving gaping portals for a hemorrhage. This complication of her pregnancy crisis had no doubt been the cause of her baby's death. Now, unless we could get this situation under control, she was in great peril from massive bleeding.

I began the basic interventions, all in my street clothes. Blanca's crisis was simply too much of an emergency to warrant me going to the dressing room to change back into scrubs. I called Dr. Kazinski to return, as well as the residents who were beginning their Christmas Day call. Telling them of my findings, they decided on an initial plan of care. We got two IV lines in, one to give blood, one to deliver fluids and medications. I started the magnesium sulfate infusion, meant to decrease the irritability at the junctions where her nerves connected with her muscles, thought to be the locus of toxemic seizures. Lab work was hastily drawn and sent off. I inserted an indwelling collection system into Blanca's bladder, returning a pathetic few drops of urine that looked more like blood than anything else. A quick check of her hematocrit on the unit showed a severely dropping red cell concentration. We called the blood bank to send us some blood to transfuse Blanca immediately.

Time was passing. Blanca was extremely subdued, and from her expression, I felt she knew that her body was in the midst of a fight for life. One of the residents took pity on me, as I was working as furiously as it was possible for a human to work. She slipped a patient gown over my dress, put on hours ago to attend a family holiday dinner party before my arrival at work. I ran to the phone and called home, hurriedly explaining that an emergency was keeping me on duty. I could tell that Bill was not in sympathy, but he told me to do what I felt was mandated by the situation. I had only moments to describe the reality that there was no other nurse to help this girl if I didn't stay. In good conscience, I could not leave.

It was close to noon before a nurse came to relieve me. By then, most of the care for Blanca was in place, and I had responsibility not only for her but also for three other patients brought up from the ER. All other labor rooms in use, I had the transporters simply line their stretchers along the hallway outside Blanca's room. I went to each patient in turn, admitting them right there in the corridor, checking to make sure their baby's heart rate was normal and helping the interns start their IVs and gather their histories.

At any other time, I would have been able to appeal to the charge nurse or other nursing staff to come help me. This Christmas morning, our numbers were pitiful, and nurses brushed past my room, aware that there was something tense going on. Overwhelmed themselves, they could not look me in the eye lest I work on their sense of guilt. I understood. I had been in their place too.

I wanted to rail at the clerks for sending me extra patients when I had the most critically ill person on the floor in my care. For them, it was merely a matter of numbers. All of the few nurses on duty had four patients. The clerks knew I only had the one and they felt it was simple justice that I get these new admits. It would have taken more energy than I had to convince them of the flaw in their thinking. I gave the new patients the absolute minimum of care necessary to ensure their safety and that of the babies they housed. Blanca continued to be my priority.

Finally, an angel arrived. It was Mercedes, a young, beautiful, and brainy nurse who thrives on challenging situations, remaining far calmer than I, a decade her senior. Along with all her other talents, she cares. She listened to the report of the morning's events, then took up the minute-to-minute activity involved in sustaining Blanca's life. Meanwhile, I tried quickly, and with some sense of clarity, to reconstruct the events of this Christmas morning in the chart for Mercedes and the others who would continue with the work of trying to save this young, grieving mother's life.

I left for home. It was surely not the happiest of holiday mornings for me. The kids were eager to show me all their treasures and to have me open my gifts. I was shaky, tired beyond anything in memory, and feeling unhappy that Bill found it so hard to understand my abandonment of our family in favor of a work situation. He is a decent man, and these hard feelings will pass. Looking at the beautiful and precious faces of my four children, I felt an overwhelming sense of gratitude that they are mine and that we all have a chance to share in each other's lives. For Blanca, Christmas will forever mean the memory of the loss of her beloved baby. God hold her child in an everlasting embrace and someday ease her grieving mother's heart.

Addendum: Later that Christmas Day, an emergency cesarean section was performed, a measure almost never taken when a baby is dead or when a mother is so unstable, except to save a life. Blanca had continued to bleed internally, and when her induction did not progress quickly, surgery became necessary. She struggled for days in the intensive care unit with the complications of one so close to death from her massive bleeding and severe pregnancy-related hypertension.

Julie, my dear friend from nursing school, came to tell me that Blanca had become conscious and alert enough to start wondering about the events of that Christmas Day.

"Where is my baby? Was my baby a boy or girl?"

These issues had been forgotten in the struggle to keep the young mother alive. Julie knew that I had been Blanca's primary nurse on readmission to our unit on that fateful Christmas morning and that I had a special interest in caring for bereaved parents.

Our nurse manager agreed that Julie and I could go to the morgue on a mission to help Blanca get the answers she needed. Once there, the attendant brought us the cold, so very cold body of what was a perfectly formed, beautiful little girl. We dressed the infant in a gown, wrapped her in blankets, and put on the little newborn stocking cap. We took pictures of her dressed like this, then unwrapped her and photographed her, arranged naturally lying on an infant blanket. We made footprint and handprint cards, name bracelets, and snipped a lock of dark hair for Blanca to have as mementos of her baby.

These we returned to the ICU where we found Blanca seated upright at the side of the bed, still weak and pale, breathing with some difficulty. We told her most gently that we knew she had wanted some news of her baby and that we had some small gifts for her to have as memories of her special little one. I know that I will never forget the sight of the young mother sitting there, staring hungrily at the pictures. With trembling fingers, she traced the other simple, tangible reminders of this child she had nurtured inside her but was never to meet in this life.

CHAPTER TWENTY-FOUR

"You seem to me like a lady, and I hate ladies."

January 15

I HAD A MENTALLY troubled woman as a patient tonight. As a rule, I like working with folks who come to us with a very different worldview. Caring for these colorful, sometimes very unusual people momentarily takes me out of my mundane, everyday existence. Not that I don't feel for these quirky people, for I do. The saddest experiences I had as a nursing student did not take place in the cancer units at a world-renowned research hospital, with people dying from catastrophic diseases. Rather, they occurred at a local cushy psychiatric hospital for the insurable insane.

I first saw Jana as the escort was moving her from the stretcher to her hospital bed in the hallway. She was thin to the point of appearing anorexic, except for the little pod of her pregnant belly. Also striking was her haircut. It was boyishly butch, about half an inch all around, contributing to her aura of a concentration camp victim. She was brought here by ambulance from a private hospital with an admission diagnosis of possible preterm labor and, incidentally, schizophrenia.

Jana was admitted to my assigned room. As I helped the transporter move the bed into place, I was struck by Jana's general air of being a well-kept, squeaky-clean, white middle-class young woman. I am used to taking care of pregnant patients with psych problems, but they are typically homeless, derelict, and dressed to prove it.

I was watching to see how floridly offbeat Jana's behavior might prove. Now she was cooperative, mildly interested in what we were doing, even asked and answered questions in a fairly appropriate manner. After monitoring her baby a bit, it could be seen that she wasn't even having a mild contraction. Her baby was doing fine, and we were essentially offering her nothing.

One of the junior residents, Dr. MacRae, came in. He performed an ultrasound scan to check for size, due date, and adequate amniotic fluid volume. Being able to measure a nice, comfortable amount of fluid in which the fetus can swim is one reassuring factor for an obstetrician trying to send a pregnant woman home. With plenty of cushioning fluid around the baby, there is less chance that the umbilical cord will get squished, causing a decrease or total shutdown of oxygen to the baby.

With everything looking favorable, Dr. MacRae decided that we would continue to monitor the baby for a bit while we waited for the return of Jana's lab results. He explained the plans to the patient. She nodded vaguely, and he left. Then the first hint that Jana was not tracking with us surfaced.

I started to replace the fetal monitors on her stomach. They had been disconnected for her ultrasound. She looked at me fiddling with the belts and leads and voiced her objections.

"Hey, you're not going to put those things back on me, are you?"

"Why, yes. Remember that Dr. MacRae told you we would watch your baby for a while to make sure everything is fine? Well, these things are necessary to do that."

"But I don't want them on. They hurt (they don't), and I don't like them. I don't much like being in a hospital. I find you condescending, and I'd just rather you didn't touch me."

One thing about psych patients: their internal world of thought is often quite out of control, and they tend to be on a collision course with the strange world of our reality that doesn't compute with theirs. They often have a great need to assert themselves as the ones in control of situations. Like the one woman who kept telling the nice female obstetrician to move along, that I was her doctor and she would only accept advice from me. In that case, for us to carry out her care, the resident and I had to assume the other's roles when interacting with the woman or she would not allow her much-needed treatments.

It struck me that Jana was trying to achieve some of that sense of control, as her present situation didn't seem to have any meaning for her. She appeared to be very disconnected from her pregnant state, even though she was at a point in her gestation when she had to be feeling her baby moving quite regularly. I had been nothing but respectful and gentle with Jana to this point. Rather than commenting on her rude remarks to me, I concentrated on appealing to her maternal instincts. I knew that she would want to cooperate in the interest of ensuring her baby's well-being.

I had no better luck with this strategy. One thing I have come to realize is that trying to appeal in a reasonable way to someone who exists in a separate plane of reality is worthless. You can't expect any of the more predictable responses from them when what you are asking doesn't make any sense in their peculiarly askew world. Once again, I regretted that I cannot seem to take the proper tack with these patients.

Next, Jana said that she was going to leave AMA, or against medical advice. Her familiarity with this medical-legal jargon told me that this was not her first instance of hospitalization. It was certainly her privilege. If there had been a problem with her pregnancy, like the one she had been transferred here with, the doctors would have tried to establish a legal hold on the basis of potential harm to her baby. Given the seemingly benign state of affairs, the lack of any indication that she was in premature labor, there was nothing to hold her here. It is no crime to be mentally disturbed, and this is not a jail. I looked on Jana's chart to see if the admitting clerk had noted a person to contact so that I could help her get in touch with someone to retrieve her.

"No," she stated baldly, "there's no one. I'll just leave, and I'll get home on my own."

I was glad she seemed to be referring to a known residence. Remembering her upscale dress on her admission here, I believed that she probably had a safe place to which she could return. But I tried again with my motherly concerns.

"Please," I coaxed her, "let me try to contact some friend or family member. It's 2:00 a.m., and it's the middle of winter. This neighborhood is a rough one. You could be in danger going out on these streets alone."

"You know," Jana replied in the curiously flat tone of some schizophrenics, "you are really starting to annoy me. You seem like a lady, and I hate ladies. Just bring me my clothes, and I'll get going."

So I did. She put on what was a stylish, slightly punk but well-made outfit and sailed out the door without a backward glance. She was seemingly oblivious to the stares of the nurses and doctors as she made her determined progress down the hallway. I fretted, thinking she was like a little lamb out in the dark with the howling wolves snapping at her heels.

On later reflection, it occurred to me that Jana had seemed to be getting off on thwarting my motherly concerns for her safety. She probably went right downstairs and called her baby daddy, or whoever, and rode home in style. I hoped so.

CHAPTER TWENTY-FIVE

"What did they think this was, some women's prison from a B movie?"

January 18

I N A PLACE like this where the patient clientele derives from the poorer, less politically connected neighborhoods in the community, there is a greater role for patient advocates. It shouldn't be the case that the patients we doctors and nurses care for have any less to say about their treatment in hospital than those who spring from the middle or affluent sectors of society. Inevitably, this is so. There are those I have worked with who have no ability to see that their education and training for the practice of medicine or nursing is challenging and enriching by virtue of our working with this population. Instead, these shortsighted people tend to treat our patients as a subspecies. In their minds, our patients are less able to participate in decisions about the treatment they are receiving by virtue of their inability to pay for their care or their lesser level of education. Sometimes, patients need some member of the health-care team to step forward and speak or act on their behalf when basic humanistic considerations have been neglected.

I learned this lesson early on in my practice when I was thrust, all unprepared, into a painful ethical dilemma. I had just started my employment here, working through my first weeks as an RN on the antepartum service, essentially a medical unit for women experiencing complicated pregnancies.

One morning, I was assigned to patient care in a four-bed room. I was all caught up in practicing new skills with medication administration, dealing with IV infusions, drawing blood from my diabetic patients to check their sugar levels, etc. I was also trying to get to know my four patients, three of whom spoke very little English. Lack of the ability to communicate freely was a great barrier to understanding what was going on for the many Hispanic women I was meeting. My five years of high school and college French were sadly unhelpful in this environment.

My one English-speaking patient, Annette McGowan, was a twenty-six-year-old woman experiencing her second pregnancy. In her first pregnancy, she had developed a blood clot that resulted in her hospitalization for all of that gestation. She was found to have a disorder that, under pregnancy conditions, made her susceptible to clot-making. She had been instructed to avoid any subsequent pregnancies, so, of course, there she was in my room, about fifteen weeks along and already experiencing a new clot.

In working with her, I came to feel that, despite her stated twenty-six years, she had in some sense the emotional age of an eight-year-old. She did not like being confined to bed and kept asking me to let her get up to the bathroom. I explained that she was on strict bed rest, that getting up might cause her to throw the clot in her leg to her heart or lungs. She didn't seem to find this a compelling reason to tolerate her confinement, and she kept begging me to let her out of bed.

"Ple-e-ease, please, please let me get up," she begged again and again, echoing the beseeching manner of working on my tender heart employed by my then-eight-year-old Matthew at home.

I knew better than to acquiesce to this. She tried to bargain with me throughout my work in the room, with the other three patients looking on with concerned expressions, not having any understanding of why the *enfermera* was being so heartless.

About ten thirty, an OB resident entered the room with a form in his hand and went to Annette's bed.

"Annette," he addressed her, "the team has reviewed your situation with the hematology service, and they told us you needed to have a medical termination of this pregnancy. You are at risk of developing more clots, any one of which could be fatal for you. I'm here to have you sign the consent for the procedure. We'll move you down to the GYN unit where you'll be induced."

I was listening to all this and was shocked to have the crisis for my patient introduced into a morning that had seen me struggling with a bunch of purely technical nursing skills. I, like my patient, had just entered the ethical big time. I wondered how Annette was going to react to the physician's news, given what I had assessed in her as some sort of developmental delay.

"What does that mean, that thing you said. . .*termina* . . .?" she queried hesitantly.

"It means you need to abort this pregnancy," he replied bluntly. "Understand? . . . abortion? It could mean your life to continue with this pregnancy."

She digested this for a moment.

"I want to talk to my family," she responded. "I could call my husband at his job. And my mother is coming to see me this afternoon after she gets off work."

Dr. Huitt did not miss a beat before his voice rose, and he told her in a most adamant tone, "*No!* You are an adult. You have to make this decision, and no one can do it for you! I need you to sign this consent now."

Oh dear. How many times had we been told as student nurses that we had an obligation to be patient advocates? We had all nodded our heads, had assured ourselves that we would surely step up to the plate in situations that demanded we act for the patient's good when circumstances compelled such action. Now, in this room, I was confronted with the need to do something, anything, to deal with this arrogant doctor. He was stepping all over our patient's right to request the counsel of her family in making this most serious decision. Yet I stood there, unsure of myself and what I should do to intervene in the drama playing out in front of my eyes. Obviously, Dr. Huitt was not looking for any input on my part.

I would have had to assert myself, something I knew at that moment I was unprepared to do. Annette, cowed by this medical heavyweight, took the form and signed it. With a sickening sense of defeat, I watched a moment later as the transporter came and got her. As I saw the gurney rolling down the hallway toward the gynecology unit, I was overcome with profound sadness. I realized that she was proceeding to the place where her baby would be forced to enter the world outside its mother's womb, with no chance of survival.

It was not that the procedure wouldn't take place, as I understood that the medical staff was recommending the termination in favor of potentially saving Annette's life. Rather, it was that the consent for the procedure was obtained in such an unconscionable manner. Here was the chance for me to act on my patient's behalf. I should have taken Dr. Huitt aside, explained my reservations about Annette's ability to make a reasoned decision based on her emotional immaturity. Furthermore, she had the absolute right to consult with her family if she wanted to in making such a serious decision.

The rest of the day, I was a walking wreck. I went home in terrible distress, aware of my terrible lack of courage and lack of ability to actualize the fundamental principles I was taught in school. I was confronted with my future as one who would assuredly be involved in other situations requiring me to intervene on behalf of my patients. I questioned whether I was up to the job. I wondered if I had chosen the wrong career, handicapped as I seemed to be by a lack of confidence in myself, unsure of when I needed to intervene, and how to intervene.

That night, I had a serious come-to-Jesus meeting with myself. I realized that I had better be prepared in future for just such drama as had been played out in that hospital room that morning. I had to be prepared to put aside my lifelong desire to avoid conflict and put my patient's needs above my own comfort zone. I must have my priorities straight and realize that some of my interventions as a nurse went beyond the simple mastering of tasks and skills. Only then could I hope to be a success in this chosen career. That was a game-changing talk I had with myself. My newfound understanding of my role as a patient advocate has stood me in good stead since that day, though inevitably there have been some touchy situations. Not every ethical dilemma has a cookie-cutter solution.

So back to the events of this morning. At 7:00 a.m., I was assigned to work in the isolation labor room. I had already completed eight hours in another area. A slight woman was just being moved over from a stretcher onto a bed when I entered this private room. Berthe Nunez had come to us from the antepartum service one floor below. She had to be isolated because she had tested positive for parasites, a not-too-uncommon finding in our patients who come here from below the border or who live in some of our less-tidy housing.

Berthe was coming to Labor and Delivery because she had started bleeding again. She had been diagnosed as having a complete placenta previa, a case of the placenta having implanted smack dab over the cervix. In such a case, she would be delivered by cesarean section when her baby was mature enough to live comfortably on the outside. Here in the hospital for weeks now, she had been shuttled back and forth between the two units. Repeatedy, she would start to experience contractions and then would begin bleeding. We would get her premature labor under control, then send her downstairs where her uterus would remain quiet for a while before the next episode of uterine cramping would begin.

If Mrs. Nunez had been at term in her pregnancy, she would have had a cesarean section by now. Her baby was not mature enough to do well independently of the womb, and we were trying to buy the infant a few precious weeks in which to prepare its lungs for life on the outside. Actually, as she came to me on this morning, she was entering into that borderline window of time when each day might find her baby testing positive for lung maturity. In some instances, the decision to operate would be taken out of our hands. With a malpositioned placenta, frank and voluminous bleeding would dictate emergency surgery whether the baby was ready to make its exit.

Berthe Nunez was a spunky, tiny Latina with Indian-looking features. She told me she was from Honduras. I looked, and there were just small streaks of bright red blood on the pad she was keeping between her legs. She had no IV line in place. On the fetal monitor that also notes contractions, I could see only isolated but fairly significant-looking activity.

Berthe started off by telling me she absolutely refused to have us start that medicine to stop labor. She knew the ropes by now, having on numerous occasions received the drug magnesium sulfate to quiet her uterine contractions. She'd been in bed for weeks now, unable to get up and walk around even once. When she'd been with us for her various bouts of premature labor, sometimes for days at a time, we had withheld food and drink except for ice chips. She was not allowed to eat on the chance that the medication would fail, then uterine contractions would strengthen and cause the cervix to open up and cause massive bleeding, thus precipitating emergency surgery. The magnesium sulfate given to this slight person had made her dizzy. It also has a burning effect as it goes through the blood vessels. Berthe was angry at the very thought of having this whole distressing process begun again.

I told her that, at the very least, we would have to restart her IV and draw some lab work. She informed me that less than one hour ago, she had many tubes of blood withdrawn while on the antepartum unit. With this information in mind, I went out of the isolation room to find an intern to start Berthe's IV.

Dr. Bellingham responded. A young man with whom I haven't had much interaction, he struck me as the sort who was already well advanced in his ego development. After he had gotten Mrs. Nunez's IV line started, he went about gathering an impressive array of different-colored specimen tubes. I explained to him that Mrs. Nunez had already had a whole panel of lab work drawn not one hour ago. Could he wait a minute while I verified with the resident that it was OK to check the computer for her current hematocrit? We could also see what other labs had been drawn and maybe save the patient being doubly stuck for the same tests.

I found Dr. Medavoy, the junior resident who was managing the care of my patient, sipping coffee in the kitchen. I told her the story about the intern waiting to draw oodles of blood, even though Mrs. Nunez had informed me that she'd just had the same done downstairs.

"Well, I don't care what the patient says!" she exclaimed irritably. I gave this frowzy-haired, serious-minded woman my most affronted look. I could not stomach such a display of arrogance. I proceeded in a frosty voice:

"I thought we could at least check the computer to see what labs were already drawn before sticking this woman unnecessarily." Medavoy thought about this for a moment.

"OK, just have the intern check the results, and we can go from there," she conceded.

Back in the isolation room, I was met by the sight of Dr. Bellingham calmly drawing tube after tube of blood from our patient's arm, not even sure what was needed. Since it was done now, I let this pass. He didn't seem like the type who could have his sense of fairness appealed to.

In came Dr. Medavoy next, and seeing the isolated contractions on the fetal monitor, she wrote the order for the mag sulfate. Mrs. Nunez, who had been watching the actions of the resident while she looked at the monitor and then began to write into the chart, knew instantly what was afoot. Right away, in fiery Spanish, she cried, "No!" She went on to tell us that she would rip out her IV line if we came near her with that stuff. Dr. Medavoy, unused to this kind of adamant objection to her treatment plans, went out and got the senior resident.

This hunt produced a physician who to this point had always been a favorite of mine. Vanessa Cordova was beautiful, with flawless ivory skin that contrasted dramatically with her silky, inky-black hair. In my dealings with her to date, she had displayed intelligence, a warm sense of humor, and spoke the prettiest Spanish. This morning, she came in and tried to explain very firmly to Mrs. Nunez that we had no choice. Bleeding was starting again because she was in premature labor, and her baby was judged too young to come yet.

Dr. Cordova argued persuasively, but the little woman remained unconvinced and staunchly refused the medicine. Soon, Dr. Cordova became irritated and told Berthe that she was jeopardizing her infant, that she couldn't understand her attitude. She castigated the young mother, telling her that she cared more for the fate of this baby than Berthe did. Then she got tough. If necessary, we could get a court order and give the medicine despite the patient's objection. Her baby was viable, and the baby's needs superseded the mother's at this moment.

Vanessa wasn't bluffing. She went out of the room and called the chief of OB medicine to get his help in obtaining a court order. In the meantime, Dr. Cordova came back in and told Berthe we could try an amniocentesis, hoping that the results would show fetal lung maturity. Then she would not have to receive the magnesium sulfate and could go ahead and be delivered by cesarean section. By now, though, it was full-blown war. Berthe refused this test as well. Drs. Medavoy and Cordova threw up their hands in disgust and left. My patient began to sob, and I felt someone had better take a different tack.

I stroked her head, and in a sympathetic voice with my best broken Spanish, I talked to her.

"Señora, I know this is a difficult time for you. You've had to be in the hospital many long weeks, away from your other three little ones. I know that you are a good mother. You have had to put up with many uncomfortable things. I don't for a minute think that you are a bad person. On the contrary, you are very brave and have come so far. I know that you want the best for your baby. I think you are simply tired and frustrated."

Berthe sobbed harder, letting out all her despair and feelings of being victimized by life. When she'd gotten that all out, I talked to her again, calmly, about the amniocentesis. I explained that they wouldn't do this procedure unless they found a safe spot, and then there was hope for an answer to all her problems. She agreed, sniffling and reluctant.

I went out of the room to find a little circle of residents, deep in their discussion of the plan for the court order. They were talking about strapping Berthe down with hard leather restraints and giving her the mag sulfate in her IV line. What did they think this was, some women's prison from a B movie? They would have had to get someone else to participate in this plan because my conscience would not allow me to play this kind of hardball. I tapped Dr. Cordova on the shoulder and told her about Berthe's change of heart about having the amnio.

Vanessa joked about this a bit. "See, it's the old story of the bad cop and the good cop. I go in and rough the patient up first. Then the nice nurse comes in and sweet-talks her into doing what we wanted all along."

I was frankly sickened by all of this. Surely most of this mess could have been avoided if just one physician had given a hint that it was possible to see things from Berthe Nunez's point of view. After all the hard words and threats, it took less than five minutes of listening, talking, and touching to obtain the patient's agreement to a plan she detested but which might buy her baby the needed time.

I called the medical social worker, Marian Cannell, and asked her to come and talk to our patient. I felt she needed a few more people to whom she could look for emotional support. When Mrs. Cannell had spent some time with Berthe, she shared with me more of the spunky young woman's story, which helped to explain today's behavior. Berthe had been compelled to leave her three children in the care of their ailing grandmother. Her husband had recently abandoned her, too overwhelmed by the pressure to house and feed his growing family. More than her personal discomfort, Berthe Nunez was terribly worried about the plight of her family at home.

Unfortunately, the preliminary results of the amniocentesis performed by Dr. Medavoy indicated continuing fetal lung immaturity. Berthe's baby needed to stay inside her for a while longer. I went back to see if she would now consent to a trial of the magnesium sulfate. Maybe it would work at a lower dosage this time. Maybe she would not be so much affected by it. She made a face at the news but agreed to receive the medicine.

I went home shortly after this. My head was full of the morning's events. I guess we all need to be reminded from time to time that we are not simply treating diseases. We are treating people with problems, not all of them of a physical nature. In this place, seeing the person as a total package is sometimes our last priority. Sometimes necessarily so, when a life hangs in the balance and time is critical. If I ever wonder about the worth of my nursing care for patients, experiences like mine today with Mrs. Nunez reconfirm for me the one great imperative—to remind those who tend to forget that a living, breathing human being so much like ourselves is the object of our ministrations.

CHAPTER TWENTY-SIX

"Everyone now knew that this was not chest pain, per se, but heartache of an entirely different sort."

January 30

TONIGHT WE RECEIVED a call from the emergency room to alert us that a patient was being transported to us, having presented to them with a history of an episode of shortness of breath and chest pain. She was coming to us for evaluation of a possible heart problem. I told Dr. Cordova, the senior resident, who made a face. We certainly have a fair number of cardiac patients, the pregnant sort. The trouble is that defining a heart ailment is not within the scope of the obstetrical resident. We have to negotiate getting a cardiac consultant to come down the hill from the main hospital in the middle of the night, and this is a struggle.

Just then they rolled Graciela Monteverde in through the entrance doors on a stretcher, still in street clothes. Apparently, she had been convincing enough about her chest pain to make the ER resident worry about a heart attack in progress, strange enough in a woman in her midtwenties. Mr. Monteverde, a young, good-looking Latino, was hanging on to his wife for dear life as they wheeled her toward us.

Both husband and wife appeared extremely agitated. My job was detaching the mister from his death grip on his spouse, giving him some reassurance, and getting him out to the waiting area so we could begin to assess his wife's problems. He was wild-eyed and gesturing dramatically.

"I want to stay with my wife and baby. No one is going to tell me to get out!" he bellowed.

That kind of talk will get people here on the phone to security, and those single-minded and self-important fellows would quickly muscle the young husband out. I got his attention, somehow, and drew him a few paces away from the crowded desk where various staff had assembled to watch this drama. No one wanted to keep him in the dark, I explained calmly. We needed a bit of time to start things with his wife. He was blubbery, and I suppose that I should have suspected drinking. I thought instead that he was simply a very emotional, caring husband, concerned that his wife was in the throes of a life-threatening problem.

The entire Monteverde family seemed to be assembled outside the double doors to the unit. They were calm and eager to get this young man under control so as not to cause trouble. I obtained his agreement to wait one hour, to go get some coffee downstairs. I promised to come and get him when we had completed his wife's admission, or if there was any serious problem.

Back in the admitting room, nurses were helping Graciela Monteverde out of her clothes. I explained to her that her husband was outside, most concerned, and that he could visit a bit later. I was surprised by her reaction to this news.

"Oh, that's OK." She shrugged fatalistically. "He's just been drinking lots."

"I see," said Vanessa Cordova in a knowing voice, having at that moment arrived to check up on the "cardiac patient."

"He's been drinking a lot," the senior resident continued. "Were you two perhaps having a family argument when your chest pain came on?"

"Yes, that was very much the case," young Mrs. Monteverde replied. She looked emotionally stressed but otherwise appeared to be a completely healthy pregnant woman. The cardiac monitor, now tracing her heart rhythm, showed a normal pattern of activity. We could not ignore the reason for her admission, however, and proceeded with the minimum cardiac workup. This meant drawing arterial blood gases, having a chest film done, and a twelve-lead EKG.

Everyone now knew that this was not chest pain, per se, but heartache of an entirely different sort. Dr. Cordova told Mrs. Monteverde, not unkindly, that the next time she should report back pain, or a migraine, sparing her the painful stick required for the blood gases. Better yet, she should think about getting into a women's support group for domestic troubles.

At this point, I happened to go out to the desk and found to my dismay that the husband was back again. Ruth, the clerk, had very unwisely called him in to take charge of his wife's modest bundle of clothing. He refused to leave again and was taking this opportunity to get dramatic, shouting his demand to see his wife and telling Ruth she was stupid, a tactical error if I ever saw one. Ruth is one powerful lady.

Again, I engaged him in conversation, walking him down the corridor, telling him that his wife was doing very well, that he should be able to visit her very soon, his baby was fine, etcetera. By now we were back down the hall at the doors to the unit. I turned him over to his family who appeared to be long-suffering individuals, very eager to please and avoid any conflagration.

He said pathetically, "I just want to tell her I'm sorry now."

This scene was all very sad. He is such a young man and seemingly already a chronic alcoholic. Very likely he repeats this cycle of drinking, arguing, abuse, remorse, and then abject apologies. There are other small children at home, and now another one coming. We'll have the social worker see Graciela in the morning, but what real good that will do until this young wife can put her foot down, I don't know. It is a sad fact that an alarmingly high percentage of pregnant women are the victims of spousal abuse while their babies are growing inside.

These Latinas for whom we care have all the more customary family afflictions of drugs, alcohol, poverty, partner abuse, etc. Further, they are typically immigrants, often don't speak the language, and have fears about seeking help through the normal avenues—police intervention, social support systems—and must fight the machismo factor. Sometimes I despair that it is at all possible to solve their difficulties, given the enormity of the stones in their pathway. How much more understandable was Graciela Monteverde's Band-Aid-like solution this night. At least she seems to have a caring family. Hopefully, they will intervene before anything more serious transpires.

CHAPTER TWENTY-SEVEN

"Don't worry. She's just all tuckered out."

February 3

I GOT A TAD passive-aggressive again, one of my worst character faults and the one I least like to acknowledge in myself. We had a fairly quiet weekend. These three consecutive twelve-hour shifts are such a challenge for me. I seem to average about five hours of suboptimal sleep between nights on duty. When Monday noon comes, I usually feel as if I have scaled some steep summit. Or been hit by a bus.

We had a very light census Saturday, and I loafed around most of the time, chatting with everyone and having a great time. I didn't feel one bit guilty because Friday I was in charge, and had low staff numbers and an endless flood of patients. I had to juggle the nurses all night, trying to concentrate them where the need was greatest and get everyone a chance to have some break. I am making progress in managing the role of team leader but don't believe I will ever assume the assignment with total confidence.

Kicking back was no problem, but by Sunday night I was feeling the need to work a bit harder to earn my nickel. My assignment, however, was babysitting a woman in the isolation room who had come in complaining of respiratory distress. She was finally, after all of us spent hours putting our high-powered minds to the problem, diagnosed as having the common cold. This put her head and shoulders, health-wise, over 90 percent of the doctors and nurses here. We have had a nasty bug circulating among ourselves for a few weeks. This is classic doctor/nurse behavior, coming to work when we are sick.

The girl with the cold went home with her boyfriend. I took an unusual and extensive break, then started looking around for something more meaningful to do. The only place on the floor that was significantly busy was the labor area. I asked my friend Cheryl, who had worked especially hard the first four hours, if she wanted to trade with me. She gratefully switched roles, as she was one of those trying to fight off the virus that was impacting numbers of our staff. In assuming her assignment, I realized how much better it was for me to be working productively. I had a busy time of it the next four hours, getting several women through their labor and off to delivery, then helping work up the new admits who came to replace them. All the labor rooms were gradually filling up by daybreak.

When the day shift arrived, Cheryl and I asked to work the last four hours together in mother-baby assessment. Every once in a while, it is a pleasure to work in this suite of rooms where the newly delivered moms and babies are brought for a brief recovery period. We watch both for about an hour to see that they have survived the rigors of birth. We check the baby from head to toe, give a shot of vitamin K to prevent any blood-clotting problems, and arrange for the first feeding. We clean mom up a bit and pay special attention to the amount of her bleeding. If dad or other family members are available, we arrange for a visit to allow for the new family unit to begin bonding.

We try to support the inexperienced mothers through their first attempt at breastfeeding. If for some reason the mother elects not to nurse her infant, or we receive a lone baby from a C-section case, we sometimes have the pleasure of giving the little one its first feeding. You cannot miss the utter bliss these eager newborns display when they get their first taste of milk. Ahhh.

I was looking forward to working in mother-baby assessment this morning, as it had been an age since the charge nurse assigned me to these rooms. This area is sometimes laughingly called mother-boring by nurses who look upon this part of their work here as pretty tame. They are accustomed to taking care of multiples of laboring women with multiples of pregnancy problems, or working in delivery and surgery, or recovering challenging postpartum or surgical patients. The issue I see with this assignment is not that it is boring, although occasionally it can be. The difficulty arises when the delivery area is hopping and the nurses begin to bring batches of mother-baby couplets here in a very short period. The staff working in this tiny two-room area can be completely bombed.

One could not have described this area as boring the morning that a woman went into cardiac arrest in here. She was admitted after a forceps delivery and had been noted to be perfectly stable. The LVN who took her first blood pressure and pulse did not think the woman looked as alert as she should. She summoned a junior resident who, after taking a look at the patient, informed Marissa, "Don't worry, she's just all tuckered out." Boy, was she tuckered out. Dr. Kwon had barely exited the room when Marissa had to call the code blue.

There was no way at that moment for anyone to understand why a healthy young woman should suddenly arrest like that. The staff went about trying to revive her, dragging the heavy-duty emergency equipment into this small congested room. Among the three or four stretchers occupied by mothers and their infants a raft of physicians swarmed, trying to save the young woman's life, so inexplicably threatened. Soon, nurses were passing newborn babies over the bed, while others continued advanced CPR on the increasingly unresponsive mother.

It is so sad to relate that, in spite of all efforts, this young woman slipped away. On autopsy, they found a massive internal hemorrhage. Somehow, in the application of forceps, perhaps, or the sheer pressure on tissues in a forceful delivery, a critical blood vessel was torn. Occurring within a compartment of her body, no sign of such bleeding was apparent to her caretakers. When she had bled enough, about the time she was admitted to mother-baby assessment, she began to lose consciousness. She was essentially gone before there was time to search for reasons for this incredible turn of events. It is shocking and dismaying to realize how many serious problems in obstetrics are related to bleeding.

Back to this morning's events, Cheryl and I had barely gotten situated when the labor rooms disgorged a sudden outpouring of patients to the delivery area. Soon, they were bringing us mother and baby twosomes faster than we could deliver their care. Before the morning was two hours gone, about twelve women delivered. We also received some solo infants whose mothers had had cesarean sections. The labor rooms were now sparsely populated.

Fortunately, there was an abundance of nurses and scrub techs to cope with the heavy business in delivery. They had additional assistance from four nurse orientees and their instructor. Cheryl and I were absorbing the impact of multiples of patients at once. We were soon treading water to keep up.

In my travels to get supplies or obtain medications, I happened to encounter various nurses sauntering about, apparently with no mission. A group was chatting in the charge nurse office, some were perusing the schedule, and some were making beds in the hallway. My ire rose because no place was busy like ours. It seemed to me that an effort was being made to avoid our end of town. It also might have been a factor that Cheryl and I were still those not-so-well-known night shift nurses and were not yet bonded with these rather aloof day folks.

As it got closer to noon, mother-baby assessment was still jammed with patients. There were some mothers with babes in arms who were parked in the corridor waiting for their chance to come to us. There was another line on the opposite side of the hallway, discharged mother-baby couplets waiting for the transporters to get to them for their journey up to their rooms on the postpartum units. No one had come to either help with this situation or relieve us to have a bit of a respite. When it's crazy-busy everywhere, breaks are forgotten. What I found difficult to stomach was the obliviousness of these nurses to the enormous patient load Cheryl and I were struggling to manage.

I approached the day charge nurse. Opting for a light tone, I said, "Izzy, I've made a quick survey. There are four patients in labor, five deliveries in progress, and we are still stuffed with mothers and babies. Couldn't you mobilize some of these folks standing around and tell them not to be afraid to 'come on down'?"

A minute later, Izzy showed up alone, and now bucking for a martyr's crown, I asked her to take over for the LVN working with patients in the other half of our suite next door. No one else showed up, and I continued to feed my feelings of resentment. One nurse, Georgette, finally showed up, not to help but to harass Izzy about some time off she was requesting. Izzy listened with half an ear while she worked over a newly delivered mom. She broke into Georgette's arm-twisting to ask her to start taking patients waiting in the hallway upstairs so as to make room for the discharged mother-baby couplets we were producing.

Now if some nurses dislike working in mother-baby recovery, they *really* loathe transporting. Georgette flounced out but soon returned with a sidekick. They were actually planning to take up one mother-baby duo together, a nice touch if it's not too busy. I blew up on the spot. "You know, instead of the two of you taking up one patient, do you suppose one of you could stay here and help Izzy? That might allow Cheryl and me to sit down for a big, fat five minutes before we go home?"

"Oh my god!" Georgette exclaimed in an affronted tone, and I knew that I had offended her. Izzy responded apologetically that she had no idea we had gone without even a short break. I had to justify my uncharacteristic display of temper, and things went downhill from there.

"I understand that, Izzy. I'm not upset with you. But there are quite a few people standing around schmoozing, checking the schedule, B-S-ing. That's fine when things are slow, but obviously, there's a lot going on here. It's impossible to miss this barrage of ours, but there seem to be quite a number of nurses who are avoiding this end of town. I think they need to get involved."

Well, that tore it. They sent us to go sit down. Cheryl was near hysterics, reenacting the affronted look on the faces of those nurses unfortunate enough to stray into my line of fire. I felt instantly contrite, not that I had asked for help, but that I had to lose my temper to get it. How much better to have gone out and buttonholed the park saunterers and put it to them nicely that we needed some assistance. I fear I'll not be getting Georgette's or Lynda's nomination for Nurse of the Year. Whoops. Once again, I was being a smart-ass.

CHAPTER
TWENTY-EIGHT

"She sounded sort of deep-down, viscerally hurting, as if nothing could assuage her pain . . ."

February 21

I AM BACK TO work after ten nights off, a mini vacation made possible by having worked quite a few holidays over the last year. Merilee told me I needed to take some time off to clear the books of this excess banked time that was owed me. I was delighted to oblige.

One of my days off was spent in class. To renew my license to practice nursing, I must complete thirty hours of education every two years. I enrolled in a class here at the Med Center that had as its content the issue of child abuse–physical, emotional, and sexual. The presenters were the psychiatrist and nurse practitioner who pretty much initiated this city's first comprehensive program to attempt to deal with this tragic problem.

It was an excellent presentation but naturally got into some areas that would be disturbing to the most hard-boiled person. Most gruesome was a long slide show of the physical signs of abuse. This portion of the morning was designed to help health-care professionals identify and separate abusive situations from the common accidents and mishaps to which kids are subject.

There was an endless catalog of the different ways we humans devise to wreak our unhappiness on vulnerable innocents. This inventory of shame was flashed up on the screen, each accompanied by a brief explanation delivered in a studiously dull monotone, as if to rob the already incomprehensible horror of any suggestion that the producers of the film were injecting their bias into the issue. Ghastly.

Almost every slide was the occasion for a swift, collective intake of breath as about two hundred nurses, social and mental-health workers watched the parade of atrocities–cigarette burns, scalding, whipping, cutting–of helpless young children. I didn't seem to be reacting too much. I purposefully halted my impulse to respond in an emotional way to every display of abuse. I had not been thinking realistically about the possible content of this day's class when I signed up for it. If I let myself feel, I wondered if I could get through the whole day.

Later in the afternoon, there were visitors–two fathers and one mother– who had molested their children. There was another mother of a child victim who was, in turn, herself an incest victim. These were very humble, contrite people who were in therapy. As members of a self-help group, they had come here as part of their personal expiation. After these visitors left, having been astonishingly frank about the circumstances of their personal tragedy, some participants in the workshop got up and expressed profound anger at these perpetrators. While they were present, however, the comments from the audience had been virtually all filled with compassion.

Not me. Not angry, that is. I felt sort of numb by this time. Later that night, it all finally struck home. An all-encompassing exhaustion engulfed me. That kind of window on some of the most miserable people in existence was more disturbing to me than I had allowed myself to realize.

One message driven home to all of the professionals in attendance was how much responsibility we bear for reporting suspected abuse. It's the law, for one thing, affecting a variety of health-care providers. In Labor and Delivery, we often overlook this issue, working as we do with couples in the extremis of the childbearing experience. We think of abuse as being something that is picked up in an emergency room or clinic setting, or in school. It is a sad fact, though, that abusive situations often occur when one family member is seen as particularly vulnerable. A pregnant woman, feeling especially emotional and dependent during the period of her baby's gestation, is all too frequently the scapegoat for unhappy husbands or lovers.

Another abuse issue that is coming to the forefront is the problem of the drug-addicted mother. Most of our patients are immigrant women from various Third World cultures. They are the least likely to take drugs, including alcohol. However, mixed in with all these women are second-generation

Chicanas, teenage runaways, and working class poor. Among this group are a significant number of substance abusers. A pregnant woman who continues to do drugs could arguably be characterized as a child abuser–the victim, her unborn and helpless child. The question of whether drug use in pregnancy is indeed child abuse gets into the very muddied waters of just what are the rights and protections of an unborn child. Can a woman be quarantined and forced to detox when it is known that she is harming her baby in utero? In our free society, we have not come to terms with this issue, even realizing the painful price that baby will pay, once born.

All this pondering of abuse problems reminds me of a deeply troubling experience I had here several years ago. I had come to work at eleven at night and had been given an assignment in a typically busy labor room. There was an older-looking Hispanic woman in the first bed, virtually wailing continuously. This behavior rapidly set my nerves on edge.

What report I got from the nurse going home gave me to understand that this fortyish woman was delivering for the first time and was uncooperative, inconsolable, and a general pain in the butt. I tried asking her a few questions– would she like some pain medication, for instance–but she didn't even acknowledge my voice. She seemed oblivious to anyone's presence around her and continued her eerie wailing. I left her side to take care of the hundred tasks demanding my attention in the disheveled and very active labor room.

As the night progressed, her behavior tickled my conscience. She was not just crying with her contractions. She sounded sort of deep-down viscerally hurting, as if nothing could assuage her pain, whatever its source. When the night OB resident came through my room to get report on the patients she would be handling, the junior resident accompanying her described my patient as "a real troll, totally uncooperative."

With a nagging feeling that something vital had been overlooked in assessing this woman's strange behavior, I found a spare moment and started paging through her chart, looking for some clue, maybe, in her prenatal record. It was with a great sense of dismay that I found this entry:

"Forty-five-year-old primipara (woman experiencing first-time birth), borderline mental retardation, impregnated while living at home with an elderly father."

Informed by this understanding, when anyone approached my patient, I was adamant in demanding that they not dismiss her as simply an irritating screamer. I explained the circumstances when necessary, eliciting a hushed sort of wide-eyed reaction that prompted a greater degree of gentleness in performing procedures. At least now we could understand the disturbing sounds this woman was making.

I never managed to penetrate the barrier this poor woman placed against me as her caregiver, no matter how solicitous I was. That saddened me a little because I would have wanted her to find some little shred of trust that these strangers surrounding her were not going to do her harm in this difficult moment. But I could understand her inability to place trust in a world that had brought her to this time and place.

CHAPTER TWENTY-NINE

". . .it feels like the floor is being staffed by two armed camps."

March 18

WE HAD A wild night, simply because so many women showed up on our doorstep who had to deliver via cesarean section. My perspective on this night was from the labor room. I was camped out in the B room, the room every nurse here hopes to avoid because it has so little space. When there are four beds in here, there is simply no room to maneuver. Some nights I feel like ripping the door off its hinges because I can't get to either the sink or linen hamper when it is open. Yet with the door closed, the room becomes unbearably claustrophobic.

Inexplicably, this is one of the two most heavily and consistently used rooms. Historically, it was decided that it was better to have four patients crammed in here as opposed to spacing out the laboring women in other available rooms. Logistically, it means less work for the physicians riding herd on these high-risk moms. With our chronic shortage of nurses, this crowded arrangement helps with staffing the labor rooms. I would venture to speculate that if one interviewed the many nurses who have come and gone, a sizable number would state that their reason for leaving was one-too-many shifts in the B labor room.

During this night's tour in the B room, three patients were produced who needed cesarean sections. Eventually, seven patients culled from the population of twenty-nine laboring women required operative deliveries, so my room was surely making its contribution. With only two RNs and two scrub technicians to run the delivery area, seven cesarean sections between midnight and 7:00 a.m. made for a phenomenal production of work. At times during the night when an emergency arose, there were two surgeries going on simultaneously. The four folks comprising the nursing delivery team were all absorbed, leaving hapless interns and medical students to attend the routine deliveries without any nursing assistance. And we had a fierce number of vaginal births, along with all the operative procedures.

Most babies will be born successfully without a nurse to assist the physician. However, with so many of our patients being in the high-risk category, it is not a good idea at all to have one person managing these births. Sometimes the mother is threatening to spit her baby out in the bed before she can be moved onto the delivery table. Sometimes the practitioner is not totally familiar with operating the equipment, or familiar with the location of instruments or supplies. Sometimes what was expected to be a routine birth develops into a big emergency. In such cases, the doctor in training desperately needs that assistant who can summon the appropriate help from a more experienced resident.

Those last few minutes before birth and the immediate time afterward are perhaps the most crucial of moments. The stress for the mother and baby is great. Likewise for the inexperienced physician, the birth event can be fraught with anxiety. We are a sought-after site for residency programs around the country that send their young doctors here to obtain a rich and concentrated experience in assisting with birth. Showing up to train with us, these "rotating" interns love the wealth of opportunity to deliver babies. They loathe the continual lack of sufficient assistive staff in the delivery rooms. I feel bad about this but realize that until this place can attract and retain more nurses, it will continue to be the reality.

No matter what is going on in the birth rooms, you would not get a scintilla of sympathy or cooperation from the resident staff when it comes to delaying an impending cesarean section, even a nonemergent one. Such determination to drive the surgical lineup is the result of the terrible shellacking in store for the unlucky senior resident who turns over to the next team any patients who should have been cut during the night. I have seen teams stay over after the end of a brutal call to do a C-section they knew should have been done during the night to avoid getting skewered by their successors.

Working at night, we seem always to be doing a bustling business in surgeries. That's human nature, I suppose. A resident might procrastinate, take a wait-and-see attitude with a case at noon, hoping the woman will progress to vaginal delivery. But with 8:00 a.m. pass-on rounds staring him or her in the face, that same senior resident cannot afford to dillydally.

Back to my night in the B room, I admitted three women who had had two to three cesarean sections in their past. Anytime a woman has had this history of operative deliveries, the chances of her needing another increase. In this institution, we are in the forefront of offering women the chance to try to deliver vaginally after having had surgery for a wide range of obstetrical indications.

We are able to offer this possibility, as most small community hospitals cannot, because we have the requisite backup in case anything untoward was to take place. Ideally, there should be obstetricians, anesthesiologists, nurses, and pediatricians in place if needed to respond urgently. Unlike our program that can provide such an array of staff when an emergency occurs, small hospitals have to make hurried phone calls to assemble the essential personnel. The minutes ticking by in an obstetrical crisis while crucial staff gathers from home or office are maddening for patients and family standing by helplessly.

When research was begun to explore the safety and efficacy of vaginal birth after a previous C-section, we participated in these multisite studies and went about recruiting patients for this effort. Many women, after being informed of the benefits and risks, opted to attempt the vaginal delivery. With a surprising degree of regularity, these women went ahead and proceeded to normal delivery, much to the mother's delight, chagrin, etc., and the senior resident's equal satisfaction. However, anytime there was a reason that a woman could not achieve a vaginal delivery in previous pregnancies, we are on alert to see if she will make it through what we call "trial of labor."

All of my previous C-section mamas were getting their trials of labor and were getting nowhere in the process. After some hours being stimulated with the drug Pitocin to produce adequate labor without any progress, each in turn had to be prepared for surgery. These were not emergencies, per se, rather patients who needed their surgery completed before 8:00 a.m. pass-on rounds.

Before I went home yesterday, I had seen Elena Rodermann, the senior resident, start off her call by seeking out those patients she felt were potential surgical candidates. I remembered her discussing various cases with her team of young residents right after the previous crew of docs departed. Elena has a reputation for cutting a lot. In fairness to her, I think she exercises safe, conservative, and knowledgeable expertise in deciding who needs an operative delivery. If she errs once in a while, it is in favor of the most prudent and beneficial outcome for mother and baby. I love that.

Now as I see her some twenty hours later, she is ragged and short-tempered. Anyone would be who was faced with so many prospective surgeries, knowing that any of our other labor patients could go sour and have to be "crashed." Her thin, expressive face was a mask of weariness as she toured each labor room and found inescapable problems in many of them.

The two nurses working in delivery were faultless in getting these surgeries going. Caroline, the delivery area team leader for tonight, is a tireless worker and one of the most skilled and experienced obstetrical nurses we have on staff. Her problem was that the small number of personnel allotted to her this night was simply inadequate to cover the avalanche of births occurring. At times, she and her staff were caught in problematic vaginal deliveries but were being pressured to "come get the next section on the table."

These nurses were repeatedly called out of rooms where births were in progress, thus abandoning their patients. Such demand meant leaving interns and medical students without assistance. The departure of their nurse bred understandable resentment in these hardworking, sometimes quite inexperienced young men and women. Why were they left alone at such a critical moment? They knew nothing of the continual pressure their nurse was under to satisfy the priorities of the resident staff to clear the surgeries out by 8:00 a.m. God, no one feels like a success under these circumstances, no matter how supremely hard he or she is working. Instead, it feels like the floor is being staffed by two armed camps.

At about 4:00 a.m., Caroline was bringing her latest postoperative patient, along with the anesthesiologist, into the recovery room directly across from my labor room. Before she had even given her report to Janis, the recovery room nurse, Elena was there wanting to know when Caroline could get the next surgery going. This candidate would be my third and last patient to need a C-section, and the sixth surgery of the night.

Caroline sagged and said, "Oh, have mercy. I need fifteen minutes to sit down, eat, and run to the bathroom." Elena made a ferocious face as if Caroline was asking for the unheard of. She exclaimed in a bitter voice, "Look, we've been up twenty-four hours and we just have to keep on going. I want this woman on the table by four thirty, and not one minute later!" And she returned exactly twenty minutes later to hound Caroline, who was already in my room to pick up the next woman for surgery.

I felt so bad. First, this was not an emergency situation. Second, that two women, both so very hardworking, intelligent, and professional, could be at odds with each other instead of admiring and encouraging each other for their Herculean efforts.

How often this scenario is played out here, with medicine waging a war—sometimes hot, sometimes cold—with nursing. Here was a perfect example in that Caroline had been doing a fantastic job, one that I am sure could be equaled by very few nurses except maybe some in a combat arena. Yet far from getting any strokes for her efforts, she was getting only guff from the obstetrical resident. No matter how hard she worked, she could only end up feeling defeated. Elena Rodermann was acting as if only her constant snapping at Caroline's heels would force her to get the patients onto the operating table. In reality, the nurse had already managed to accomplish so much under trying circumstances. And they wonder why nurses continue to leave service here the way they so consistently do.

Because this unsatisfactory situation repeats itself so frequently, I asked Merilee, our charge nurse, if this issue could be brought up for discussion at the monthly perinatal department meeting. The chief of perinatal medicine is there, as well as Janelle Blankenship, our nurse manager, the chief of OB anesthesia, and other potentates. Surely all these intelligent people could reach a better understanding of the respective challenges facing the nurses, the obstetrical house staff, and the anesthesiology residents so that everyone could hope to win. As things stand, ill will is the result of the nagging tensions existing between the three groups. Whether they want to admit it, medicine has a role to play in the persistent inability of this unit to retain nursing staff. Tonight's events are a graphic example of the problem.

It is completely unnecessary that we view each other as adversaries of some sort. We are all involved in the same effort, doing difficult work under difficult circumstances. The medical staff is here to obtain education and training from a nationally recognized and stellar physician faculty. The agonies they sometimes endure will later pay off in rewarding careers and handsome salaries. For the nurses, while the pay is not meager, it isn't lavish. What keeps us here has more to do with the challenge of the work and the satisfaction of taking care of a colorful patient population that genuinely needs our care.

But we are not here to be abused by anyone. What I ask myself again and again is why these challenges don't cause us to bond with each other, instead of driving a wedge between us? I suspect that the answer lies in that dismal realm of human behavior wherein one group in a perceived power position, under an excruciating load of stress, has to find some more vulnerable target for the offloading of its tension.

CHAPTER THIRTY

". . .it would have turned my face magenta with embarrassment."

April 3

A FELLOW NURSE CAME to me with a wonderful story this morning. I was so delighted that she shared this with me. I was tired and cranky after another trying night, and it was at the very moment that I wanted more than anything to be away that Althea stopped by my labor room to give me the perfect gift: a good laugh, and another reminder that we meet so many good people in this work.

It seems that one of Althea's patients today was a deaf woman in labor. Mr. Hortensky, the patient's husband, was himself both deaf and mute. He had joined his wife and was giving very tender and solicitous support to her. It was something to watch as he coached her intently in sign language.

Sometime during the morning, Mr. Hortensky drew Althea aside and handed her a note that he had scribbled on a sheet of paper toweling from the dispenser near the sink. On it appeared this message:

"bleep . . . little water"

For bleep, you may substitute an enormously crude and offensive street-slang word for the female genitalia. Now if Mr. Hortensky had been able to say this word aloud to me, it would have turned my face magenta with embarrassment. I remember being taunted by having this word flung in my face by an older teenage boy in my neighborhood when I was just beginning that uncomfortable entry into puberty at age twelve. Today, I cringe when this word is used in casual conversation. In the situation today in Althea's room, she accepted the novel communication from Mr. Hortensky, who was smiling in a friendly manner as he handed it to her.

After staring solemnly at the shocking note for a minute, Althea looked up to find the concerned husband continuing to regard her in a hopeful manner. What could she surmise but that the crudity he had penned was the only word Mr. Hortensky had ever learned to indicate the anatomy in question? It turned out that this very decent fellow was trying to let Althea know that his wife's bag of waters had broken and that she was now lying on fluid-soaked linen. He wanted to get Althea's help in making his wife more comfortable. He meant, she intuited, nothing disrespectful.

Still, the note was a shock. It had the effect on Althea of making her desperately want to laugh. It was not unlike the situation when someone breaks wind in church, and everyone struggles to remain dignified and oblivious. The more one tries not to laugh, the greater the difficulty in refraining. Althea was forced to move hastily to the window, turn her back on Mr. Hortensky and his wife, and attempt to get her wayward giggles under control.

When she felt more composed, Althea returned to her patient's bedside and began changing the soaked pad. She thought she had herself together. Midway through this effort, she was overcome with a fresh and urgent desire to laugh, as she could not help thinking of the incongruity of Mr. Hortensky's gentleness and his amazing note. She scurried to the window again. She knew that, unable to hear, this very special couple must have been mystified by the antics of their nurse who kept hovering by the window with quaking shoulders.

The beauty of this episode was the rapidity with which Althea, who is sometimes a little on the brusque side, assessed Mr. Hortensky's inherent gentlemanliness in the face of his astonishing note. Yeah, Althea!

CHAPTER THIRTY-ONE

". . .there ensued a kind of Keystone Kops effect, as Loretta seemed to be having one of her off nights."

March 24

ANTEPARTUM PROBLEMS TONIGHT. Events can shift rapidly here. I might end up in the morning with a totally different set of patients than the ones with whom I begin this shift. One resident, Dr. McAdams, who right now is feeling slightly disenchanted with the thousands of obstetrical cases he's been involved in, tells me that working in this room restores to him the sense of being a doctor. The reason for this feeling, he explained to me, is based on the variety of reasons women are sent here to this long galley-like room.

There are women whose pregnancies are complicated by any and every kind of medical problem. There is Mrs. Arbeit, who was born with a tangled mess of arteries and veins in her head, and will require the most delicate management of her pregnancy and delivery. Julia Carranza is a class F diabetic, and her pregnancy is a train wreck in progress. There are also perfectly healthy women for whom pregnancy becomes a major threat to their health, like the women whose placentas are implanted imperfectly. They risk massive and life-threatening hemorrhage as their pregnancy progresses. There is also a continuous stream of post-cesarean section patients coming to this room for recovery, most of whose care is routine, but each coming to us with the potential for an array of complications.

I was particularly glad to be here tonight because last night I had two of these women as patients during their labor in the LICU. Gloria Morales and Jennifer Quinn had both been diagnosed as having severe pregnancy-induced hypertension. Both young teenage mothers had tolerated their discomfort with a great deal of grace, and both had delivered tiny infants later this morning. The babies were doing very well in spite of having to enter the world prematurely due to their mothers' illness.

It's very tough for these particular women. They have to spend at least twenty-four hours in this recovery room getting infused with medicine through their IV line to prevent seizures. Once delivered, the effects of their severe brand of toxemia begin to subside day by day, but early in the postpartum period, they are prone to various problems that demand careful assessment. They suffer confinement to bed, the discomfort of the catheter placed in their bladder to ensure their kidneys are functioning OK, and then the burning, irritating effect the antiseizure medication has on their blood vessels.

One issue we tend to overlook is that these women are separated from their newborn babies for an extensive period. That is a terrible ordeal, one I know would have had me crawling over the bed rails. As a new mother, I was always haunting the nursery windows between feedings, so I can imagine how deprived these young mothers feel with their babies several floors away and completely unattainable. In the press of the skilled doctoring and nursing that goes into the care of these women whose well-being is often in a tenuous state, we aren't very sensitive to this issue. I get caught up like everyone else in all the interventions involved in their care. Then some shy young girl like Gloria motions me over and asks with touching uncertainty, *"Por favor, Señorita, cómo esta mi bebé?"*

At that moment, I am taken back in time and can remember the intensely maternal feelings I had in the hours following the birth of my own children. I get on the phone to the nursery and at least get a report on how the little one is doing. If at all possible, arrangements are made to bring the newborns here for a visit. If that is not an option, we get a photo for mom to cling to while she waits out her confinement.

Tonight, as always in this six-bed room, I had a partner nurse to handle the raft of problems facing us. Caroline and I make a great team of two. When we work together, things hum, so smoothly do we pick up on each other's needs as well as those of our patients. We started off shuffling a few patients over to other units, as their particular problems had already been stabilized and we needed to make space for new admissions.

We had only enough time to clear the clutter when new candidates began arriving to take their place. I began to feel a little overwhelmed, wishing for a few moments to regroup and get organized. Luckily, several rather comical things came my way to help restore my equilibrium and make an otherwise hectic night more of a pleasure.

One of the patients who rolled in was a huge, and I mean *huge* African American woman. Mrs. Latisha Carnes had a triplet pregnancy, but sadly, one of the babies was already known to have died. She had been up and down between our unit and the antepartum service one floor below us. Mrs. Carnes kept going into premature labor, as is so typical in multiple gestations. Now she was back again for the same complaint, and the mound of her belly was totally impressive. Before she had been hospitalized, Mrs. Carnes had weighed in at a mean 310 pounds.

Latisha Carnes turned out to be a funny, bright, but somewhat odd woman. She was massively uncomfortable for several reasons. She was experiencing intermittent, mildly painful contractions. In addition, with a womb now housing triplets and pushing up on her diaphragm, our new patient had to sit upright in bed to breathe.

I talked to her a bit while Caroline and I struggled to get monitor belts around this monumental abdomen—no small feat. I asked Latisha if her triplet pregnancy was a natural phenomenon or had she perhaps been taking a fertility drug.

"Oh, no, honey," she responded in a booming voice filled with rich, good-natured humor. "No high-tech sex for me!"

Caroline and I both enjoyed a good laugh at this and the many other earthy-whacky things Mrs. Carnes entertained us with as we went about getting her treatments started. It occurred to me that with the kind of patients we generally see—non-English speaking, in pain, emotional because of the labor and birth experience, hostile sometimes—we don't see much humor or wit. On the other hand, because of the high-stress atmosphere prevailing in this unit, the long hours, the press of so many life-and-death issues, there is often on the part of staff an excessive need to relieve internal pressure with laughter. Some of it is wildly inappropriate—the kind of thing that makes *Saturday Night Live* funny.

Back to this night's events. As I was working with Mrs. Carnes, I heard a sort of fluttering noise outside the window. I wondered if this might be the helicopter that regularly brings patients to this medical center from outlying hospitals unable to cope with various OB emergencies. Since the room I was assigned to would be one of the more likely places an OB patient might come, mentally I geared up. Sure enough, about ten minutes later, Dr. McAdams came in to tell Caroline and me that we were to prepare for a new patient. She had been transported here from another outlying county hospital that did not provide obstetrical services. This woman was some variety of bleeder and had been placed in a mast suit prior to helicopter transport.

A mast suit. Caroline and I exchanged a look that conveyed the message, "Oh great. A mast suit. This could be a supreme disaster."

A mast suit, or shock trousers as they are sometimes called, is a device used by hospitals and paramedics working in the field for persons who are experiencing massive bleeding. When inflated, this suit prevents blood from circulating, except minimally, to the lower extremities. The idea is to shift blood to the body's most critical organs—the heart, lungs, and brain. The body has its own internal system to do this very thing, but the mast suit amps up the lifesaving effort.

We have had occasion to use the mast suit here in Labor and Delivery for those critical cases when a woman is bleeding out during or following a cesarean section, or hemorrhaging in the midst of a vaginal birth. Thus, the term "mast suit" called up in my mind a critical, emergent event. This on a night when Caroline and I, as well as Dr. McAdams, had our hands full with a raft of other patients' problems. We would have to prioritize the incoming patient's needs, as a life might be in the balance. If the mast suit lady was truly critical, I was sure that other nursing and medical staff would pour in to help.

Moments later, the "critical" patient arrived on a stretcher. She looked remarkably alert, pink cheeked, and merely a bit shaky. Mrs. Armendariz had a mask hanging around her neck to administer oxygen. Lying alongside her were two packets of whole blood. She had been disengaged from the mast suit. Whew!

First, I looked to see what the source of this reputed bleeding might be. There was only a speck of fresh blood on the pad she had between her legs. Dr. McAdams, who arrived just then, said that apparently she was fine. The hasty ultrasound scan he'd done as she came through the double doors showed no placenta previa, a marginal or low-lying placenta at most.

Assured that Mrs. Armendariz was in no danger, Caroline began to admit her, and I concerned myself with those two units of blood. Blood is precious, hard to obtain in adequate quantities, and must be used within a certain time frame once out of refrigeration. The docs in that other hospital, concerned as they had seemed to be that this woman might begin to hemorrhage massively during her helicopter flight, had sent the blood along as a precaution. But now, with the paramedics gone and no information on her accompanying papers, I had no idea how long this blood had been out of cold storage.

According to our protocol, blood cannot be used for another patient after it has been out of refrigeration for more than thirty minutes. I was pretty sure that this blood was now useless and would have to be discarded. I thought this was an enormous waste, especially in light of my growing sense that the other hospital had somehow panicked, making a big hoopla about a relatively minor complaint. I called the blood bank, and they concurred that this blood was now unusable. I should send it to them, and they would document the situation.

Through the busy night, I wanted to get a look at the note from the physician who transferred this patient to us. I hoped to reconstruct the events there that had precipitated his calling for helicopter transport and the mast suit business. For too many hours, there were so many routine tasks pulling at me. After checking Mrs. Armendariz's hematocrit (percentage of red blood cells to plasma) and finding it to be a healthy 37 percent and continuing to note the slight streaks of blood on her pad during the night, I had to divide my time between her care and that of the other five patients in the room.

One other thing came up. The unfortunate Mr. Armendariz had to drive here posthaste from that hospital out in the valley. Surely he was panic-stricken, thinking his wife had some life-threatening problem to initiate the trip by helicopter. As soon as I knew Mrs. Armendariz was stable, I told our crack visitor information person to call down to the waiting area and get word to her husband to come up and be reassured that his loved one was fine. There ensued a sort of Keystone Kops effect, as Loretta seemed to be having one of her off nights. Two more times I asked her specifically to try to get in touch with the husband. On my third try, she responded inexplicably, "Oh sure. I will call him back. He came up, but it was right before my three-thirty visitor rounds, so I told him to go back down and wait."

Bloody hell. "Yes, Loretta. Please go and get him back here right now."

The look on that man's face when he walked in and saw his wife, all apple cheeked and smiling shyly, told the whole story. Tears ran freely down his cheeks. He completely disregarded his long and nerve-wracking wait. He was so completely overjoyed to find that his wife was going to be all right.

Finally, minutes prior to the day shift's arrival when all my tasky jobs were completed, I dug back in the mast suit woman's chart and there found a puzzling story. The emergency room physician at the valley hospital described her as coming into the ER and being observed to have a "gush of bright red blood from the vagina." Then a little further in his transfer note to us, he calculated the estimated blood loss to that point as being 10 cc. *10 cc.* That's what we might collect in a test tube for lab tests. That's nothing. I looked for any documentation of further evidence of bleeding, but that was it.

Now there is admittedly one big problem with an obstetrical patient with any amount of vaginal bleeding. No one dares stick a hand into that vagina for an exam. Such an exam in a true case of placenta previa could precipitate a massive bleed and, concomitantly, grave harm, even death, for the fetus and mother. The answer is to have an ultrasound so the location of the placenta can be visualized in relation to the cervix. I can believe that the ER docs over there had to wonder if this woman wasn't possibly a previa. That would be prudent judgment. But it seemed to me that the mast suit, the helicopter, and the packs of blood they sent along were a tad dramatic under the circumstances for a woman who was exhibiting no active bleeding.

I had to remind myself that what is to us routine, accustomed as we are to dealing on a constant basis with every complication of pregnancy known to medicine, is for others quite scary. I remember several years ago receiving a patient from this same hospital. She was a mother who had come to them ready to deliver and was exhibiting some elevated blood pressures. The staff there, though not experienced in the treatment of obstetric problems, had started an infusion of magnesium sulfate through her IV line that is the standard treatment for pregnancy-induced hypertension. After her delivery, they sent the woman and her little one in an ambulance to us, accompanied by a registered nurse from their ER.

As I met her and the paramedics on entry to this unit, the nurse gave me report on her patient. Her breathless tone conveyed her feeling that she was pretty caught up in the drama of shepherding this woman on her trip to this medical center. I politely listened to this and then explained that the patient would be taken back to the delivery area to be checked by a physician. I started to disconnect the magnesium sulfate infusion because it had come hanging on an expensive pump, and I knew the paramedics were already getting antsy to leave.

"But you don't seem to understand!" this nurse exclaimed, her voice all worked up and shaky with emotion. "This woman is a *toxemia* patient!"

The visiting nurse could have no way of knowing that her newly delivered mother, who by all that we could glean from the record of her vital signs and lab work, merited a diagnosis of a mild case of this disease entity. Patients with mild toxemia are seen here in great numbers, and we do not get our blood pressure up when dealing with their care. I employed my best diplomatic efforts to reassure the nurse that she could safely turn her over to us. She left then, plainly worried that she had not been able to convey to us the serious nature of the woman's condition. I know that I sound disgustingly smug. Secretly, I wanted to giggle in her face. Instead, I waited until she was out the door.

CHAPTER THIRTY-TWO

". . . sometimes we are humbled and taught the meaning of dignity and courage by families who have none of the amenities of life we consider our inherent birthright."

March 25

RECENTLY, I UNDERTOOK something that is quite a departure from what I have been doing. I have consistently worked a few hours of overtime here. The little bit of extra pay is great, as well as my effort to fill in the blanks and staff the unit a little more comfortably for the four hours a week I devote to this effort. My husband has started a new business venture, and we need all the loose change we can come by. I don't mind working extra a bit, but to do so at this medical center, a nurse must go through a per diem pool, sort of an in-house registry. The nursing pool has made it a habit to change its requirements every other month, and I am tired of being whipsawed by this bureaucracy.

One of my friends here in Labor and Delivery works overtime at a lovely community hospital that is about ten minutes distance from my home. It happens to be the hospital in which I delivered my son, Patrick, our youngest. Tracy has been urging me to try to join her there to pick up the few extra shifts a month that I intend to work.

I have vacillated a lot about looking into this prospect. Many of us who have worked exclusively in a large public health facility like this worry that we have lost the social skills necessary to get along in a private hospital setting. Finally, I got up my nerve and went over to have an interview. They seemed impressed with my credentials and hired me on the spot.

Part of me does want to peek into the world of nursing in the private sector. I saw lots of it in my final two years of nursing school when I rotated through six different private hospitals for my clinical experience. These places differ so vastly from the city hospital in which I now work.

The hospital in which I will begin a short orientation soon is not a teaching hospital. All the patients there are under the care of a postgraduate physician in private practice. I have seen the abysmal rudeness, condescension, and chauvinism that certain doctors direct at the nursing staff in these much cleaner, nicely appointed, and very expensive places. I know that I have a very low boiling point for that sort of treatment at this time in my life, so I have to ask myself what I would do in the face of such behavior toward myself. Tracy doesn't complain of being mistreated in her experience at this cushy labor and delivery unit and thinks I would find myself very comfortable. "Easy peasy," she encouraged me.

Recently I was talking with an old friend from nursing school who went almost immediately upon graduation into the critical care department. Today, Kathy Donnelly works in the cardiac intensive care unit at another well-respected hospital in this community. She takes care of many patients undergoing open heart surgery. It is part of her role to meet these patients before their surgery to let them know what to expect when they arrive at the ICU following this major surgical procedure.

She related to me an incident that has had a disturbing effect on her morale. She was seated at the bedside of a very nervous, older gentleman. She was holding his hand for reassurance as she gently went about explaining what was going to happen the next morning, letting him know that she would be there when he opened his eyes from the anesthesia.

A physician appeared in the doorway. It was the anesthesiologist, coming to talk to this same man, introduce himself, and give his spiel prior to meeting this patient in the operating room. He did not even excuse himself to Kathy, interrupted her in midsentence, and, not looking her in the eye, addressed the room air. "I'll need ten minutes with Mr. Smith."

Kathy was stunned by this abysmal rudeness but could not think of an appropriate rejoinder. She was confronted at that moment with the longstanding and inherent inequities between nursing and medicine. She stood up and left the room, unable to come up with the words she wanted to say to this arrogant jerk. The whole thing made her sick at heart. We talked about what happened, and I told her it would be best to develop a prepared response if such a thing were to occur again. I have much the same problem in being able to think on my feet in such circumstances.

I once asked a friend, an older oh-so-wise woman who is a marriage and family counselor, how to handle scenes like this. During her training while working on her masters in counseling, she was a crisis intervention intern at a large city hospital. There, she routinely dealt with people facing the trauma of modern living–car accidents, shootings, fire victims, catastrophic events. Betty was called to the ER to help with the distress some paramedics were experiencing when they had to bring in children who had been caught on the railroad tracks by a train barreling down on them.

An influential older physician did not agree with her handling of the situation. He chose to start dressing her down in the midst of the emergency room, in front of a raft of staff, patients, and families.

"What did you do?" I asked nervously, picturing this distressing scene.

"I gestured him to follow me to an exam room," Betty replied. "Once there, I told him, 'I don't allow *anyone* to talk to me that way.'" He was taken aback, and the trash talk ended.

Wow. What powerful words. They diffused the situation with the abusive physician, and I have never forgotten this story.

I worry that, in accepting this new position, I may be setting the scene where I would have to use those words. However, allowing my hesitancy get in the way of taking on a new challenge seems foolish, especially since the problem may never develop. I think I'm ready for a slight change now, as much as I love my work here in the high-risk obstetrical unit.

What exactly am I looking for in this new work experience besides the princely amount of cash per hour they are going to pay me? I am pretty confident of my overall skill in obstetrical nursing, but there is, and always will be, room for improvement. Looking at my personal deficiencies, I can say that I need to grow in the subtle area of management, of gaining confidence in my judgment without the pillar of constant physician presence to lean on. Several of my acquaintances among the midwifery staff have told me that until I have worked in a small community hospital, until I have admitted patients and assessed them while the docs are at the office or home in bed, I have not stretched myself to my limits. The private docs rely on the report of the obstetrical nurse to make a decision whether to come to the hospital or send the patient home.

Most of my experience to date has been in a setting where the physicians are physically present at all times. If I see a problem with a patient, I have the ability to summon a resident within seconds, minutes. There is no doubt that there is enough stress here due to the volume and degree of crisis that we face almost daily. Yet there is a safety net in the presence of so much medical staff, especially since some emergencies in obstetrics require almost instant intervention.

Selfishly speaking, I suppose that as long as I have to be working extra hours each week, I might as well be a little less overworked, get paid exceedingly well, and have a chance to polish up a few of my skills. Most of the patients at the private hospital have had the benefit of childbirth preparation classes. They aren't conversing with their nurses in a foreign language, and their expectations of their treatment in hospital are profoundly different than those of our typical Latino immigrant family. The nurses wear attractive pink-flowered scrubs (pink has always been rather flattering to me). The labor rooms are decorated with lovely wallpaper. The whole place is faultlessly clean.

None of these lures would tempt me to give up my work here. I still walk in through the ER waiting room at night, packed to the walls with droves of people who have only this place to seek for their care. Husbands with wives on their arm, walking back and forth while she goes through early labor; roly-poly grandmothers with Indian features chasing after toddlers who are hyper, being up long past their bedtime; an occasional bag lady or gentleman shuffling along, hoping to find a warm hideaway to put up for the night if the security guard doesn't spot them.

This motley crew still gets to me. I know that that young girl who is straining to tolerate her contractions as she paces up and down the floor in her inexpensive cotton smock will soon be coming up to us on a stretcher. She will be scared, in great pain, unsure what to expect, and having problems with the language. She will be wondering just what all these gringo medical folks are going to do to her. I can offer this girl something, because her poverty and vulnerability only make it more important that I be a good nurse for her.

It's sometimes dismaying to hear a resident or an intern refer to our patients as "bozos" or "trolls." I wonder how charming and attractive any of us would be if we had to endure the very marginal existence some if our patients have had? Thank goodness there are enough people working here who are able to respond to the fundamental decency of these patients, enough doctors and nurses who feel compassion for our clients and insist on top-rate treatment for these poor women and their infants. We have endless opportunities to act as patient advocates. And sometimes we are humbled and taught the meaning of dignity and courage by families who have none of the amenities of life we consider our inherent birthright.

I cannot see how I could ever derive the same satisfaction from caring for women who are being cosseted in cheerful, quiet surroundings, accompanied most times by a loving support person. But perhaps I am too hasty. I was once one of those very women, and I sure appreciated the loving touch and expert skills of some very special nurses who took care of me in my time of need. Maybe this is the real lesson I am meant to learn, that when a person is hurting and feeling vulnerable, it matters not the other circumstances of their lives.

CHAPTER THIRTY-THREE

"In working with them one learns to appreciate what is inherently fine in the human spirit."

May 3

WE ARE HAVING a lovely, uncharacteristically quiet night, so I have the luxury of trying to collect my thoughts. I am in the midst of my grueling thirty-six-hour weekend stint. Even if it's kind of mild like this one has been so far, I still build up a sleep deficit. By Monday afternoon at twelve when I get off, my body screams in protest at the abuse to which I have subjected it. Also, I've begun my occasional moonlighting job at the nearby private hospital. I'm working there this coming Monday night, so who knows what kind of zombie I'll be when that is over.

I have such mixed feelings about that other job. I have survived enough new, threatening work situations to know that I can plan on being uncomfortable for several more months until I've become acclimated. It's often the small things, like learning where all the widgets are located and who your well-wishers are and who are . . . well, not. I would dearly love to leap over the uneasiness and uncertainty of this period, but that is not part of the deal.

The few times I've worked there so far have been OK. It's only myself and one other nurse, with an additional nurse at home on call, set to come in if we get a flurry of patients or need to do a cesarean section. With only the two of us, it's far more insular there. Luckily, I've been paired with friendly, welcoming nurses. I can believe that if I were on duty for eight hours with someone with a difficult personality, such isolation and intimacy could be uncomfortable. Those nice nurses I've met so far have warned me that that will ultimately be my fate. There are some temperamental folks, both doctors and nurses, who will be testing me soon.

I've been on my best behavior, being the new kid on the block. I've pretty much been keeping quiet and being a listener, which is, I think, a good strategy when beginning new relationships. Both nurses who have partnered with me so far, Joan and Angela, seemed happy to have a fresh ear to listen to their favorite and wildly amusing stories about the unit. Figuring heavily in their tales were the ten or so obstetricians who form the medical staff of the department there, right down to whose wife is a brat and why Dr. So-and-So is not speaking to Nurse Whosit. These anecdotes impress me with how much freedom I have here at this hospital with such numbers of people, continuously changing. If I find one resident or some nurse irritating or difficult to get along with, I turn around and there are flocks of bright, witty, charming folks to make my day.

The other insight I have had into the workings of the maternity unit at the other hospital is that so much emphasis is placed on preserving the image of the doctor as being totally in control. Everything must go fine, and there can be no cracks in the armor. It comes as no surprise to me that the affluent couples who are the clientele just eat up that sense of security, that assurance that with Dr. Fishbate at the helm, nothing could ever go awry.

I was just as ignorant, just as all-trusting as a pregnant woman receiving obstetrical care. No matter that, with my third child, my urbane, courtly obstetrician let me languish in labor for over ten hours without once coming by to stick his head in the room. This impersonal touch might have been OK if he were at home keeping track of my labor. But, no, the nurse told me that he was sleeping down the hallway. That nurse did everything for me except for his running in at the last second to grab my son barehanded, resulting in a nasty laceration from the lack of controlled delivery.

I was still so everlastingly grateful in my postpartum euphoria that I could not thank the man enough. The nurse who had given me such constant and solicitous care remained in the background, and I remember now with shame that she went thankless. She must have wanted to throw up. She had her revenge in time, though. It was the inspiration of her professional and gentle manner that led me ultimately to choose this work. Later in my stay, on the night before I went home, an unduly chatty nurse's aide let slip that my obstetrician, who had treated me in such princely fashion throughout my prenatal care, was the scourge of the nursing staff. He was notorious for venting his temper if they called him one minute before the baby was set to come out.

I can't say I've seen any of that cavalier attitude in the few times I've been on duty at the new place. The population of pregnant women in the white well-insured community this hospital serves has shrunk. There is a great deal of cosseting the small patient pool who have now become "consumers," discriminating shoppers for obstetrical care. Those private docs get in there to give personal care to their patients, and I cannot fault any one of them with having a blasé attitude toward their largely affluent patients.

I am determined not to be a naysayer about this new job because there are pressing reasons why I should settle in and be happy there. They pay me well, the surroundings are pleasant, and so far they seem grateful to see me coming in the door. In general, the workload is about one-twentieth of my current pace at the public hospital. Thus, I can moonlight and not be so terribly worn out.

It's odd. When I graduated from nursing school, I wanted to come to the city hospital because it seemed the best place for an anxious, shy person like myself to go through that baptism of fire, the reality shock endured by new nurses in one's first work experience out of school. I figured it was like a war zone down here, and it would be a case of either shoot or be shot.

And so it was. There was no way for me to hang back, diffident and unsure of myself, when there was such an incredible load of patients needing care. I stumbled, fumbled, went home in tears, lost sleep, took my baby steps, had my first little successes, and gradually came to have a sense of my own value, strengths, and skills.

I had always planned, as soon as I had gleaned all I could from this place, to exit it for the nicer environment and easier pace at a community hospital like the one in which I am currently moonlighting. It never occurred to me that I would fall in love with our population of poor immigrant mothers and other assorted oddballs, that caring for such impoverished and relatively powerless people would give me such enormous satisfaction. All my notions of what would satisfy me in my work as an obstetrical nurse were turned on end.

I am by no means alone in feeling this way. Most nurses with whom I work here at the city hospital share these sentiments, though they could each find work in vastly more pleasant and less stressful places. The poor have a certain dignity, and in working with them, one learns to appreciate what is inherently fine in the human spirit. I had to come here to find this lesson. If you'd tried to sell me these ideas before I came here, I'd have suspected you were smoking some funny cigarettes.

CHAPTER THIRTY-FOUR

". . . found myself struck . . . by the stark terror I saw in the eyes of what appeared to be just a young child in the adjoining bed."

May 4

THE PHENOMENON CONTINUES. When I came back at eleven tonight, my friend Roz told me that beginning at noon there were no patients in labor, and only two women were being treated for premature labor in the antepartum problems unit. I cannot honestly begin to convey how bizarre it is to have so few patients. It is much more customary to wonder how in the world so many women could all be delivering at once.

This week begins an annual affair here at the medical center to promote a sense of appreciation for the nurses' efforts during the year. It coincides with the national week celebrating the American nurse. Our nursing department makes the arrangements and, theoretically, all of us are supposed to be involved. There are free educational events and, oh, sometimes a little fair, a 10-K run, an awards banquet, and so on. In my mind, it has always meant a cake arriving on the unit, brought up by the nursing supervisor. They want to be careful about this custom because it too easily lends itself to the reference "Let them eat cake."

It's very tempting to develop a cynical attitude about what are undoubtedly very sincere aspirations on the part of the nursing administration to give us a sense of being valued. The problem is that the great majority of nurses involved in these festivities are ones who don't assume the direct, hands-on care of patients, the very ones for whom the week's activities are planned. In a huge facility like this, with several separate hospitals on the campus, it's hard to develop a sense of group identity. The physical plant is pretty grim, and there is very little budget for making things comfortable, let alone attractive. What remains is the work and the varying kinds of rewards that accrue for doing a difficult job in less-than-appealing surroundings.

It is not the fault of the hospital administration that there are so few of the frills that make private hospital work much more alluring. When I was a student doing a one-day stint in the emergency room at a local, prestigious community hospital, the staff nurse I was shadowing took me to the nurses' lounge for some coffee. Wow! The place looked like the VIP suite at the Hyatt Regency. "The ER docs donated funds to create this for the nurses," she explained proudly, "because of all the support we give them."

There's none of that here at the city hospital, and never will be. Even if you are the best, brightest, hardest-working nurse in the history of the hospital, you could leave here after working thirty years, and one month later, the sands would have shifted, new docs arrived for internship or residency, the ever-changing roster of nurses would have been juggled, and you would be old "what's her name?" That sounds lonely even as I write it, but I am only being realistic. It is best to understand that the rewards are nearly all internal here.

Back to Nurse Recognition Week. I have been invited as part of the activities to read a paper I wrote earlier this year, a case study on a patient for whom I cared here in Labor and Delivery. Six of these papers were selected and submitted to a citywide competition.

When some of my fellow nurses urged me to write this paper, knowing that my first degree was in English, I'd chosen one of our more famous patients this past year. She came close to losing her life not only once but rather over and over due to complications from placenta previa. Antonia Aceves had been at home waiting to come in for a scheduled cesarean section when she started to bleed.

Before Mrs. Aceves reached the hospital, she had sustained a dramatic hemorrhage. In the course of her emergency surgery, she had to have almost a total volume replacement of her blood, something like five quarts. My only connection with her amounted to bringing some of the many, many packs of blood that she was having poured into her. Other nurses played a crucial role in her care, including those who assisted with her cesarean section and the immediate hysterectomy that followed. She was transferred postoperatively to the ICU in the main hospital because of her quite precarious condition. There, expert nurses continued to help restore her to health, as well as those in our much smaller intensive care unit here in this hospital when she was stable enough to return to us.

I kept in touch with Dr. Moreno, the senior resident who performed her surgery and followed her daily through her various remissions. Thankfully, her baby was saved and did fine, going home with the family within a few days of birth. Mrs. Aceves eventually rejoined her family after a long six-week ordeal in this med center, her ultimate fate in question many times over during her recovery.

To me, Antonia Aceves was a vivid example of the utterly overwhelming catastrophe that can ensue when a complication of pregnancy occurs even in this enlightened age of high-tech medicine. As a child, I watched in horrified amazement as my mother was carried to the family car by my father, bleeding from a premature separation of the placenta. I remember, with the ghoulish fascination of a child, bringing the neighborhood kids in to survey the spectacle of impressive amounts of blood spattered on the bathroom and kitchen walls and floors of our small home. My brother Michael was born prematurely by emergency cesarean section, weighing a mere three and a half pounds in an era when not much could be done for such tiny ones except to give warmth and comfort. I remember that my mother came home to a very shaky recovery, pale as parchment and weakened for the next year of her life from her ordeal.

In researching Mrs. Aceves's chart to start writing my paper, it appeared to me that she received almost fifty units of blood and various blood products. Her chart was inches thick from the pink blood request sheets. She stayed in intensive care long enough to exhibit signs of ICU psychosis. This mental disorder is a natural outcome from the patient's sequestration in a small room without windows to the outside, deprived of natural light, surrounded by rafts of beeping machinery, and bereft of much human contact or activity.

This pretty-famous patient of ours nearly died from acute respiratory distress syndrome, a vicious complication involving the lungs when a person is clinging so tenuously to life. It was even posited that she'd suffered a myocardial infarct, what we think of as a heart attack, due to the deprivation of oxygen to the heart muscle during her acute loss of blood. It was a day-to-day effort keeping this young mother from succumbing to the aftermath of what was initially only a hemorrhage.

When I finally sat down to put all this information together for a case study presentation, I found some difficulty getting going. After several fruitless fits and starts, I realized that the reason I was stuck was that my involvement with Antonia Aceves was mostly intellectual. I was interested in her and her ordeal, but honestly speaking, she was not my patient. Other physicians and nurses were the direct participants in her care. I had to ultimately abandon this project because it would never have rung true.

I began, instead, to retrace in my memory my involvement with hundreds of women over the past few years. I asked myself which of these many patients

I could most truly claim as my own, someone whose outcome had been directly impacted by my involvement. Then it became easy.

I could never, never forget little thirteen-year-old Carla, whom I first discovered in that horrid B labor room. She was surrounded by three other patients: a heroin abuser chained to her bed because she was in custody, a gray-haired woman having her twelfth baby, and another woman screaming hysterically who proceeded to plop her baby out amid ferocious howls in the bed next to the frightened teenager. I had come across the hall to find the cause of such screeching and found myself instead struck by the stark terror I saw in the eyes of what appeared to be just a young child in the adjoining bed.

Anita, the labor room nurse, left to accompany the newly delivered and now quiescent mother and baby en route to the delivery area for their postpartum care. I walked over and picked up the youngster's chart. Thirteen. That did it. Sometimes we care for early teens who are little streetwise toughies, but this girl looked more like a ten-year-old. I could not bear to have Carla stay in these bizarre surroundings. Another time when every bed on the unit was full, there might not be a choice of where to care for this youngster. That night, at that moment, we were not so stuffed with laboring women. I felt that someone had to realize that there was emotional trauma to be considered in Carla's case. We simply had to do better.

I found the third-year resident James Milligan and told him about the situation. He was in charge of the LICU, but there were no patients currently admitted there. He agreed to move Carla to a space there and let me give one-to one care to the teenager as long as no seriously ill woman needed a spot. Carla's mother, who remained at her daughter's bedside, helped me move the bed over to the complex labor area. Once in a quiet and private place, with her pain soon ameliorated by a blessedly fine epidural block, Carla fell asleep.

As the hours of the night passed and we developed a bit of mutual trust, her mother shared Carla's story with me. Her daughter had been repeatedly raped by a group of older boys who had accosted her on her way to the neighborhood market. Carla was too ashamed to tell her parents, and her pregnancy remained undetected. Later, her mother, increasingly suspicious, thought to observe her daughter's swelling abdomen while she slept and saw the baby's movement. What utter heartache, trying to uncover the grim truth, trying somehow to help her child deal with a pregnancy at age thirteen, and some weeks later having to bring her here to be with her through labor and birth.

Once we nurses and doctors had identified and recognized the needs of this special patient, things changed dramatically. Dr. Milligan was very receptive to my suggestions for Carla's continuing care. Only he was to examine her, and then only infrequently and with extra consideration for her natural sense of modesty. He explained everything he was going to do with sensitivity and performed exams with consummate gentleness.

When it came time for her to deliver, James took Carla back to the delivery room himself. Such personal attention was quite a departure from the norm around here. Residents do not assist with routine birth. That is the province of interns, medical students, and midwives. As he became involved and aware in Carla's peculiar situation, I think James had come to see that, out of all the population of women presenting that night with a host of challenging obstetrical and medical problems, Carla was very likely his most needy patient.

I'll never, never forget that night. I can recall everything, even down to the quality of light that I kept dim so that Carla could sleep. How her mother and I stood on either side of her bed and both shed tears after she shared with me the crime that had brought them both to us that night. How Carla listened so intently to my explanation of what to do when it came time to push. How she held on to my hand and her mother's, and pushed like a little trooper. How I kept thinking that my daughter Nicole was this child's age and wondering what problems Carla's experience of birth based on such violent events might breed in the young girl's future and that of her baby.

As Carla was being moved to the delivery room, one of my fellow nurses was at the door of the LICU. She reminded me in a ticked-off voice that she had a patient who needed to be admitted to this area. She had come over some hours ago and didn't appear very impressed with my explanation that we were holding off admits until the teenager delivered. So I told her to bring on the patient and thus missed my chance to be with Carla and her mother for the birth of her little daughter. I saw the trio of infant, child mother, and new grandmother as they passed the LICU doors on their way to recovery.

Sometimes there are situations people have to face that are so heartbreakingly unfair, so fraught with psychic pain that one wonders if they will ever recover. Those of us on the periphery who are compelled to watch such agony can only embrace them with our care, try to pass what comfort we can. I knew that on another night, I might come across another Carla for whom even the small degree of compassionate treatment she had received would not be possible due to the press of so many sick patients. That was the horrible, shameful truth.

CHAPTER THIRTY-FIVE

"You're only a nurse. You're standing still, going nowhere."

May 29

S OMEONE LEFT A journal around
the unit, and an article I read in it posed
some sticky, rather thought-provoking questions. This was an editorial essay
written by some politically elevated nurse executive who seemed to be saying
that

a. nurses complain mightily about their poor pay, lack of professional
   status, lack of recognition, and just about everything else;
b. nurses ought to stop griping and remember how modern nursing
   derived from the efforts of altruistic, heroic women whose characters
   put contemporary nurses to shame;
c. anyone who has to ask for respect doesn't deserve it.

And so on.

Well, those are some very powerful statements that, on first reading, make
me want to affirm at least some elements of them. There are such complexities
surrounding the professional status of nurses. I think it is wrong to ascribe a
cause-and-effect relationship between the behavior of modern nurses (as the
author seems to believe, frustrated, impotent, and self-centered) and the lack of
respect we so often find ourselves experiencing. I will agree that there is truly a

big problem in this area of receiving the proper regard as a profession. It is just as certain that the outcome we would like to see will not happen overnight. Where to even begin in the effort to achieve the respect I believe we so very much deserve as a group?

Nursing has a hard row to hoe, as do most female-dominated careers. In this country, medicine, formerly a totally male-dominated profession, has been elevated to top status as a career. In some manner, its practitioners might be considered an informal American aristocracy. I've met some of their princes right here in Labor and Delivery. Nurses were historically the helpmates of physicians. As we struggle for our professional validation, we sometimes find our medical compatriots quite stingy when it comes to sharing a portion of their exalted status with us.

In recent decades, women found entry into a wide variety of career possibilities that had been closed to them. Nursing took some blows to its pride as many bright and ambitious women who formerly might have joined its ranks opted for careers with better pay and professional status. This societal shift should have been a healthy means of ridding ourselves of all but the committed. Instead, applications to nursing schools dropped precipitously, and many schools had to lower admission standards to fill slots.

In our nursing milieu, we hear from time to time some very lofty praise about the value of the nurse's work by, for instance, our hospital and nursing administration. But then when something very concrete comes up like contract negotiations, the threat of strikes, or requests for shared governance, we run into a blockade set up by those same entities. We become the enemy and are made to feel like a pack of nasty, bitching lowlifes.

I had a very interesting discussion recently with my in-laws about their attitudes toward nursing as a profession. They never expressed their dismay when I announced that I was planning to enroll in a local college nursing program. However, when their daughter took a similar path after watching my journey through school and entrance into practice, they were most unhappy. I asked them, after they made some very uncomplimentary comments about her plans, to tell me why they had these objections to Janet's wanting to become a nurse.

"Every nurse I knew was a hard-living, heavy-drinking, foul-mouthed slut," proffered my mother-in-law.

"If she wants a career in the medical field, she ought to just go on and become a doctor," stated my father-in-law disdainfully.

These statements drew a picture for me of what many of their generation viewed as the low social status of this career.

I know that my in-laws come from a different time in which good women pursued a very limited array of career choices (i.e., teaching, secretarial work) before settling into being wives and mothers. My mother, as well as her two sisters, became nurses during the WWII era but returned swiftly to private life as soon as the war ended. Mom explained to me that she had had no desire to practice as a nurse but allowed her parents to push her into nurse "training," as it was called. Having lived through the Great Depression, her parents wanted their daughters to have work they could pursue if the need arose. She was happy to escape to a woman's traditional role as speedily as possible once she met my father, a recovering wounded war veteran.

My story is quite the opposite. Having graduated from college with a degree in English, I had no real notion of what I was going to do other than some vague idea of a career in teaching. I started a master's program in English Lit and found that I had taken the wrong path. Sitting in the library researching some obscure writer whose work I wasn't interested in totally turned me off. I abandoned this pursuit to accompany my husband, a young second lieutenant with orders to ship out for Vietnam, to his training site at an army installation in the Midwest. During his training, he was found to be unfit to send overseas due to a health issue, and we completed his army obligation while he assisted with the orientation of other unlucky soldiers going to Vietnam. We had our first child there in the army hospital, and I had my initial experience with the work of nurses. It would be five or six years later that that seminal experience during childbirth, as well as subsequent births, solidified for me the sense of the work I was truly meant to do.

It was about this same time that many more women were obtaining college degrees, and there was a growing sense that women were capable of performing in many different fields that previously were barred to them. After WWII, women who had stepped into men's shoes to perform jobs that had previously been exclusively in the male domain saw the work world with new eyes. They found that they enjoyed the sense of prowess, pay, and independence that derived from such work. Society was becoming more materialistic, and a two-paycheck family slowly became the norm. Divorce lost much of its social stigma, and more women found themselves in the situation of being heads of households. They needed a decent-paying job to make up for the loss of the husband's income.

In our profession, although small as an overall percentage, more men are choosing to enter the field of nursing. I believe that men's joining our ranks has helped spur the demand for better pay and less sense of subservience for the nurse. Growing calls for the bachelor's degree as entry level education for nurses, though not entirely realized, added to the sense that the nurse should be recognized as a professional rather than simply an adjunct to the physician. The expanding arena of advanced practice for nurses—nurse practitioners, nurse anesthetists, nurse midwives—opened up new possibilities for nurses, in recognition of more complex responsibilities that could be managed well by nurses.

In the real everyday world of the nurse, there has been some movement toward a lessening of the deep divide that has existed between the medical staff and the nurses with whom they interact. This shift parallels somewhat a societal change in which the workplace and workers are protected from the abuse of those who are perceived to be in positions of relative power. There is more emphasis on the team, with recognition that all contribute to the best outcomes for patients.

I myself have been subjected to very little overt abuse, verbal or otherwise. Maybe this is because I am slightly older than the young doctors I deal with here, and they hesitate to unload on me in the way that I have seen them do with younger, more vulnerable members of our nursing staff. Overall, though, I would unhesitatingly say that there is a world of improvement that needs to be achieved in this area. I have seen physicians talk to nurses in a manner that would not be tolerated in any comparable work situation. Sometimes the nurse sticks up for herself and demands an apology, letting the offender know that such behavior will have consequences. More often, she is paralyzed by the abuse. There is a lag in this physician-nurse relationship, perhaps due to the lingering understanding that nurses were historically under the thumb of medicine. Unfortunately, it was part of the role of the nurse to be self-effacing even when confronted by almost pathologically rude behavior.

More and more, nurses have given notice that such abuse will not be endured. To be fair, there are many docs who have the innate decency to treat everyone with respect, from the custodian to the chief of medicine. Certainly, I have seen some policing among themselves. One night an extremely attractive, newly married nurse was working in the LICU with one of the junior residents. JoAnn noticed that Dr. Emory was in need of some assistance with a procedure, and she said to him, "Would you like me to get you a pack of sterile towels?" In response, he looked at her with a leering grin and said, "No, but I would like you to. . ." He went on to suggest a blatant and astonishingly sexual service that she could render to him. This sick behavior seemingly came out of nowhere.

I don't know if he thought he was being funny, or what. He had the bad judgment to make this crude remark within hearing range of Dr. Boardman, his senior resident, and another third-year resident, both males. They jumped all over him and really dressed him down. Dr. Emory later left this residency.

This unfortunate incident was handled about as well as it probably could have been, yet there is definitely an old-boy network among physicians, which widens to include female docs. It's difficult for them to police each other's behavior. They recognize that at some time in the future, they just might have to depend on the good graces, lack of critical judgment, or outright mercy of their peers if some behavior or action of theirs renders them vulnerable to liability.

I can understand that it's a delicate problem, calling a fellow physician to task for some crummy behavior, but who else is going to do it? If that crummy behavior is directed unjustly at a nurse, who is going to brave that old-boy network and call the perpetrator on his or her behavior? It takes someone with a very clear sense of self-worth to do that, and it is in that very area of self-worth and self-esteem that so many women have difficulties in professional practice.

As a new nurse on this unit, I had occasion to be involved in a surgical case, acting as circulating nurse in a cesarean section. The circulating nurse is the member of the operating team who remains unsterile, able to move around the periphery of the operating arena. He or she is the one to get whatever must be added to the sterile field after everyone else is gowned and gloved and hovering over the patient. Additionally, the circulating nurse is supposed to watch everything that is transpiring around the sterile procedure and intervene when something is not being performed according to surgical protocol. I don't think most surgeons view the circulator as having this additional role, seeing the nurse as the one to simply carry out requests from the operating staff, or the one to fetch and carry.

As the end of this case drew near, the surgeon Dr. Rorcas, who was a notoriously temperamental fellow, stopped sewing and turned for no apparent reason to vent his spleen on the innocent scrub nurse who had been minding her business and doing a quietly efficient job. Grace had warned me at the beginning of the case to be careful, that Rorcas was on the warpath. She had been walking on eggshells through the whole operation, being extra careful not to set him off. In the classic way of abusers, he needed no real excuse to begin. He verbally insulted Grace at length, ridiculed her accent, derided her skills and intelligence, and actually called her a clown. He went on with this tirade while the intern Dr. Meed stood silent and tense and the anesthesiologist played deaf and dumb behind his little drape.

Oh god, I was still so new and had never seen anything like this. Moreover, I was a desperately shy and unassertive woman. But there are some situations that just cannot be passed over. I felt compelled to do something. Grace was quietly weeping, trying to hang on until the finish of this miserable case. I walked around the operating table until I could catch Dr. Rorcas's eye and shook my head, as if to say, "No more." He went back to supervising Dr. Meed's placement of the last stitches.

After the case, Dr. Rorcas was standing at the side of the room showing the young intern how to complete the operative report. I went over to him and told him I thought he had been a tremendous bully. My knees were shaking, both as an effect of the ugly scene I had just witnessed and because this was my first occasion to take a physician to task for his behavior.

"Why don't you pick on someone your own size?" I asked him. "You treated her cruelly."

He replied disdainfully, "Oh, so I'm supposed to care about the feelings of every humanoid that walks around on two feet?" Further, that he only treated people the way they deserved to be treated. He then turned his back on me in a blatant gesture of utter contempt for my opinion of his actions, which I considered to be an almost psychotic diatribe against the totally blameless scrub nurse.

It would have been out of character for Dr. Meed, the intern, who was dependent on the good evaluation of the third-year resident for his continuing success in his residency, to tell Dr. Rorcas to behave himself. I could see from the conflict in his expression that sensitive Dr. Meed was in a very tough position. He was stricken with pain, though, as I watched the final few minutes of this wretched case.

After he and I had seen our patient to the recovery room, Dr. Meed sought out Grace. She was sitting with head resting on her crossed arms in the break room. Without mentioning what had happened, Dr. Meed spoke quietly to her.

"Grace, I want to personally thank you for the fine job you did in that last case. I really appreciated the help you gave us."

This display of regard was such unprecedented behavior, complimenting the scrub nurse who often seems like part of the wallpaper in the many operative procedures performed in this unit every day. I could see that Dr. Meed was trying to make up for his silence in the operating room. He was touched by her plight, as powerless as he felt to do anything about it. I felt sick that such behavior as Dr. Rorcas had exhibited could silently pass into the night, unexamined by any but the few of us present. To do nothing, I felt, was to remain complicit in the crime that had taken place.

I thought about what I should do. I ended up writing a detailed description of the events and slipped it under the door of the office of the staff physician who had administrative responsibility for the overall affairs of the perinatal service. I agonized about whether I was just a tattletale and would be perceived as an agitator. I took some reassurance from knowing that Dr. Jessup was a caring and fair person, and had maintained good relationships with the L & D nurses since her own days as intern and resident.

Apparently, when Dr. Jessup read my letter, she turned it over to the physician who oversees the residency program here. He called Dr. Rorcas and Dr. Meed into his office, handed them my letter to read, and asked them to comment on the truth of its contents. When Dr. Rorcas responded that the information was basically true, he was reprimanded verbally, as was Dr. Meed.

They were told that no physician was ever to treat any of the staff here in such a manner, no matter the circumstances.

How do I know this? Because Dr. Portman, the physician who did the reprimanding, called me at home to discuss this whole sad affair. But having stressed that the reprimand was a stern one, and that a note would be placed in their files and would follow them for all of their residency and beyond, Dr. Portman qualified his remarks by telling me that brutish Dr. Rorcas was "one of our brightest young men," and that, in spite of his totally unacceptable behavior, we could all learn something of value from this experience.

I was dreading my next meeting with Rorcas, which came just nights later. He was seated in the alcove near the front desk along with several other residents and didn't see me approaching, able to hear him joking about the inefficacy of some nurse who had "written him up." A few hours later, when he came into the PAR where I was responsible for one of his diabetic postsurgical patients, he looked over my chart entries. Making no reference to previous events, he told me that I had taken good care of his patient and that my notes were in excellent order. Strange, untypical behavior for this arrogant shit heel, but I accepted it without comment.

For the remainder of his residency, Dr. Rorcas treated me with scrupulously correct behavior. No reference was ever made to the incident that had produced our conflict on that awful night. I doubt very much that he knew anything of my conversation with Dr. Portman, or that I knew there had been consequences for him—albeit a hand slap—but at least some sort of embarrassment.

I have had a great relationship with Dr. Meed. He's a senior resident now, almost ready to go into practice. I think this deeply conservative member of a somewhat fundamentalist faith was troubled by the events of that long-ago night, and his sense of decency was somewhat mollified by the consequences for Dr. Rorcas and himself, that such abuse did not go unremarked or unpunished. Yet he never referred to the incident again, which was strange to me, who tends to talk things through to exhaustion. Perhaps a gender issue at work. Or perhaps such discussion would have meant trespassing the subtle barrier that docs hold up against the too-close scrutiny of their behavior as a group.

I have diverged a bit (and at length) from my original topic, which had to do with the article on nursing and our problems in achieving respect. I think many nurses have a pretty clear fix on the value of our work for the patient. We know that nurses are not doctors, that each group has something unique and distinct to offer people in their times of sickness and distress. Many times our efforts intertwine and overlap with each other. We do not have to be at war, although at times our behavior, individually or collectively, smacks of belligerence or disdain. For nurses, like almost all groups in a perceived subordinate role, there is a great deal of room for feelings of resentment, bitterness, impotency, frustration, etc.

Almost every year when a national survey seeks to discover which profession has the highest degree of trust among the American public, nursing is voted number one. We should relish and cherish this regard, and work hard to be perceived as skilled, knowledgeable, and caring practitioners. Thus might change the portrayal of many nurses in the media (i.e., sitcoms and soaps) in which nurses are cast as bits of fluff or aging harridans who hang out at the workstation answering the telephone. The stereotype of nurses as possessing more cleavage than brains will have a better chance of disappearing into the rearview mirror.

In reality, most of us have a multiplicity of skills, performing many of the roles that were formerly the exclusive province of the physician. A good nurse uses her head and hands and heart to make a difference in his or her patient's outcome. We usually practice in a setting where there are far too many persons to care for, and many times endure stress that would fell a less committed individual. However, no one should suggest that nursing is a sacred calling, one for which we ought to sacrifice ourselves for the common good. For some, nursing may be a vocation; for most, it is a career, albeit one I believe that has great significance. Nurses are no different than any other group in seeking to have adequate recognition and compensation for the value of the service they perform.

Last month we had the painters here to refurbish the walls a bit, and I did something I'd wanted to do for years. I approached two of the white-suited gentlemen in the hallway. One was rolling paint on the ceiling in a very relaxed manner. Another was peering at the newly painted surface and pointing out any missed spots to his comrade. At that moment, the two painters had to make way for a crew of nurses and doctors hurrying a patient in a bed through the corridor on the way to emergency surgery. When that drama played out and things returned to normal, I approached the men in white and asked if they would mind answering a terrifically nosy question. How much did our med center painters get paid these days?

Mr. Spotterman laughed good-naturedly. "You'd be surprised. Not as much as the electricians, plumbers, or carpenters!" Then he went on to quote an hourly wage slightly higher than that of the nurses working on the day shift. "But remember," he cautioned me in a serious tone of voice, "we really had to be *trained* for this job!"

It's very hard for me to understand this. Painting and working with electrical problems, plumbing, or building materials are surely necessary and desirable services that must be performed periodically. How much more important should the nurse's role be perceived and valued? The stress, the responsibility for lives, the skills, education, critical judgment, etc., all are operating at a vastly higher level. You just can't sell me on the idea that it's strictly the law of the market place, the law of supply and demand that dictates this disproportionate state of affairs. There is a fundamental flaw in our value system that says a painter of walls is to be compensated more than the man or woman who paints iodine solution on a patient's belly as he is prepared for surgery, then goes on to assist in so many other ways with keeping that patient safe and well.

Just the other morning, Tracy, one of my young nurse acquaintances, related a run-in she had with an intern who was here from another state getting experience in obstetrics for a month. I don't recall the circumstances that precipitated his comment to her that "You're only a nurse. You're standing still, going nowhere. I'm a doctor, on the other hand. I'll be going places. You ought to be thinking about doing more with yourself."

Tracy's reply to him was probably incomprehensible based on the insensitivity he had displayed to that point. Tracy told him that he knew nothing about her and her motives in doing the work she had chosen. That he obviously had no understanding of what nurses do and the possible satisfaction to be derived from this work.

Every time I come to work, I have the opportunity to be involved, if only fleetingly, in some of the most intense moments in peoples' lives. My patients are almost always in a vulnerable state in which their personal resources are being tested to the maximum. I could be insensitive to this, just performing tasks, carrying out orders, some complex and some mundane. Yet really being a nurse calls for so much more in terms of judgment, integration of knowledge, and regard for the whole person, body and spirit.

Sometimes I do my work, giving much less than it's possible for me to give. I perform skills and complete tasks in rote fashion. Then there are those other times when I can almost sense myself working, thinking, giving with a kind of identification with these poor women and their ordeal that takes us out of the everyday run of affairs and demonstrates how human beings who were strangers a moment before can have a special bond. Those times when I forgot what I was about were times when both the patient and I lost. When I really do the work of the true nurse, there is such an enormous, deep-down sense of satisfaction that no one can take away my sense of self-respect.

It's this underlying sense of my own worth, and the worth of my work to my patients, that allows me to push down my natural dismay when some tormented creature, in the throes of transition contractions, urps up her burrito dinner all over me. What's more important, my fastidious nose or her feelings of shame that she has contravened all the rules of *norteamericano* etiquette? I've seen the look of personal failure on the face of a patient when another nurse or physician responds with an "Aw, shit" to a similar incident. Cleaning up the mess and reassuring her that I don't think any less of her because of this very understandable betrayal by her body allows me to serve her without in any way being servile.

In my fantasies, I look down the road to a time when nursing gets its act together and promotes such respect for this profession that men and women are pounding on the doors of higher education wanting to enter the profession. Being a perennial optimist, I think greater respect for our profession can occur, but it will take some concerted effort. More political involvement. More self-governance to improve our own practice. More advocacy to ensure that patients are not victimized by incompetent or mean-spirited doctors or nurses. Less willingness to accept abusive treatment or condescension from any member of the health-care team. Less willingness to be told by nursing tower dwellers what is important to focus on in delivering decent and knowledgeable patient care.

I am so very proud that I willingly chose this work after I made a false step in my younger years toward academia. I was sitting in a Victorian Lit class in the first three weeks of a master's program when it came to me that this wasn't what I wanted to do at all. It took me some years of living to come to the realization of what I was really attracted to in a career. I have never regretted one minute of what is many times difficult and stress-laden work. I don't for one minute think I'm going nowhere. Honey, I've arrived.

CHAPTER THIRTY-SIX

"With a look of blinding tenderness and compassion, Jaime put his hand on the man's shoulder . . . and in dulcet Spanish began to inform him of his loss."

June 28

TONIGHT IS JAIME Bautista's last few hours of call as a senior resident in the high-risk obstetrical unit. In July, he will be leaving this institution where he spent four years of residency, as well as his student years in the School of Medicine. He is entering private practice as an obstetrician/gynecologist in one of our local communities. Jaime is one of the nurses' all-time favorites as a person and as a physician, and we planned a celebration to honor the completion of his work on our unit.

Even if a senior resident isn't our favorite, if they have been, in fact, not the most pleasant of MDs to work with, the nurses will recognize the doctor's last call by having some sort of celebration, a cake at least. We applaud the monumental effort that goes into surviving this grueling residency. The senior residents have come to expect this accolade from the L & D nurses, and we would not wish to wound even the greatest cheeseball in history by failing to recognize their graduation. Hey, we're that kind of group.

We have such affection for Jaime, though, and everyone is eager to give him a lavish send-off. A gentle giant, he resembles a Mexican American panda bear. His dealings with his fellow physicians, the nurses, his patients, indeed everyone, are uniformly calm and considerate. I have never seen him raise his voice in anger, no matter what the stress or provocation. He is the ideal teacher, and one can see how junior residents and interns blossom when he is leading his team.

One of the most poignant moments in my recollection of Jaime's stay here took place in the midst of a great tragedy. That morning, we received a frantic call from the ER to let us know they were bringing up a pregnant woman in full-blown cardiac arrest. The scene in the LICU was unbelievable as physicians and nurses rushed in to help. I caught a glimpse of this Latina mother looking gray, unmoving, and lifeless. After a moment, it was impossible to see as the staff surrounded her bed and did everything we know how to do to save a life that is slipping away. Checking for a baby's heartbeat, it was apparent that the little one was lost. After about thirty minutes of working over the woman with absolutely no response, she was pronounced dead.

It turned out that this woman had come to the hospital a while back with a fairly common pregnancy complaint, a urinary tract infection. She had gone home with antibiotics to treat her problem. That morning, she had called her husband at work to tell him that she was feeling terrible, and that he would have to come home to take her back to the hospital. En route, she had complained of increasing difficulty in getting her breath. As he pulled into the parking lot, her husband could not arouse her. After an appalled staff had checked her in the ER, they had rushed her up to us on the chance that the baby could be salvaged, if not the mother. It was too late for both. She was ultimately diagnosed to have been the victim of septic shock, an overwhelming system collapse that had grown out of the infection that had spread from her urinary tract into her blood.

As staff began the grim tasks of postmortem care, the lobby clerk came in to tell us that the woman's husband was outside our doors, wanting to see his wife. Jaime, who was then the third-year resident, went out of the LICU and met the anxious gentleman as he entered the unit. With a look of blinding tenderness and compassion, Jaime put his hand on the man's shoulder, leaned in close, and in dulcet Spanish began to inform him of his loss. The husband began to sob, and Jaime engulfed him with his not unsubstantial frame. That has to be the most god-awful part of being a physician. Jaime was so visibly moved by the tragic plight of this immigrant husband whom he had never met until that anguished moment.

So tonight, in honor of this good man, we rolled out a long curl of butcher paper and penned in colorful bold letters: "Good Luck, Jaime!" Each nurse adopted a letter and devoted it to some amusing or admirable aspect of the Jaime we all knew and loved. Dana took the *J* and wrote, "J is for jalapeños! Hey, Jaime, I'm hot for your bod!" which eventually made the unassuming and somewhat portly young man blush rosily, then laugh wholeheartedly when he read it. The mental picture of the stunningly beautiful, tall Dana next to the short, stocky resident was incongruous, yet there is definitely something very attractive, I think, about a man who is so genuinely good at heart.

At about 1:00 a.m., Dr. Felikian, the third-year resident, had knocked on the door of the senior sleep room and got Jaime up to "Come to the LICU, there's a red blanket footling breech on the way up." As Jaime passed by the break room door, he glanced inside at the pack of nurses, residents, and assorted staff who were waiting for him with barely contained excitement. A shout of "Good-bye, Jaime! Yeah, Jaime!" went up. He sheepishly came forward, aware now that the RB was the traditional ruse used to get seniors out of bed for their farewell party.

At the end of the lavish spread of food, cake, ice cream, and faux champagne (sparkling apple cider), Jaime got up on a chair and slowly scanned the butcher paper banner we had tacked up. He silently read the various remarks– complimentary, amusing, even ribald. Then he carefully pulled the banner down at each scotch-taped end and just as carefully rolled it up. He thanked us in his customary quiet way. There were not a few tears in the room.

I know that, if my childbearing years were not in the past, Jaime is one person I would unhesitatingly seek out for obstetrical care. His patients will be fortunate to have such a fine, knowledgeable, and skilled man to attend to their needs. Have a good life, Jaime! You so deserve it.

CHAPTER THIRTY-SEVEN

"Farnaz is practical in the extreme and leaves the esoteric style of nursing to the hotshots."

July 10

I AM TEAMED IN the PAR/antepartum problems room tonight with Farnaz, a remarkable nurse who comes from the Middle East. She is a strange mixture of intelligence and naiveté, of super-organizational skills and little foibles. When I first started working here, a newly oriented staff nurse, Farnaz was tough getting used to. She had a fully realized concept of how to run the PAR, put together over years of experience. She rapidly brought new nurses under her regime, expecting all newcomers to assimilate into her system.

Being rather shy, and many times feeling overwhelmed at the beginning, I was content to accept Farnaz's lead. Still, it was aggravating to have her, for instance, flip on the overhead lights moments after I'd turned them down so that some desperately tired woman could try to sleep. Or listen to the sometimes abrupt and managing way she had with patients. Or watch her shoo visitors out the door when the patients wanted to chat about their new babies, their surgery, etc.

As I came to know Farnaz over that first year, I realized that she was quite kind in her unique way. If you proved willing to work, work being her god, she quickly became your friend. In time, she shared with me some great stories about this unit in the years before I came. This room has a limit of six patients, and when there are six, it's a crush. When Farnaz started working here, however, they would admit up to *nine* women, and she was the only nurse giving care. In those bad old days, a separate team of nurses worked in the PAR and LICU, and the regular labor and delivery nurses never set foot in the door.

Farnaz told me that she would start at one end of the PAR to take vital signs—blood pressure, pulse, and respirations, sometimes a temperature. By the time she made her way across the room to the ninth patient, it was past time to start all over again. The funniest stories were of the way women behaved when it was the practice to try and stop premature labor with an alcohol infusion—nothing like trying to care for a bunch of drunken women. The only way I can envision nine patients in this long corridor-like room would involve removing all the consoles that house the fetal monitors. That makes sense, because I believe in those days this equipment was not in use.

The other nurses in the unit ignored Farnaz completely and never took pity on her overworked state. It irritated the charge nurse when compelled to come into the room to relieve her for a much-deserved dinner break. She flounced in, Farnaz recounted, with a retinue of LVNs or nursing assistants to help her do the same work Farnaz did alone. Under such demanding and stressful conditions, Farnaz learned to be highly organized simply to survive.

Now she is a wonder to watch as she comes into the PAR at the beginning of the night shift. You can see her surveying the room while she receives report from the two evening shift nurses. As soon as they are out the door, she starts in, shifting around the beds until she has each patient situated for the maximum of efficiency, the minimum of duplicated steps. She shakes her head at the debris left behind by much younger nurses who have not been able to cope with the often grueling load of tasks to be accomplished in this complex care area. Before many minutes have passed, every surface is spotlessly clean, the counters denuded of all clutter.

Farnaz is practical in the extreme and leaves the esoteric style of nursing to the hotshots. She gets right down to what has to be handled, short term, and sets up a plan for more long-term objectives. It does not matter if there are critically ill patients. She gives the nurse who partners with her a great deal of confidence that, no matter how complex the assignment, it is manageable.

She isn't the most sensitive soul, I suppose, as she relates to our patients, even though she calls them all "darlink." Maybe in the Middle Eastern culture from which she springs, they haven't heard of reflective listening. ("For God's sake, Nurse Jones, why won't someone tell me whether my growth is malignant?" "I hear a lot of anxiety in your voice, Mr. Smith. Tell me what your feelings are about this.") But Farnaz is one who will get a woman off damp or blood-soaked sheets onto fresh linen, or move a long-term patient from a niggling narrow stretcher onto a more comfortable bed.

One odd thing I have observed while working with Farnaz has to do with charting. It is impossible to read her nurse's notes, the ones entered at the end of our shift or before a patient is discharged from the PAR. After working with Farnaz for many months, I realized that this problem was related to the indecipherable scribble she produced. Further, the note took up the same space in the record—exactly three lines—whether this was a routine postoperative case or the care of a woman with an enormity of problems and interventions. Another organizational strategy?

Was I being so very OCD with my extensive and detailed summary notes? I couldn't help myself, even if I had to stay over at times to complete my charting. I don't think Farnaz spent one second worrying about the content or worth of her charting, recognizing that few ever scrutinize nursing notes unless something goes gravely amiss. Not much ever goes amiss when Farnaz is rendering care.

I have learned a lot from Farnaz, because a lack of organizational skills was my besetting personal defect when I embarked on this career. You can't just want to help patients. You have to actualize nursing concepts so that they do something concrete to promote patients' well-being. Farnaz is past master of getting the job done.

The other thing I have learned in my association with this wonderful woman is not to necessarily trust my first, even second judgment about people. So many times I have found a fascinating person, albeit different from myself, beyond my first impression.

CHAPTER THIRTY-EIGHT

". . .while the fetal heart rate was diving in a very ominous way, contributing to our sense that we might be listening to this child's last heartbeats."

August 14

T HIS HAS BEEN the oddest month. The annual summer flood of patients is in progress. We all know it's coming, but no one addresses the fact that more babies seem to deliver between July and December, and that perhaps we need to staff more people for this barrage. Also, each July sees the entrance of twelve new OB-GYN interns who are largely unfamiliar with the service and need to be mentored in a whole raft of new skills and knowledge. The experienced staff here, physicians and nurses, will have to strain to be patient while they learn and grow in their grasp of the work.

In the face of this yearly crush, we have had a sudden and dramatic loss of nursing staff. This personnel dilemma is due in part to a clustering of pregnancies. It is also due to nurses simply getting fed up with the enormity of the workload here and bailing out. Many nurses, as I do, have children home from school for the summer and want to take their annual vacation during this prime family time. This phenomenon adds to the paucity of numbers on the schedule. I know that the two weeks I was away in July helped me refresh myself for the inevitable battering I would take when I returned.

When I came back to work, as expected, it was to a stream of very taxing nights. Often the entire team of doctors and nurses spent every moment totally on the run, not sitting down for five minutes, getting through on quick gulps of rotgut coffee. I felt very bad for the uninitiated, the nurses fresh out of nursing school who were trying to learn to be labor and delivery nurses under these conditions. How could anyone cope with the inevitable challenges of beginning one's first job as a licensed nurse under the oppressive stress here, with the constant banging of the double doors as yet another woman was wheeled onto the unit to have her child?

I particularly worried about a group of six student nurses whom I taught at the beginning of summer. They are here from four-year bachelor's degree programs, heading into their last year of nursing school. They came to get good, practical skills under true-to-life conditions. Boy, it can't get much more real than this.

They have performed so admirably, working side by side with the nursing staff and helping us get through the long, hot summer. Teaching them, orienting them to this unit, was perfect for me. I like to teach for short spells, as was the case for the four nights I spent with these nursing students. I helped one young girl through what was for her the sheer terror of holding a live, wiggling newborn for the first time. I provided a crash course in obstetrical Spanish. I attempted to prepare them emotionally for some of the inevitably shocking things they would see in an emergency. After a bit, though, I get tired of hearing myself talk and I want to get back to my patients. I know that full-time teaching is probably not for me, but it is a nice compliment that our nurse manager thought I would make a good instructor and role model for these soon-to-graduate students.

One of the most upsetting incidents I have ever been involved in as a nurse, as a person, occurred a few nights back while I was working as part of the delivery team. We had a moderately busy time of it and were just grabbing some coffee in a lull when, from our station in the break room, we heard the call that a "crash" cesarean section was going back to surgery from the LICU. Up we sprang and met the physicians as they were pulling the patient's bed into the corridor and heading for the delivery area.

"What have you got for us?" I quizzed the two residents.

"We have a fifteen-year-old here," Dr. Medavoy, the night OB resident said in a breathless voice. "Her scalp sample came back 7.01, and now the baby is having wicked late decels."

7.01. That value was the pH of the baby's blood, a highly acidic state indicating a seriously oxygen-compromised infant, one theoretically heading into a terminal stage.

As this little scene was taking place, an anesthesia resident brushed past us, walking in the opposite direction toward the labor rooms. It struck me as odd that he seemed to be ignoring us. An anesthesiologist is crucial to the staging of an emergency cesarean section because nothing can be done, surgically speaking, until the patient is numbed or put to sleep. General anesthesia, rapidly induced, was called for in this most critical situation.

Dr. Morrisey was stepping around us as we continued to wheel the bed forward, talking as we pushed. I was concerned enough to ask, just in case this man was unaware, whether this was indeed a "crash." The anesthesia resident continued walking toward the other end of the unit in the face of Dr. Medavoy's excited affirmative.

Dr. Morrisey's ignoring our drama could mean only one thing, I decided. He must have known that his partner, the second anesthesia doc, was sleeping in the call room located next door to the surgical suite. Still, it was odd that he would leave such an emergency for his partner to handle alone. When feasible, the two of them would typically come in to assist one another in starting the case, at least until the baby was out.

Once in the operating room, things became frantic. The two obstetrical residents, Drs. Medavoy and Bart Randal, who were the type to get rather excited under stressful circumstances, kept yelling for things to be done. They seemed unable in their hyper state to perceive that all these things were being handled by the efficient nurses, scrub techs, and the intern. The main problem, though, was that there was no anesthesiologist to put the young girl under, and they screamed at me to get someone, somehow, stat.

I had already knocked on the door of the anesthesia call room where I had supposed the resident was sleeping. No response, so I opened the door to find empty cots with mussed sheets. I then called on the intercom system to the labor desk and told Ruth and Jerome to get ahold of the anesthesia docs and get them back here instantly. With no one showing up, and the whole OR team now listening tensely to the slow descent of the baby's heart rate, I ran to the call box again and asked where the missing docs were. "Can't find them," responded the clerks.

Frantic now, myself, I ran out into the empty delivery area corridor and yelled at the top of my lungs, "We need anesthesia help in the OR!" I thought they might be in one of the deliveries ongoing at the moment. Nothing. I rushed to the operating room to tell them the bad news.

The ominous sound of the failing fetal heart rate sickened me. An intern, wanting to assist but helpless to do anything meaningful, put an oxygen mask over the young and terrified girl's face. What happened next shook everyone to the core. Drs. Medavoy and Randal, not knowing whether they would be getting any help before this baby perished inside its young mother, went ahead and cut this girl after rapidly infiltrating the general incision line with local anesthesia. She was completely awake and surely could not have received but a whisker of numbing. Every cell in my body protested hearing her reaction to the excruciating pain, as evidenced by her heartrending screams as she felt herself being opened up from just below her belly button down to her pelvis.

It was truly the most awful moment I have ever experienced. The pain was so intense that the young girl cried out that she was dying. All my coworkers—OB surgeons, the intern, nurses, scrub techs, and the pediatric team here to resuscitate the infant, were being equally traumatized by what they had to do to this girl to try to save her baby's life.

The anesthesia resident eventually arrived, long minutes after the baby was out and the pediatric docs and nurses were valiantly trying to give the very limp and colorless baby a chance at life. He strolled in, looked at no one in the room, and in a seemingly dispassionate manner proceeded to intubate the girl and put her to sleep. He expressed not one word of apology or explanation for his strange absence. The air sizzled with tension, but no one spoke. Above their surgical masks, Dr. Medavoy and Dr. Randal appeared to be in the grip of terminal rage.

Later, I sought out the other anesthesia resident, Dr. Monteverde, a quiet Filipina, who told me what happened from her perspective. She had been awakened earlier with a request from the OB resident to place an epidural for a patient who was pushing prematurely, thereby developing a swollen cervix and impeding her progress in labor. As she was in the midst of this procedure, her partner, Evan Morrisey, had come over to the labor room in which she was working to tell her that she was needed urgently in surgery. That she was up for the next case. She told him, "No way," that she was in the middle of the epidural and that he should return to the OR stat and do what was needed. So I was not mistaken in believing that Dr. Morrisey was very much aware that surgery was going forward, an emergency at that.

There were so many witnesses to the events of this night that I felt sure that this guy's head was going to roll. I had yet to see a physician booted out of medicine, but I felt that this man's behavior surely merited the strongest sort of censure. Even knowing how medicine circles its wagons around most instances of physician malfeasance, there were too many of us present when this outrage was perpetrated on a totally innocent victim, all unnecessarily. Patrick Finelli, the intern, was in favor of performing castration on this guy, using room air for anesthesia.

I went over to the recovery room several hours later to visit the new mother whose small baby was at the moment fighting for its life in the NICU. I worried so that the experience she had undergone would leave her indelibly shattered for life, but she seemed uncommonly at peace. She remembered the pain but rationalized it so heroically. "Was *para mi bebé*," she stated, "to save *la vida de mi bebé*," her sweet little Madonna-like face transformed with a beatific smile. I can't help thinking that she will be a good mother, in spite of her youth, and if her baby is spared.

All of this is recalled to me tonight because, as it happens, I am the circulating nurse in a cesarean section in which Evan Morrisey is rendering anesthesia. He stands before me garbed in the deep burgundy scrubs that differentiate the anesthesia team from the usual frumpy blues and greens of the surgical or OB team's attire. His Rolex gleams on his well-tanned arm. He is tall and strikingly handsome, chatting casually through the course of this routine operation with the nurse anesthetist about his investments—"penny stocks, IRAs, and Daddy's trust fund." His other theme is the array of jobs he can get that pay a lot and don't require much effort. "Why do big open heart cases when you can do a couple of gall bladders and hip replacements and get the same amount of money?" It's not too difficult to scan this man's character.

My god, I would have trouble sleeping at night if I knew I had been the author of some other human being's agony. I am still having nightmares about what went on in this very room just a few nights past. He ought to be arrested.

Addendum: As it turned out to my chagrin, nothing happened to this physician. The events of the surgery in which I participated with Dr. Morrisey were reported to the anesthesia department by Drs. Medavoy and Randal. On being questioned, Dr. Morrisey responded that he did not realize there was an emergency in progress, or, of course, he would have responded promptly. There is not one person involved who gives this account any credence, but I suppose it is difficult to punish someone on such a serious charge if there is a shred of chance that he might be telling the truth.

I did not hear about the surprising results of this investigation until a few months later when Dr. Medavoy was back on our unit as part of her regular third-year rotation. In discussing this mess with me, she just shook her head at the inefficacy of the medical brass in punishing this bent guy for his crime.

I've decided to let my anger go. I cannot see what is in another person's heart, and the only behavior I can try to control is my own. I know that, many times, human justice is very flawed. I have a personal belief that there is some dimension of universal justice in which all of our inadequate human efforts are made whole.

Dr. Morrisey will have to live with himself. What goes around comes around. Evan, I'd be on the lookout.

CHAPTER THIRTY-NINE

"I am beginning to feel uneasy about the implications of all this."

August 16

SOMETHING HAPPENED TONIGHT that shook us. At about 1:00 a.m., Ruth called Merilee to come to the desk. "We've used every last bed," Ruth informed Merilee. "And the ER has called up three more labor patients. Where are we going to put them?"

It has been apparent for some time that this department, as currently set up, can no longer handle the consistently heavy numbers of women arriving on our doorstep for maternity care. We have tried to adjust to the situation, opening up storage areas and turning them into labor rooms. Now we are sacrificing one side of the mother-baby assessment suite for the same purpose. But finally, there is a limit to such accommodation. This was the night we had all known was coming but had hoped would not—the night when a laboring patient would arrive with no bed available to put her in.

Merilee told me about the situation when she came to my labor room to see if I had any potential deliveries on the horizon. "There's a woman sitting out by the desk for whom I have no bed," she said forlornly. "And she is definitely having contractions."

I explained to Merilee that I did have one multip (woman with a history of previous deliveries) who might be expected to go back to delivery within the hour. "Well, let's pray someone vacates a bed soon," she commented before moving on.

Fate stepped in and twenty minutes later I was calling for an intern to take my frantic patient back to delivery to have her baby. As I helped push the bed past the desk, I saw three pregnant women seated side by side in molded vinyl chairs just to the left of the labor desk. When I returned, after handing my patient over to the delivery team, I asked Ruth to tell me which of the three women most needed to be in a bed and have her baby monitored.

"The woman in the middle, probably," the clerk responded. "She's a diabetic, but she didn't have any prenatal care."

Trust Ruth. Even though she is only the clerk, she has helped admit a million pregnant patients and she has learned from experience how to triage problems expertly. I went over to the little lineup of women sitting in their "labor chairs" and told the middle patient, Mrs. Guadalupe Cano, that she was coming with me. It was hard to avoid the poignant looks I received from the other two patients who must have wondered why I was passing over them. One had a contraction that doubled her up even as I stood there.

In my labor room, Mrs. Cano settled her massive girth into the bed. She was forty-five, with streaks of silver shot through her long, unkempt hair. Her feet were not clean, which told me that Mrs. Cano was not paying good attention to her diabetes. Most diabetics take scrupulous care of their feet, as problems of circulation are often seen first in the lower extremities. That and the fact that she had sought no prenatal care made me wonder how much Guadalupe Cano was in denial, or simply how ignorant she was of the health threat with which she was living.

I fought to get elastic belts around the huge belly of my new patient. I then began to search for the baby's heartbeat by moving the fetal cardiac transducer over the brown expanse of my new patient's abdomen. I tried all the common locations where the baby's heart reflects the sound waves that allow us to count the beats that appear as a tracing on the fetal monitor strip. No luck, so I tried some of the uncommon sites that work when the baby is in an unusual position. I was not initially too concerned with my lack of success. It is often a challenge to pick up the heartbeat when a mother has a six-inch fat pad to help obscure the signal. When I had spent over ten minutes trying to find baby's heartbeat with no luck, I decided I needed some help.

I went out into the corridor and intercepted Dr. Georgia Hodgeman. "Can you come see the new patient in the A labor room? I'm not sure, but we may be in trouble here. Better bring the scanner."

The tired resident pulled the ultrasound machine from down the hallway behind her, asking me what I knew about Mrs. Cano. I filled her in as we entered the room. Dr. Hodgeman greeted Mrs. Cano in the perfect Spanish she had learned as a medical student in Guadalajara, Mexico. She did not hint at any problem as she folded back the sheet and squirted a healthy glob of transducer gel on the woman's impressive belly. There was no sense alarming her when it might turn out that the baby's heart rate was normal, just difficult to find.

Georgia was solemn of face when, some minutes later, she pushed the monitor screen into a position where Mrs. Cano could see it. "Guadalupe," she addressed the patient quietly. "I think you know what I am about to tell you. How long have you sensed that your baby wasn't moving?"

Oh god. I hadn't been looking for this, in spite of all the forewarnings. Mrs. Cano wasn't ready to deal with the fact that her baby was dead either. She had a stubborn and angry look on her face as Georgia began to show her the facts as the little monitor screen revealed them.

"See,"–she pointed to a spot on the monitor–"here is your baby's heart, but it is not moving at all."

"No, no, *doctora*," Mrs. Cano protested angrily. "My baby was moving today. In fact, I can feel my baby moving right now."

"Let me show you something else," Georgia continued, not insensitively, trying to get our patient to face the sad truth. "Here are the little scalp bones. The way they look here, I can see that your baby has not been alive for some time. I'm sorry, but you have to know the truth."

Mrs. Cano was adamant that there was a mistake. During the time that Dr. Hodgeman continued taking Guadalupe's history and doing the physical for this diabetic Latina, she had to listen to protestations that we were wrong, that the baby was still OK. Finally, dispiritedly, Georgia Hodgeman left.

Mrs. Cano continued to swear that her baby was alive and that we just weren't finding her baby's heartbeat. I agreed to her request that she be allowed to have the fetal monitor transducer so that she could find the baby's heart herself. Pitifully, she kept up this fruitless exercise for a full ten minutes before she let go of the equipment. Thereafter, she lay wide-eyed and stricken looking.

When her lab work results came back, Mrs. Cano's blood sugar was in the high 300s. Amazingly high. Now was not the time to take this woman to task for her failure to seek medical treatment during this complicated pregnancy. Here one could see the vast difference between cultures at work. I think most of the American population of pregnant women who became pregnant at forty-five years of age, diabetics on top of that, would be on the physician's doorstep almost from the moment of conception, if not before. But maybe it was not a cultural thing at all, just the great human tendency toward denial of unpalatable truths, that somehow all will work out fine in spite of the worst.

Later in the morning, with Merilee's help, we were able to juggle the patients around a bit and move Mrs. Cano to the private room we reserve for patients laboring with a fetal demise. This plan was a reflection of the decency and selflessness of our charge nurse. Merilee had to look out for the welfare of the continuing population of laboring women forced to wait on chairs near the desk until a bed was freed up by someone going to delivery or was discharged home.

I'd like to think that this phenomenon of no beds for patients is a onetime fluke, that we will never see this situation again. What are we going to do if this begins a trend that continues? Even if space could be arranged, there are simply not enough physicians or nurses to see safely to the needs of all these high-risk pregnant women. Our census has gradually grown over this past year to double what it was in the past. We aren't able to train enough new nurses to plump up the staff needed to do the job effectively. Instead of being able to utilize the newly oriented nurses to relieve what was the impossible workload for the veteran nursing staff, we have to spread out the newcomers to help with the great influx of new patients. I am beginning to feel most uneasy about the implications of all this.

CHAPTER FORTY

". . .like snatching life from the yawning jaws of death."

August 19

I CAME TO WORK tonight more wasted from tiredness than I ever should. Bill and I had some friends from college visiting for whom we had to clean and cook. The effort it took to atone for my typical casual style of housekeeping ate into the time that I usually spend resting between work shifts. I thought somehow that I would luck out and have a reasonable night, even though there has not been one of those in recent memory.

When I came through the double doors after dressing in scrubs in the locker room, there seemed to be tension permeating the atmosphere, a sense that something heavy was in progress. I had asked to work in delivery tonight to follow up with the students I had taught earlier this summer. I was not destined to see them for even a few moments. Instead, I ended up sequestered in surgery for long hours, with no real sense of what was going on around me in the remainder of the delivery area with its six birth rooms and several ORs. Anita Ewald, the relief charge nurse, asked me to go directly to the operating room where a very critical patient was about to have a hysterectomy.

It was a surprise to me, having understood that I was being sent to assist the circulating nurse in the OR, to have Miranda gratefully turn the whole case over to me. She made her exit as soon as she had given me report. The patient, who was on the point of being prepped and readied for general anesthesia, was in a very tenuous position. Mrs. Cortina had not left the operating room after a crash cesarean section for a bleeding placenta previa. After the baby had been delivered, the placenta was found to have grown into the muscular wall of the uterus, instead of only being adherent to the inner lining of the womb. This situation resulted in further massive bleeding for an already compromised person. The placenta was inextricably locked in place and would continue hemorrhaging, thus dictating a second surgery to remove the uterus.

During the initial surgery, when parts of the placenta appeared to explode out of the uterus under pressure from the built-up fluids, those present said that a tremendous volume of blood was lost. Mrs. Cortina's hematocrit, or red cell concentration, dropped to 16 percent, half of what it should be. This kind of systemic crisis makes everyone in the operating room extremely tense, because even though the patient can be transfused quickly, if the body gets too blood depleted before replacement kicks in, shock and death can occur.

The OB surgeons had called for blood to transfuse the patient stat. Then commenced an endless succession of trips back and forth to the pneumatic tube where we receive incoming packs of blood from the storage bank in the main hospital. Because of the life-threatening hemorrhage, the surgeons wanted not only units of packed red cells but also whole blood containing important clotting factors, and fresh frozen plasma and platelets. The Red Cross had to be contacted for the whole blood because it is such a precious item.

As circulating nurse, I was on the run for the three hours this procedure took. A cesarean hysterectomy is quite a different prospect from the more typical operation done to remove a woman's uterus when not associated with pregnancy. The operation Mrs. Cortina was having was intended to deal with her disastrous hemorrhage, the principal reason such surgery is attempted.

Whenever we hear that a patient is having a cesarean hysterectomy, it calls up the specter of death. A C-hys is almost always associated with some complication of delivery and is in itself a source of heavy bleeding for patients already compromised by heavy blood loss. Circulating these cases is one of the greatest challenges for an obstetrical nurse, and I had never had responsibility for this procedure from start to finish. I was feeling quite pressured, to say the least. My adrenalin load was instantaneous, and my initial sluggishness from sleep deprivation fled precipitously.

Fortunately, Brad Antonia was the scrub tech for this case, and he is very experienced and confident about his abilities in such complex surgeries. Working together, we kept on our toes and did not fall behind with the part we were playing. As the difficult case went on, I began to think that, yes, we would be able to keep up with the fire of demands from the surgical team.

Still, the case was such a challenge. There was a variety of equipment needed with which I was barely familiar, if not completely unacquainted. I was told to get special retractors that we did not keep in L & D. I had to request them from downstairs in the gynecology surgical unit and arrange for someone to get them. Then clips to clamp bleeding vessels were requested, another item that I had never been asked to provide, along with a ton of sponges in all sizes. I could not bear the thought that any lack of knowledge or skill on my part might jeopardize the outcome for our stunningly critical patient.

Brad and I had to keep the most accurate count of all the little and big pieces of blood-soaked gauze, what are called sponges, because the operating site was a well of red. It would be easy for the surgeons to leave a sponge inside. So full of free-flowing blood was Mrs. Cortina's belly, the surgeons at times were stuffing the area with big, green linen towels to absorb the blood. They needed to visualize the target areas that required cauterization and suturing, and the continuous outpouring of the patient's blood was obscuring the targeted surgical site.

As each sponge or towel was packed inside, Brad would call it out to me, as in, "Green towel in the right gutter." I immediately noted it on the tally board on the wall. As it was removed, I crossed it off. When the docs were closing the peritoneal cavity, Brad and I did our count of all the sponges and were able to tell them to stop and find one that was missing.

The senior resident Dr. Melcher did not believe that the sponge was still inside the patient's belly and displayed his great irritation at our interrupting him. He told us to search for the missing item on the tiled floor, which was itself a sea of red. So tightly had Brad and I maintained our sponge count, we asked him to check inside for a small piece of gauze the size of a cotton ball. Reluctantly, he hunted for a bit and eventually produced the missing sponge, which, if left inside, could have caused a massive infection.

The anesthesiologist Dr. Eisenstadt was understandably a bundle of nerves. He had to try and evaluate this critically ill woman and keep her somehow systemically stable while her surgery proceeded. The nurse anesthetist helped him, and I did what I could. We read the paperwork accompanying each pack of blood with him to ensure that the blood was compatible with Mrs. Cortina. I ran for the bits of equipment for which he was yelling.

Thank God for the help of sympathetic nurses who heard about the pressure I was under and came to assist me. They made calls to the blood bank, scurried downstairs to the GYN surgery unit for some exotic instrument, and checked the pneumatic tube for incoming packs of blood. I could not have responded to the furious fire of demands from the surgical team without this support.

As the operation was nearing completion, the traditional argument began: whether to send this woman to our PAR or instead to our small ICU downstairs for her recovery. Mrs. Cortina would most definitely be going on a ventilator. Our nurses are trained to recover surgical patients, and some of our postoperative patients are pretty sick. However, we are not intensive care nurses and are not schooled in managing the intubated patient. From the docs' perspective, they want to keep their very sickest patients nearby where they can maintain a careful watch over them. They don't feel comfortable running up and down the flights of stairs between L & D and the ICU, pulled between the rafts of high-risk laboring women and their one critical patient. The result for our PAR nurses is that they end up caring for the very unstable, desperately compromised woman, and the patient is only transferred to the ICU when she is more on the mend. Go figure.

And so it was. Rebeka and Andrea, the recovery room nurses, had to shove one of their six high-risk moms out in the hall, send her to the ICU, and admit this extremely critical surgical patient. I came too and tried to clear up the paperwork mess that was now reaching mammoth proportions. It proved a hopeless task. The surgeons were too busy to complete their part, and I would have to finish this documentation later.

The last thing I did was try my best to get Dr. Eisenstadt to deal with the unit of whole blood that I had at last received at his adamant request. One of the nurses who had been helping me delivered it as we were exiting the OR with Mrs. Cortina and the anesthesiologist. Once in the PAR, minutes were ticking away as he fiddled with this and that. We had strong-armed the Red Cross to give us this blood in the first place. If it was not hung within a half hour, per our protocol, it could not be returned to cold storage for use with another hemorrhaging patient.

I quietly reminded the young man of this fact, and he snapped at me for my efforts. Ordinarily, I would find it hard not to take this kind of treatment personally, but Dr. Eisenstadt clearly was under phenomenal pressure trying to make sure that Mrs. Cortina did not go out on us. I did not feel it was the right moment to tell him he was being an ass. He came over in a few minutes to apologize. I have known some docs who thrive on acute stress and responsibility like we are experiencing this morning, the challenge of a difficult case. This quite tense young resident is not one of that breed. I'm not a drama magnet myself, and I can forgive him for his very human reaction to this enormous pressure. After all, this was about Mrs. Cortina, not Dr. Eisenstadt or me.

I went back to the operating room to try and replenish it, as it had been virtually stripped clean in our big case. In the meantime, Anita brought back another patient for a cesarean section and put her in the adjoining OR. Her young patient Marilyn Brown had been forced to wait until Mrs. Cortina's emergency surgery was completed. This delay would prove to be most unfortunate. Marilyn had a very unusual story, for she was born with no anal opening. A rectum was fashioned surgically over the course of many operations, and yet she still had problems with the anatomy.

When Marilyn was admitted earlier in the evening in very early labor, the main issue for the obstetrical team was trying to decide whether she could attempt a trial of labor, knowing that only a thin wall of membrane separated her vagina and this very iffy rectum of hers. Could she deliver a baby through such delicate tissue, earned for the patient at such cost over a lifetime? An emergency medical consult had taken place shortly after her arrival. The specialist had advised the obstetricians that under no circumstances were they to attempt a vaginal delivery. Such a birth might destroy the carefully constructed tissue that was allowing Marilyn a somewhat normal life.

I was busy stocking my operating room, while Anita was setting Marilyn up for surgery next door. Minutes later, the ordinarily unflappable Anita shrieked for me to come quickly. What I saw absolutely horrified me. Marilyn's baby's head was not only crowning but was also starting the bulge that immediately precedes delivery. It seemed to me that whatever damage to be done had already occurred, but I flew to the intercom and told them to get the senior resident *now,* that his patient was on the point of delivering.

Anita and I were already setting up for a delivery when Dr. Melcher, who had made it back to the OR in an instant, yelled at us. "Absolutely not! We're crashing her now! I want her put down *now!*" he bellowed at the anesthesiologist.

How could they get this baby up through the birth canal when it was practically hanging out? But we got the surgery going in lightning-fast time, and by god, the infant was out in less than five minutes. Time will have to tell whether damage was done to Marilyn Brown's plumbing in all of this.

Without the tension of these two very hectic and urgent cases, I was now reeling with exhaustion. My body protested that I could do no more. Though I was not sick in the usual sense, I was too goofy to be a responsible caregiver. We were so short-staffed, though, that it would have been criminal to ask to leave. I went out of a delivery where an intern was instructing a medical student on the intricacies of episiotomy repair. I stumbled over to the kitchen and gulped down hot coffee in the ten minutes of break that I was to receive in the thirteen hours I worked this date.

I had asked to work the last few hours in delivery as the day shift team of nurses came on. Hopefully, the pace would slow down and they would be better staffed, or at least fresh. I thought that maybe I could do the one thing I have never done before on duty–lay my head down and sleep for a half hour or so. By seven forty-five, having had no respite in which to return to the PAR, I went over to the recovery room to try and complete the paperwork for Mrs. Cortina's two surgical procedures. What did I find but the nurses and doctors pushing this desperately ill woman out of the PAR door to return to surgery. They knew that she was bleeding internally because the size of her abdomen had increased in girth hour by hour through the night. She would have to be opened up to try and stop the bleeding as a last ditch effort to keep her alive.

I became alert as if I'd just awakened from a terrific sleep. I volunteered to circulate the case, even though it was not my turn. I had become personally interested in Mrs. Cortina's fate, even though I had not exchanged one word with her to date. I knew that she was in grave peril of losing her life. Somehow, I cared so much about the outcome for her. I wanted to play my part in this continuing effort to sustain her, even given the seeming hopelessness of the situation.

This time, I was to be in the operating room for four hours. Poor Mrs. Cortina had even more massive bleeding than before, if that was possible. She was most likely a victim of "washout syndrome." Even though blood was being poured into her to replace what was flowing out of her blood vessels and tissue, her body had lost its natural clotting factors, which meant that blood was draining internally from a multiplicity of sites.

I am not knowledgeable enough to describe what measures were being attempted by the surgeons to deal with this critical situation. They had requested emergent help from the gynecology-oncology staff physician on call, as this gentleman had so much experience with massive bleeding during surgery to treat pelvic cancers. I left off any attempt to see what was being done in the red well that was Mrs. Cortina's surgical site. I was too busy trying to keep track of all the sponges and linen being used to staunch the bleeding. Forty extra-large sponges were used, seventy smaller ones, and then those hefty green linen towels. I was continually occupied as well with fetching and carrying the stuff that was needed. Circulating is such a humbling role.

The degree of stress was so apparent for all involved, and as the saying goes, the shit does tend to roll downhill. When any venting of frustration took place, it was Benjamin Grady, the scrub tech, and George Faulkes, the hapless third-year resident, who caught hell. The unspoken thought in every mind present was that this furious labor, this Herculean effort on the part of each member of the surgical team, was very likely to end with the woman's demise.

When the end of the case was in sight, as they were packing Mrs. Cortina's abdomen with roll upon roll of sterile gauze, the same argument about our recovery room versus the ICU started up again. I guess the docs felt that now this woman definitely merited intensive care nursing, and could no longer justify keeping her in our unit. So then they began to wonder, out loud, if she should go to our small four-bed ICU downstairs, or should she be transported to the surgical ICU in the main hospital up the hill?

Dr. Meese, the head of OB anesthesia who had stepped in to supervise his resident during this difficult case and who makes a life's career of belittling everyone with less than his admittedly high degree of knowledge, offered his opinion. He said Mrs. Cortina had better go to the surgical ICU where she might have a prayer of getting decent care with nurses who know how to take care of sick people!

Dr. Brandon, the gynecology-oncology surgeon, the one who had been summoned to lend his expertise with our bleeding operative emergency, disagreed quietly.

"I don't recommend that course. I find that too many of our patients go up the hill to obtain less-than-optimum treatment. At times, I've gone up there to find my patient without anyone but a medical student sitting at the bedside, peering curiously at the chart with the woman languishing, unattended. In our ICU, though small, we know ours, and they get much more personalized attention."

Well, that left Dr. Meese without much to say for once, so utterly beyond argument was the calm conviction in highly respected Dr. Brandon's voice.

Down in the ICU, it was long past the end of my shift, and I began to feel the accumulated effects of this marathon session. I had three separate operative reports to complete, and I stared in dismay at questions about events that had transpired before I even arrived on the scene. The nursing supervisor, Mrs. Janes, had come to the ICU to make sure that things were proceeding smoothly with the admission of this critical patient. She saw the look on my face, took pity on me, and helped me plow through the records debris until some semblance of order in the paperwork prevailed. Bless her!

The senior resident Dr. Melcher, in my previous estimation a complete toad, arrogant and condescending to just about everyone, for once earned my compassion. Now on his feet for more than twenty-eight hours, handling patients in crisis and performing difficult, challenging and anxiety-producing surgery, he was white as a sheet and looked to be on the verge of passing out. He will have to remain here, nevertheless, to watch over this so-tenuous situation with Mrs. Cortina.

Addendum: On my return to work tonight, after sleeping nine hours straight, it was to the news that Mrs. Cortina was stabilizing nicely and would not be leaving a young family motherless. I think this was one case we could all look to as having demanded all we were worth, and was some sort of miracle even, like snatching life from the yawning jaws of death.

CHAPTER FORTY-ONE

"Many might have shrugged this decidedly unpleasant task off onto others."

September 27

I AM BY NO means the only nurse here who is involved in unusual, memorable incidents. I believe each nurse or doctor who stays here for any length of time has their personal treasure trove of adventures. In slow moments, we delight in sharing these experiences with one another.

I was chatting with Merilee the other night, remarking about just this phenomenon, when she treated me to what she believes is her special "most memorable moment." To me, her story combined elements of both dark comedy and tragedy, the absurd realities of trying to deliver care under what sometimes reaches pressure cooker conditions. In such a setting as ours, both heroes and antiheroes are produced, depending on how individuals face the stressors they encounter.

One of our routinely chaotic nights was in progress, and Merilee was doing her best as the charge nurse to cope. Merilee can handle an excruciating degree of stress, remaining admirably calm. She is continually on the move, navigating the unit and inspiring everyone by working harder than five people. She seldom sits down except to scribble some necessary bit of paperwork. She remains nonjudgmental in the face of staff behavior far less professional than her own. Merilee still stops here and there to coach a scared teenager or admire a newborn for proud parents. She also speaks beautiful Spanish, having grown up in a neighborhood of some diversity, though her own antecedents are blond-haired, blue-eyed Norwegians.

Early in the morning on the day of this episode, Merilee was called back to the delivery area to intervene in a perplexing situation. An African American mother, who had the great misfortune to deliver a stillborn infant, was complaining bitterly that we had lost her baby. It took Merilee a bit of time to establish the facts, puzzling as this story sounded. We constantly worry that, in the midst of delivering close to fifty babies every twenty-four hours, we will mix up some infants. We follow strict practices for identifying mothers with their babies. However, the infant in question was deceased, sadly. No chance for a case of mistaken identity. So where was this upset and angry woman's baby, for the body was nowhere to be found in the delivery room?

The events up until the moment Merilee came upon the scene demonstrate the disarray made inevitable when multiples of babies are being born with medical and nursing staff stretched to the limit, and beyond. This particular patient was brought back to delivery by an intern. He had nursing assistance only until a crash cesarean section was brought to the OR. His nurse had to make a hasty exit to lend a hand in the emergency.

The intern put the patient's stillborn baby in the infant warmer, wrapped in green surgical towels, and set about doing the mother's episiotomy repair. When the stitching was completed, he wanted to return to the labor area to catch up on his backlog of "scutwork," the traditional code name for the tedious, unglamorous tasks relegated to the first-year resident. He stepped over to a nearby delivery room in which another birth was minutes away from taking place. He commended his patient to the care of the overwhelmed LVN who was running between two adjoining delivery rooms, trying to meet the needs of doctors and patients experiencing impending birth.

At some point, the nurse sprang free and came to see the woman with the stillborn child. Jasmine, knowing the reams of paperwork and detail involved in finalizing the postmortem care for both mother and baby, decided to do the most expedient thing. She moved the woman off the delivery table and onto a stretcher, then placed her in the hallway. The delivery room could then be cleaned and made ready for another patient on the brink of giving birth. Jazzy left to run back to see what was happening with the other two births.

A short time later, the drowsy mother awoke and expressed a desire to hold her stillborn infant, which previously she had declined to do. Such a change of heart is common happenstance with grief-stricken parents. Their first shock upon giving birth to a dead baby must be given some time to diminish. Eventually, though, both mother and father come to the realization that, though their infant is not alive, they are indeed parents. They want to see, touch, and hold their baby whose destiny is so profoundly different from that of other fortunate families. The nurse who had recently moved mom into the hallway returned to continue her care and was completely perplexed to find that there was simply no baby. At this point, Merilee was called to mediate in this painful situation.

It took Merilee a while to reconstruct events herself. When she was in possession of all the facts, an explanation, really the only feasible explanation, came to her. She called the nursing supervisor in the nursing administration office. She told Miss Graffing that, in all likelihood, the body of this little one, unable to protest with the newborn's usual vigor and noise, had been unknowingly thrown down the linen chute with the rest of the surgical linen from this case by the housekeeper.

And so Merilee and Miss Graffing went to the basement where all the linen descends from eight floors of patient care areas. They began to go through bag after bag of linen, soiled with the debris of human illness. In their minds, Merilee remembered, they were sure that the baby was among this incredible mountain of stuff. Yet some macabre realities the human spirit refuses to admit. Thus, when they unfurled yet another in an endless number of linen bags and the body of the little dead baby fell out, they both shrieked hysterically. The body landed on Merilee's white nursing clogs.

Is it possible for anyone to get beyond the bizarre and even somewhat disturbing facts of this story and see the beauty and special heroism of this wonderful woman? She lent her intelligence, her persistence and sense of duty to solving a mystery that was causing great distress to one of our patients. She did not let the seemingly appalling prospect of searching through a whole linen chute full of dirty sheets and towels dissuade her, though many might have shrugged this decidedly unpleasant task off onto others. She took the silent, peaceful body of the little black infant back to the delivery area, wrapped it in baby blankets, and returned to put it in the arms of our grief-stricken mother.

I would suggest that my charge nurse, Merilee, was acting in the noble tradition of another nurse named Florence Nightingale, a woman of genteel birth who took nurses to the battlefields of the Crimean War to care for the wounded and dying, work that formerly had been left to prostitutes.

CHAPTER FORTY-TWO

"This work I do has the most profound rewards, and I had just received an especially precious one."

September 30

IT'S 11:35, AND I am in mother-baby assessment waiting for our first mother-infant couplet to arrive. Last night I spent twelve hours straight in the B labor room, and surely I've cut years off my stay in purgatory by participating in the events that took place there. Four patients were crammed into that impossibly small space, as usual. I'd somehow had a premonition that I was going to be assigned there as I drove in to work. Instead of feeling oppressed and picked on for this assignment, as I sometimes do, I gave myself a good talking to. If I was going to be in the B room, I would make the best of it for my own sake and that of my patients.

Sure enough, as Merilee read the assignments, my fate was to be the nurse in the killer B room. Moreover, she related, there was a "screamer" in there. Great. Women who let the pain of labor get to them to the extent that they lose all vestige of control and scream at the top of their lungs make a difficult experience hell for themselves, their fellow patients, and also the nurses and physicians. I could hear this patient going berserk with a contraction as I approached the cramped and tense labor room that was to be my home for the next twelve hours.

It turned out that this particular woman, Dinorah Acevedo, had been in labor for over twenty-four hours, her achingly slow progress being forced along with the contraction-enhancing drug, Pitocin. The anesthesiology team had twice attempted to place an epidural block. These attempts to alleviate the tortured woman's pain had been unsuccessful after both tries. It was thought that she must have some unusual anatomical impediment that prevented the placement of the anesthesia.

Other pain relief measures were forthcoming. At intervals, Mrs. Acevedo had received doses of narcotics to take the edge off of her pain. In her case, the Demerol she had received had a paradoxical effect. The drug seemed to loosen her already tenuous grip on her emotions, and she had proceeded to react to each of her subsequent pains with the animal-like screeching I was now hearing. Her long-suffering husband tried to help her keep control, but Dinorah was inconsolable.

After beginning my turn with her care, I came to believe that Dinorah was close to the edge of overwhelming physical and psychological exhaustion. Such decompensation was the result of her prolonged labor and her excited reaction to the onset of each contraction—thrashing around, screaming, sobbing from the gut. It was impossible to keep the linen straightened beneath her body, and it disturbed me to see her lying with skin directly touching the vinyl mattress of the labor bed. My attempts to straighten the bed linen were futile. One pain later, the sheets were in disarray, and I had to give up this fruitless effort.

She did better when I stood at her side, held her hand, and coaxed her to breathe through her contractions. However, the moment I had to step away to do something for one of my other three patients, Mrs. Acevedo would revert to unfettered wildness. Finally, her husband said he was going to take a break, and left. He never returned. This abandonment was a sad defeat for both. I could understand that it was torture to watch your loved one in terrible pain, making only minute progress. But I could not totally forgive Mr. Acevedo for leaving Dinorah to her fate, as he knew that I could not be with her minute to minute.

I checked her after a time and could feel the lip of her cervix slightly swollen and hugging the head of her infant as it tried to move down. She was a bit more dilated this hour. She had a terrific urge to push, and my exam had revealed the reason for this. The baby's head, really just the soft scalp tissue, was swollen and bulging past the thick rim of the cervix.

When the head is down like this, women feel as if they are about to defecate. Like Mrs. Acevedo, they become doubly agitated. No adult can tolerate this feeling of losing control of a basic body function. Inevitably, most women who have not had an enema on admission for labor will expel some feces during the passage of their baby through the birth canal. If more women understood this, they'd be begging for those enemas. Some years ago, the decision was made here to forego the practice of administering enemas as a routine.

We nurses try to minimize the embarrassment our patients feel when this point in their labor or delivery comes. I know that women seldom anticipate this eventuality when they are thinking forward to their birth experience. For the staff, we can sometimes predict the advent of the next delivery by the strength of the odor coming from the labor room.

Back to Mrs. Acevedo and her ordeal, I began to wonder if this protracted labor was due to a disproportion between her pelvis and the baby's head. Her baby had been judged by ultrasound scan to be almost four kilos, large for a first pregnancy. Then finally, miraculously, she edged forward to complete dilation, and I was coaching her to bear down with her contractions. She stopped screaming and pushed ferociously. I had the supreme satisfaction of calling an intern and helping take her back to hand over to the delivery team. I was happy for her, and intensely happy for my other patients and myself at the prospect of a much more tranquil atmosphere in the B labor room.

Opposite Mrs. Acevedo's now-vacant bed was a woman who was to become one of my all-time favorites as a patient. Glenda Jordan was a late-thirties African American who had her hair tucked into a spotless, white-frilled cap. She too was having a protracted labor, but she had made herself stay calm. How she managed to do this in the circumstances she found herself enduring in my labor room, I could not fathom. She was down-to-earth and commonsensical, obviously having talked to herself a lot before coming to us to have her baby.

"I'm only going to do this once," she related to me as we finally had a chance to get to know each other. "I want to do it right."

Glenda was polite, but not fawning, and was very appreciative of all my efforts to promote her comfort. When that was impossible, she accepted what pain she had to bear very philosophically. Once, when she thanked me for some bit of help I'd given her, I had to compliment her.

"I'm so impressed with how you are handling what has been a long, slow ordeal under sometimes hellish conditions."

"Well, the support of a sister means so much" was her quiet response.

I don't believe I was ever so gifted by a patient in my years of supporting laboring patients as I was by these words—her acknowledgement that, beyond skin color, culture, education, or social status, women attending each other in the act of giving birth are sisters. This work I do has the most profound rewards, and I had just received an especially precious one.

One of my interventions on Glenda's behalf did not result in the amelioration of her painful, slow-moving labor as I wanted. I saw the effort she was making to withstand the distress of her contractions, something she had endured for many long hours. I have often been witness to the beneficial effect of a good epidural in relaxing a woman's tension, which I believe can be a factor in the failure to progress in labor. Dr. McAdams, one of my favorite senior residents, came through on a survey of our labor patients, and he agreed with the plan to help Glenda with her pain via anesthesia.

The epidural placement was successful in one way, as the pain of Glenda's contractions abated dramatically. However, she was almost immediately made uncomfortable by one of the common side effects of this treatment, hers being in the crescendo range as opposed to the more typical whisper. She began to shiver uncontrollably, not from chills as we typically think of this phenomenon, but from some systemic reaction to the anesthesia. The poor woman exchanged one awful torture for another. Would that it were not so.

Glenda did not have an easy time of it even when she was completely dilated and ready to push. Exhaustion was a factor, and she pushed more or less ineffectively for the two hours allowed before we must try some other stratagem to assist with achieving birth. In coaching her, I could see the baby's head moving down with each contraction, but in between pains, it would retract. When Bruce McAdams came in to respond to my call for an evaluation of Glenda's lack of progress, he agreed with me that what was called for here was a vacuum delivery.

A vacuum extraction is a way to help a mom who has reached complete dilation, is pushing, but is having trouble getting the baby out. When she bears down with her muscles, the head moves forward, but as soon as the pain subsides, the baby's head retreats to its previous position. A suction cup can be applied to the baby's scalp, and when attached to a vacuum pump system, each push of the mother advances the head a bit. Little by little, the vacuum system helps maintain the baby in the forward position. Glenda Jordan had the perfect situation for having an assisted birth by vacuum.

I went in search of the delivery area team leader. Imelda, as well as another nurse, Lorraine, was luckily available to assist with Glenda's birth. Vacuum extraction is considered a somewhat complex procedure, as well as demanding nursing assistance to help with the vacuum equipment. I sought to elicit whatever extra attention these two capable and kind nurses could afford my patient. Imelda accompanied me back to my room so that she could meet Glenda and move her back to the delivery room.

As I continued to work in the B labor room, I was thinking of my patient, so quietly courageous, happy for her that she must now be delivered and enjoying the reward of seeing her long-awaited baby. Finally, it was time for me to go home. I was walking down the corridor when I nearly bumped into Lorraine, who was hurrying along with a solemn look on her face.

"What's happened?" I asked with an uneasy feeling.

She motioned for me to wait, and then caught up with Bruce McAdams who'd left the delivery room after a successful birth by vacuum extraction. "Could you come back, Dr. McAdams?" Lorraine requested. "Something is terribly wrong with the baby."

I was stunned. Throughout the labor period, no matter how long and painful for Glenda, the fetal heart tracing was consistently benign, without a hint of baby stress. Lorraine could not say what was wrong, just that the pediatricians were working with the little newborn girl and were preparing to transport her downstairs to intensive care. I left, needing to hustle down the road to our neighborhood kindergarten to pick up my little guy. I was praying that the baby wizards from the special care nursery would work their magic and turn things around for Baby Girl Jordan.

Shortly after I arrived tonight, Dr. Crosswaite, the second-year resident who had assisted with the vacuum delivery, came into mother-baby assessment to inform me that Glenda's baby had died early in the afternoon. I felt physically ill and had to sit down abruptly. How could this be? It turned out that the baby had a condition known as hypoplastic lung, in which case the little air sacks that inflate to allow normal breathing are underdeveloped, rigid and unable to expand properly. As long as Glenda's baby was inside her, she was able to thrive and grow, oxygenation being effected through placental delivery. Once born, it was immediately evident how very ill equipped this little girl was to survive on her own.

The nurses had to bring our gentle, strong, newly delivered mother down to the NICU to share some brief moments with her little daughter, even as she was in the last moments of life. I could only try to imagine the depths of shock and sorrow Glenda must have felt. It struck me as one of those strange ironies of this puzzling life. Dinah Acevedo, my patient who had lost all semblance of decorum and had become almost animal-like in her behavior during labor, was now holding her baby in her arms. My utterly stoic and gentle mother with the frilled white cap was now grieving with empty arms. Not that any mother should have to endure this tragic loss.

As I was still reeling from this painful news, a call came to the desk. Glenda Jordan was wide awake at this late hour and felt moved to call us in Labor and Delivery. Ruth, our clerk, came to tell me that Mrs. Jordan had wanted to relay her appreciation to all the staff who had cared for her. She mentioned special thanks for Dr. McAdams, who had remained with her to explain events so sensitively, and for me, the nurse who had supported her through the long hours of her labor. What utter generosity of spirit to think of us in the midst of her great pain.

She was now being cared for in the gynecology unit so that she would not be subjected to the sights and sounds of all the newly delivered mothers and babies in the postpartum ward. I went up on my morning break, knowing that somehow Glenda Jordan and I needed to go one step further in this friendship of ours that had been forged so quickly in the stress of her labor.

As I pushed through the swinging doors and entered the GYN unit, I saw Glenda down the hall. She was pacing along as she pushed her IV pole ahead of her, her frilled white cap still in place. There was about her an aura of barely restrained hyperactivity. She turned as I called her name and waited for me to catch up to her. Our arms went around each other; our tears were quiet, and somehow so healing.

We went into her room and were immediately faced with the stark reality of being a patient in a public institution like this. No privacy was afforded due to the presence of three gynecology patients looking on with abashed expressions, Hispanic women awed at the sight of the nurse in blue scrubs and the woman in the white cap sitting together with clasped hands, dabbing at swollen eyes with tissue.

Our conversation only confirmed for me my earlier impression that Glenda Jordan was one very special woman. She shared so much with me in our half hour together. A deeply spiritual person, she was already deriving some consolation from her belief in a better world for her innocent daughter. I tried to respond with what little wisdom I could contribute, never having faced the depth of pain this good woman was experiencing. Thank God she had a large and loving family to surround her with affection and support. As close as we were at this moment, I knew that this was inevitably the extent of our friendship. Still, we had connected in much more than a superficial way, and I don't think I will ever forget our time together. God willing, I will derive some personal lessons from watching the way Glenda Jordan dealt with the stress of her labor and the incomprehensible pain of her loss.

CHAPTER FORTY-THREE

"He was hunched over the desk, writing a copious note into the woman's chart, even as events were still in such desperate progress."

October 6

MY BIRTHDAY. I had a personal fiasco in that I had slept only three hours between two twelve-hour shifts. When I got home at noon, my children informed me that their dad had hurt his eye badly the night before doing some work in the garage after I'd gone to the hospital. He had been up all night and had just barely fallen asleep. I didn't wake him, but I had the sinking feeling that I wasn't fated to sleep much, just as I was nearly reeling from lack of sleep myself. I went to bed but told my oldest child to wake me if her dad needed me.

Sure enough, two hours later, she got me up, saying she didn't like the look of that eye. He was in obvious pain, his eye inflamed and very teary. I couldn't visualize any laceration, but my daughter was sure she'd seen a big cut in there. I concentrated my efforts on convincing him that he needed to see a doctor. He was stubborn and put me off, saying that he was too tired and needed to sleep a couple of more hours. Meanwhile, I was completely awake and stayed up.

Finally, I woke him at five o'clock and told him he needed a good kick in the rump. That eye had to be seen. I took him to the local urgent care center, and it turned out that he had a moderate corneal abrasion. Not too much was needed to proceed to a cure. They inserted antibiotic ointment and bandaged the eye. By then, it was 7:00 p.m., and I was due to be back on duty at eleven. I finished my wifely duties heating soup for him, and my motherly duties bathing the little guy.

The house was so quiet, the kids always so subdued when one of us is ill. I'm sure they tend to take our fitness and ability to perform our usual grown-up roles for granted. Then when one of us caves to some purely human fallibility, they are so uneasy. At any rate, I got one fat hour of sleep to put in the bank for the coming twelve hours. Here I am at 6:00 a.m., feeling better than I have a right to feel but borderline decompensating as I care for my three patients in the LICU.

But then, consider the fate of one patient of ours who at this very minute is lying near death in our postanesthesia recovery room, and my lack of sleep becomes a minuscule irritation. Twenty-five-year-old Maria Larios delivered by cesarean section earlier yesterday evening and was now diagnosed as being in DIC, or having disseminated intravascular coagulopathy. This complicated situation meant that her body had lost its ability to fight internal hemorrhaging by use of her clotting system. She had exhausted all of her platelets in a severe hemorrhage during her surgery and now was bleeding from many sites within her body. She was in grave condition.

To control her problem, to try to get on top of it, Mrs. Larios was given many transfusions of whole blood and blood products. One of the nurses caring for her reported that she was spitting up frothy blood, which could have implied pulmonary edema. In such a case, her heart could not handle her circulating fluid volume, the result of the many liters of fluids pushed into her to sustain life, resulting in back pressure on the lungs. The other possibility was that, due to her clotting disorder, she was simply hemorrhaging into her lungs.

There was a cardiac resident here for consultation, and he judged that Maria was getting more critical by the minute. He wanted her transferred to the ICU up the hill where he could monitor her closely. She was being readied for this transfer when she stopped breathing and her heart stopped beating.

We are not experienced ICU nurses here, most of us. I often ask myself how I would perform if I were caring for a patient who suddenly arrested. We all train in the basics of cardiac life support, but in the more acute case of cardiac arrest in a health-care facility, the interventions are complex, and the nurse must be ready to respond with immediacy to a bevy of demands for equipment and medications. When I slipped over to the PAR for a moment's brief observation, I saw that the PAR nurses and Merilee were remaining remarkably calm. They were responding to the fire of orders from the five or six OB residents, the anesthesiologist, and the cardiologist involved in the resuscitation.

Maria Larios was revived momentarily but went on to code several more times. How unimaginably difficult this situation was for everyone involved, including the five patients in the PAR. From their hospital beds, these patients could not help seeing the fury of activity as the medical and nursing staff tried so desperately to save this young mother's life. I knew this was a bad one.

Over in the LICU where I had returned to my three patients, Dr. Zendejas, the night OB resident, came in and slumped dispiritedly in a chair with his head in his hands. He exclaimed to me, "I feel sick. That jerk probably killed that poor woman!"

Horror-struck, I asked, "Who?"

"The anesthesiologist. You don't give a totally critical patient who is marginally clinging to life a dose of Pentothal. He just sent her over the edge."

Later, when someone had a chance to examine the blood gases that had been drawn before this alleged insult, it was apparent that our patient was virtually beyond help. We will never know now if the Pentothal the anesthesiologist gave was the ultimate precipitator of death, or if the situation was sadly inevitable. Another resident told me later, "You don't give a woman whose entire vascular tone is desperately trying to help circulate a red cell concentration of 12 percent a medication that totally drops out what tone she had!"

What was striking to me, speaking of the human dynamics of the emergency, was the behavior of the anesthesiologist in question as the drama in the PAR ensued. While the OB and cardiology residents were resuscitating the woman over and over, the gentleman who gave the patient the Pentothal was not in the midst of them helping, as one would expect. Instead, he was hunched over the desk writing a copious note into the woman's chart, even as events were still in such desperate progress. Strange.

It's impossible for anyone to second-guess with crystal-clear accuracy the true source of this gravely compromised young mother's demise. One of our very wisest nurses, Anita Ewald, felt that perhaps the critical situation should have been assessed much earlier on. She could have gone to the ICU where her worsening metabolic decompensation could have been attacked. But there is still the specter of the DIC issue, the loss of the person's entire clotting system in the wake of a severe and unresolving hemorrhage. Perhaps Mrs. Larios was beyond help no matter what the human intervention.

Whatever the case, we all felt a horrible sense of loss and defeat. It isn't that we don't face death in this unit, because we see the death of the very smallest and vulnerable. But a young mother, dying as a result of a condition of pregnancy and whatever possible mismanagement on our part here, is just an astounding tragedy. And the human tragedy goes on in the lives of the husband and newborn baby, and the other little ones at home.

Apparently, the husband and family of our critically ill patient showed up in the midst of the second arrest. They were turned away from the PAR where at least ten doctors and nurses were working on her. The family was taken down the hall to wait in an empty labor room. Merilee and Anita tried to show sensitivity to their plight, finding them chairs and explaining what was happening. No physician was able to come for over an hour. How do you tell a man who was previously sent home with the news that his wife was ill, but stable, that she's dying down the hall? I'm coward enough to be relieved that I wasn't there.

CHAPTER FORTY-FOUR

"The OB and anesthesia docs squabbled in a very territorial way about whose fault this undesirable outcome was . . ."

October 14

IN REPORT TONIGHT, I found my assignment to be that of team leader in delivery. I scribbled the names of the various RNs, scrub techs, and nursing assistants who would make up my staff on a sheet of paper toweling. Merilee continued with report, noting which delivery rooms had births or surgery in progress. "There's a Down patient in delivery room 5," she said, "but I was told she delivered."

I had heard about a young girl being cared for here several days ago. A fifteen-year-old with Down syndrome, this teenager was believed to have become pregnant while attending a school for the handicapped. Virtually incapable of coherent speech, the young Latina's pregnancy went undetected for many months. She was initially brought to our unit in premature labor, and she had continued to dilate in spite of all medical treatment designed to stop her labor.

I had been off for a few days and had only a smattering of knowledge of this situation. In any case, I could believe that giving care to this special teenager had been quite a challenge for her nurses and doctors. I was relieved to hear that the delivery was a fact, and that this poor girl's ordeal was largely over.

Still, as team leader, I felt it was my place to assume the most problematic delivery, so I went to room 5 after assigning staff to other jobs. I was putting on my face mask at the sink when I heard the most horrific scream from inside the delivery room. I rushed in.

All eyes turned to me. The young girl was struggling furiously, her stubby legs escaping the metal stirrups. A very distressed-looking middle-aged woman and younger girl, possibly a sister, were attempting to soothe and restrain the little one, who was nevertheless all over the table.

The pediatric resuscitation team was standing by, looking frustrated. The senior resident Sandra Spellman was seated on a stool at the foot of the delivery table. She turned to me and said, in a voice strained and weary, "Got any ideas on how to deliver this one, Natalie? I'm fresh out."

Just then, another contraction came. Most women, when completely dilated, have a natural and overwhelming urge to bear down with their pain. Our patient Miriyam Castenada, when faced with the stunning and, to her, incomprehensible pain of a contraction, would not push. Instead, she thrashed about wildly and bellowed with outrage at nature's cruel trickery. Who could blame her, totally incapable of understanding the strange and awful events in progress?

I could see, based on the length of the fetal monitor strip, that over forty minutes had passed in this room. Usually, if a patient gets stuck like this in delivery, we figure that we miscalculated the time of birth. Due to the demand for birth rooms, we cannot tie them up indefinitely, and we would take the woman back for a period of time pushing in the labor room. But in the face of the complete inability of little Miriyam to cooperate, along with the seeming stubbornness of this infant in making its entrance into the world, a cesarean birth seemed inevitable.

Sandra Spellman, whose decision it would be to wait or go ahead and operate, was expending the extra effort in this case to achieve a vaginal birth because she wanted at almost any cost to avoid surgery. Down patients are special. It isn't just that they have unusual needs because of their mental disabilities; often there is heart and other organ involvement. Sandra would really have preferred not to do surgery.

The decision was ultimately taken out of her hands. After a few more of these ineffectual and extremely distressing contractions, the baby's heart rate took a huge dive and refused to convert to normal. Now we had to set up for a crash cesarean section, shove all the delivery stuff out in the hall, bring out the surgical packs, get a tube to drain the bladder into this terrified and wiggling girl, get both the surgeons gowned and gloved, and slap some iodine prep on the tiny belly. The room was a mass of organized upheaval as we strained to do all this with the sound of that diminishing beep . . . beep . . . . .beep of the baby's heart lending impetus to our efforts.

In the midst of the bedlam, I looked up to see Miriyam's mother and sister standing rooted to the ground, fear and confusion written across their faces. We had completely forgotten them in our haste to prepare for surgery. I led them out of the room, commandeered a kind gentleman from the instrument room to see them to the waiting area and explain about the surgery, and then raced back to resume my surgical role.

The two anesthesiologists were sweating and cursing. Miriyam had pulled out her IV line in her agitation. It was proving difficult to restrain her sufficiently to work on her arm. Her veins were tiny, and they had to jab her repeatedly to get this crucial line in, adding to her distress. But she could not be put to sleep without an IV line, and finally, with Sandra and the junior resident berating the anesthesiologists continuously, the crucial IV tubing was in place. This sort of scene would be incomprehensible, I'm sure, to the lay bystander. With a baby's life on the line, the stress was like electricity crackling in the air. I understood all the acting out.

Finally, Miriyam was asleep, and the surgery proceeded rapidly. A tiny but squalling infant girl was delivered. Superficially, she appeared completely normal, just a few weeks early. We could relax. Or so we thought.

Our new mother's organs were all quite small, as they were visualized sitting in her abdominal cavity. Her uterus was a pale, malleable pancake. Typically the uterus, a thick, rosy, blood-filled muscle, must contract into a tight ball to squeeze off the gaping holes left when the placenta shears off the wall of the womb after delivery. Miriyam's tiny uterus remained limp, opalescent. However, it did not bleed a lot, as a flaccid uterus usually does.

Now here was an ethical dilemma. Everyone in this room could see that here seemed a possible opportunity to take out this handicapped teenager's uterus and prevent a reoccurrence of another distressing pregnancy like this one. Severe and nonresolving uterine flaccidity would be a perfectly respectable indication for a cesarean hysterectomy. Moreover, it would be so compassionate, Sandra said.

Yet the senior resident couldn't come to an easy decision. The surgical bed was virtually free of blood, and life-threatening hemorrhage was typically the rationale for taking out a woman's uterus in the prime of her reproductive life. The young and serious-minded Dr. Spellman was faced with a most perplexing quandary.

Sandra asked me to call for the attending staff physician to come to the OR so that he could consult on this issue. Dr. Yuri, an experienced member of the obstetrical faculty and an expert perinatologist, would be the one to guide Sandra in making this difficult ethical decision. He was, so I thought, sleeping down the hall in the attending physician's call room, available this night for just such iffy situations. I got on the intercom and asked the desk clerk to wake up Dr. Yuri and request that he come to room 5.

In a minute, Jerome buzzed me back. Dr. Yuri was not available.

"Now wait a minute!" exclaimed Sandra, overhearing this conversation. "That's impossible! Call him back and tell him to get his behind down here!"

Another relay between me, Jerome, and Dr. Yuri produced the response that Dr. Yuri was, inexplicably, outside the hospital some fifteen to twenty minutes away, and would only come for a life-and-death situation. I will delete the exact string of curse words this evoked from Dr. Spellman.

"Well, I'm unwilling to yank this girl's uterus without staff concurrence. God, what a bloody shame," she sighed.

Miriyam did not have a very easy postsurgical course either. She was not coming out of the anesthesia normally. Who knows what systemic peculiarities the little almond-eyed girl possessed? The OB and anesthesia docs squabbled in a very territorial way over whose fault this undesirable outcome was, as the anesthesiologist continued to inflate Miriyam's lungs with a breathing bag in the recovery room.

Addendum: I called down to the ICU tonight when I got here to see how this special patient of ours was doing. Miriyam had gone to intensive care to be ventilated on a respirator. Lily, the intensive care nurse who was seeing to Miriyam's well-being, told me the happy news.

"Gosh, she's fine. So spunky. She ended up spitting out her airway this evening on her own. She'll do."

CHAPTER FORTY-FIVE

"Maybe the enormity of his form will have a self-limiting effect on his career."

October 19

I LIKE MOST OF the young obstetricians in training with whom I work. There is the monthly invasion of rotating interns and medical students coming here for a taste of obstetrics, though they will go on to specialize in other fields. It is impossible to get to know this passing parade of individuals terribly well, but most are well mannered and eager to learn. Like the med student who came to my labor room shortly after eleven thirty last evening, and coming up to me, remarked,

"Oh, great, you're here. Now I know it's going to be a good night."

Then there are our proprietary interns, or first-year OB-GYN residents. They will be finishing their beginning year of specialization in the field of women's health and will be staying here for three more years of residency. One gets to know them well over this longer period of association, at least professionally.

They also get to know me, which is important when I approach them with my ideas about what is going on with our patients. Having seen my practice, they usually are respectful of my input, and we most often work together to get the patient's needs met. Sometimes there is a bonus in having time and inclination for exchanges on a less formal level, laughing about an amusing incident, discussing life, work, and people. Only some seem to want to share that much of themselves, making us real persons to each other.

An example for illustration. I have worked with Jane Gernowski, a likable resident who had been a nurse in a former career. In her third year of residency, she became pregnant for the first time and was gone for her six-week maternity leave this past spring. She will have to extend her residency by this same six-week period at the end of her education here. On return, she spoke with me about her trials as a new mother.

"When I go into private practice, I'll never be cavalier about the effort new moms go through. Just getting started with breastfeeding was a challenge. My baby couldn't get the hang of it, which was surely mostly my ineptness. Then came the cracked nipples. There is no pain quite like that. I'm trying to pump my milk here at work, which turns out to be next to impossible. Thank God my husband is such a support, emotionally and otherwise. Another blessing was the lactation nurse who got me through my ordeal with breastfeeding. The memory of her expertise and endless patience, well, that will stay with me forever."

Sharing such life experiences, relating to each other's problems and successes, create a bond, breaking down some of those walls that exist between doctors and nurses and making us real persons to each other. Such camaraderie lends a truly pleasurable dimension to this often difficult work. Another benefit of our more benign and supportive interactions is the breeding of respect for each other's professions.

But there are those few who, by some truly scummy behavior, just kill any chance that we can have a mutually respectful relationship. There is Dr. Melcher, who has recently been preaching to us about righteous living based on the Talmud. Last week he sent me jokingly down to a labor room to try and locate the baby's heartbeat on a new admission. He found it amusing that I almost took this request seriously until the patient's nurse let me know not to bother. The baby was deceased. What could he have been thinking? I only know that Dr. Melcher does not stay up at night worrying about my lack of esteem for him.

But I am not one of that subset of nurses who are doctor haters. My uncle Gerry is one of the finest persons I know and recently retired after forty-eight years in practice as a family doctor. His patients were so fortunate in having this decent, very knowledgeable, sensitive man to care for their families. It sickens me to see someone masquerading as a member of this honorable profession when he or she has no business caring for vulnerable persons such as we routinely treat here.

The other night I was working in the overflow labor room, which until early morning had not housed laboring women. Rather, it was used to recover a stream of postsurgical cases. At around 5:00 a.m., when the last postop patient was trundled off to her room upstairs, I started accepting labor patients again.

The first customer was a woman in the middle stage of labor. I waited a bit, but no one came to see her, doctor-wise. I did as much as I could–started her IV, drew her lab work, spun her hematocrit, and did a vaginal exam. The night OB resident Dr. Genovese arrived at last. He thanked me for going ahead and getting things started.

Soon they brought me my second patient, a frail-looking black woman who acted somewhat oddly. She was curled up in a fetal position, seemingly sound asleep. The transporter said that Mrs. Beulah McMasters was a mother many times over. When they had checked her in the ER, Beulah was dilated to three centimeters. Her baby was coming a little early by about four weeks.

When I tried to get Mrs. McMasters to respond to me so that I could get her turned over, apply monitors, and get a history, she flopped on her back and snored. She was very much alive, however, as I found with her next contraction. Beulah was squirrelly and kept wanting to pee. I watch this kind of patient assiduously. I have learned that those women who (a) act squirrelly or (b) keep feeling pressure on either their bladder or their rectum are women whose labors are progressing at the speed of light.

At this point, a second-year resident, Gordon Crockett, one of the few doctors I have worked with who is significantly overweight, stepped into the room. He said, "Hi, Beulah, how's it going?" in a facetious voice. Beulah responded with a grunt, and Gordon just smiled, winked at me, then turned and exited the room. I thought he was going to get her chart. He astonished me by returning in a matter of minutes with a completed written workup, including an entry on the graphic chart we use to plot a woman's progress in labor.

The mark Dr. Crockett had made indicated that, by his exam, this woman was still the three centimeters she had measured in the ER. He had never gotten within six feet of Beulah McMasters. Instead of the usual physical exam and history taking that go into the workup of a new patient, Gordon had just copied the information that the midwife downstairs in the ER had noted in her thorough workup. Mainly, I was disturbed that he had stated as a fact that he had found Beulah to be still three centimeters dilated. He was giving all those who followed in his wake the mistaken impression that she was in early labor. Just by her behavior, I could guess that she was nearing time for delivery.

I fumed over this, but luckily an intern walked in just then. I asked him to please examine Mrs. McMasters, as she was becoming more agitated by the second. He was putting on a glove as I lifted the sheet, and we both stared at an amniotic sac bulging ominously. It was filled with some murky-looking, green meconium-stained fluid. The membrane was tense and threatening to blow, which it did as the force of a contraction ripped through our patient.

The two of us hastened down the hall, the intern pulling the bed as I was pushing it. We were trying to get Beulah to the delivery room so that the pediatric team could come and assist with the care of a somewhat premature, potentially at-risk infant. I was so disgusted. Beulah's care and that of her premature baby could have proceeded much less frantically if lazy, unprincipled Dr. Crockett had done his job even minimally.

What tricks will he be up to as he pursues his career in medicine if he is pulling this kind of scam now? I looked him straight in the eye as I swung past him, seated on his throne at the resident desk. I wanted to convey to him that I had his full measure as a man and that he should at least get off his prodigious behind and show some concern for his patient. He returned my pointed stare balefully.

I'm not sure that I could prove what I surely knew to be true about what had transpired. I did tell his colleague, pleasant, bland Dr. Thomson, that Gordon had copied the workup and manufactured the vaginal exam on Beulah's chart. The first-year resident looked at me without changing expression. They will trash each other among themselves, but they are not likely to admit the folly of another colleague to anyone else.

Come to think of it, it's very hard to listen to the complaints of the physicians when they are directed at nurses. I guess it is simply human nature to want to protect those who form one's peer group. I know I was most offended recently when a few of the residents were complaining about their inability to get a cesarean section on the operating table. They attributed the problem to "nursing dystocia." My hackles instantly went up at this cut to the universally hardworking delivery staff. It could have been true that there was a "Nurse Crockett" who was dragging her feet on getting a patient to surgery. The point is, I guess, to not make generalizations about groups.

After tonight's business, I've decided to watch Dr. Crockett more carefully in my dealings with him for the next two years, armed with my knowledge that his manner of practice might prove unsafe for his patients. If he is inclined to abuse his oath as a physician again, I will think about asking him what he is about to be behaving in such a way. If he were to respond with indifference, I would have to take it further. There are faculty here who bear responsibility for the residency program. It would be better if Dr. Crockett were found out now when there is a little more pressure that could be brought to bear. In private practice, controls are much more tenuous, and the public has to rely on the basic integrity of the physician community to ensure honest and reputable care.

One thing about Dr. Crockett. If I were one of his future patients and this three-hundred-pound man with hands the size of hams approached me with the intention of performing any sort of exam, I'd think really quickly about searching out a less imposing sort of OB-GYN practitioner. Maybe the enormity of his form will have a self-limiting effect on his career in women's health.

CHAPTER FORTY-SIX

"Somehow in my heart I knew that the last moments he and I had spent with the vital young woman we knew as Juana had taken place moments before her delivery."

October 27

CHICKEN POX. A relatively innocuous childhood virus. Since I took care of Juana Benitez, chicken pox will forever have a completely different meaning for me. As it did for her.

Wednesday, I met Juana as I took over her care from the nurse attending her in the isolation labor room. A seventeen-year-old just days from her eighteenth birthday, pregnant with her first baby, she had contracted the varicella virus from an unknown source. She and her equally young husband had only been in this country for a few months, living with his uncle while he tried to find work. Juana looked miserable when I met her and listened to Roz's report. Covered with spots, some scabbed over and some water-filled vesicles, Juana looked at me with shy eyes.

James Currie, the junior resident, was scribbling something in Juana's chart. He told me, "She's probably going to be discharged to the antepartum service. She's had PIH (pregnancy-induced hypertension) ruled out." Well, not exactly, as things turned out.

Roz continued telling me of all the events that had transpired since Juana's admission earlier in the week. Besides the great discomfort from the flu-like symptoms with her chickenpox and the irritating itching over her little, swollen body, she had been exhibiting some slightly elevated blood pressures. She also had persistent protein in her urine, a lot of it. However, Juana's other lab work did not seem consistent with the pregnancy-related blood pressure disease. It was a confusing picture.

The senior resident on this team, Andrea Martinez, had judged Juana stable enough to send to an isolation room one floor below us, but she wanted to double-check with her attending physician. Dr. Elise Markham showed up shortly, and I went outside the labor room to listen to the conversation surrounding the issue of Juana's diagnosis. Inquiring minds want to know.

After reviewing all the findings, Dr. Markham was convinced that Juana qualified as a toxemia patient. The question was whether to call her mild or severe. Dr. Martinez, the senior resident who was handing over Juana's care to the new team, was leaning in the direction of downplaying the severity of disease, if any, for our patient. I don't think there is too much evidence-based research on the interplay between chicken pox and PIH, but Andrea was thinking that somehow the protein in the girl's urine, a marker for rating the severity of PIH, could be attributed to the virus. She told me to allow Juana up to the bathroom and get her some real food for breakfast. She was writing orders for her to leave this area for the less acute unit where more stable pregnant women are observed.

I happily went about freeing Juana from the constraints of the last few days. I helped her totter to the bathroom, made up her bed with crisp, clean linen, and got her a tray from the food cart. After polishing off everything in sight with gusto, Juana settled in to page through old copies of fashion magazines I had filched from the break room. Though the shy young wife spoke not one word of English, I supposed that pretty clothes were a universal female language of sorts. Juana busied herself for a half-hour paging through *Glamour* and *Vogue*. All these normal activities encouraged me to think that she was doing fine, as well as could be expected for one who had contracted chicken pox as a young adult. Late onset typically produces a much harsher version of the childhood virus.

One reason the physician staff was hoping to temporize was to ensure that Juana's baby had the best chance to be born without contracting the varicella virus. Such a development could be very damaging to the health and well-being of a newborn. Then Dr. Horst, the attending obstetrician for the current twenty-four hours of call, happened to stop by the unit. When she heard about Juana's situation, she was not happy about the management plan of the resident staff. Belinda Horst disagreed with the senior resident's suggestion that somehow Juana's persistent spilling of protein in her urine could be explained by causes other than toxemia.

"Pregnancy-induced hypertension is a whole syndrome of symptoms, not just high blood pressure," Dr. Horst lectured the team of residents as they sat reviewing Juana's case. "Her proteinuria has me very concerned. I feel we need to deliver her, and expeditiously." For the remainder of the four hours I spent with Juana this day before leaving at eleven, her fate remained in limbo while the medical staff awaited the final decision of an even more senior perinatologist, and possibly a consult from the communicable disease service.

Two days passed. Back on duty to work some overtime during daytime hours, I found myself once again assigned to the isolation labor room. Upon entering this smallish private suite, I found Juana in the throes of labor. In the interim since we were last together, her blood pressure had skyrocketed, and the results from repeated lab tests showed a worsening case of toxemia. She was now diagnosed as having the more severe form of this disease, and we were inducing her labor. How miserable for this young woman, laboring, still feeling the malaise from her chicken pox, and now suffering from what still in modern days can be a devastating illness of pregnancy.

Catherine, the nurse I was relieving this morning, told me of Juana's most recent problems. Like all laboring patients with toxemia, she had been receiving the standard dose of magnesium sulfate by a pump to prevent the possibility of seizures. Nevertheless, this drug had to be discontinued some five or six hours ago, as Juana responded to the infusion with profound nausea, dizziness, and shortness of breath. She still appeared to be uncommonly lethargic and limp in muscle tone, typical of one who has received the mag sulfate for an extended period, or one who has mistakenly received a too-large dose. Neither of these explanations fit in Juana's case, who had merely been receiving the lowest dose considered therapeutic. Strange. Lab results attested to the fact that levels of the drug were very reasonable. Perhaps she was having some idiosyncratic reaction to the drug, possibly one related to her physiologic state of being infected with the varicella virus.

As I assumed Juana's care again, I watched her contractions as they caused her great pain. She was denied the blessed relief of an epidural, as the anesthesia and obstetric docs worried that the chickenpox virus might somehow travel via the tubing that delivered the numbing substance upward to the brain, causing encephalitis. Likewise, the medical staff wanted at all costs to achieve a vaginal birth, lessening any prospect that baby might contract its mother's infection during a surgical delivery. As Juana appeared sicker and sicker throughout my time as her nurse, I regretted this prohibition. If the chickenpox wasn't dictating the decisions about Juana's treatment so much, I believe she would have been in the operating room hours ago.

She put up with each labor pain heroically. Hector, her equally young husband, had arrived and was giving her what tender support he could. Juana would turn to each of us with a sad, resigned expression as her contractions started. Unable to receive even a narcotic for the pain, based on her strange and persistent muscular lethargy, my heart went out to this sweet, suffering girl.

Juana's blood pressure was alarmingly high, at times registering 210/110. Even though she wished to remain on her back, Hector and I had to encourage her time and again to stay on her left side, which was the only position to maintain blood pressures that were even minimally acceptable. I put pillows behind her back and between her knees to add what small bit of comfort I could.

I was in this quiet, sequestered room with what I knew to be a very, very sick patient. Wouldn't you know it? We were involved at this very moment with another young woman who was sick with another infectious disease, the ten-day or "hard" measles. This patient was already delivered and was isolated in another bigger labor room that had been given over to the sole care of the now very compromised mother. She was experiencing acute respiratory distress, and our OB docs were heavily involved in trying to get on top of what was potentially a life-ending complication, consulting extensively with the pulmonary and communicable disease services.

Still, I left my isolation labor room repeatedly to summon the residents to assess Juana's condition. At least she was making slow progress toward complete dilatation. This news was hopeful, in that her toxemia could only begin to improve once her baby was born. I tried to impress Drs. Chan and Moraga, the junior residents on this team, with my concerns about Juana's continuing muscular lethargy. It had been hours since the magnesium sulfate infusion had been discontinued. It was inexplicable that Juana should still be affected by this drug, and yet what else could be the cause of her persistently sluggish body movements and her slurred speech? Dr. Moraga told me to have another mag sulfate level drawn, which I did.

Two hours later, Juana began to complain of pain at the base of her head. Again, I went in search of Dr. Moraga to report this new development. The third-year resident's harassed response left me most troubled. "Your guess is as good as mine, Nattie," she told me.

So next I sought out the senior resident Janet Kirkpatrick. "You know, Janet, I feel that I am in that room with a *very* sick girl. Not only is she having this strange neck pain but also her urine output is only borderline acceptable. And her pressure is off the scale."

Dr. Kirkpatrick, a tiny, dynamic African American resident whom I greatly respect, came into Juana's room and checked over the situation. She commented that perhaps Juana's urine output was artificially decreased due to the pressure of the descending head of her infant on her urine-collecting tubes.

"She's getting pretty close to delivery. We'll bolus her with some normal saline and see if her output picks up. If she's still behind after delivery, we may have to put in a Swanz."

Janet was referring to a tube inserted into a chamber of the heart and then into the circulation to the lungs that helps physicians decide how critically ill patients are managing their circulating fluid volume.

I understood what was going on in Janet Kirkpatrick's mind. It was much like my train of thought. We both had cared for many women with severe toxemia. Most times, although giving us plenty of anxious moments while seeing them through their labor and birth, such patients begin to resolve their crisis in the first day or two after delivery. Juana was nearing the end point of labor. We were both praying that relief from the young woman's torture was near and that we would be seeing her slowly begin the trek back to robust health.

Now Juana was completely dilated by my exam. As exhausted as she was, I felt like a brute having to encourage her to push. Over and over, Hector and I had to physically prop her in the upright position for pushing, as she seemed to have no strength to keep from slumping over. Hector and I exchanged looks over her head, each of us so distressed that there was nothing we could do for her except help her to get her baby delivered. He counted to ten in Spanish as each contraction began. I tried to reassure them both that her ordeal was nearing its finish, as she slowly, inexorably brought her baby down the birth canal.

I had been in this room with this sweet couple for six hours straight. I went out into the hallway and sought out a passing rover nurse. I simply had to leave for a moment to visit the restroom. When Ingrid heard my request to watch Juana for a moment, she told me to go and get something to eat and have a few moments of respite. I was grateful for this thought but cautioned her:

"If I hear you calling for a doctor to deliver Juana, I'll be back. This delivery is going to require some extra help. Be sure to call the pediatric resuscitation team to run upstairs for this birth as well. This baby is surely going to come out stressed."

I had barely heated my soup in the kitchen next door to Juana's room when I heard Ingrid calling for the physicians to come to the isolation room for delivery. I hurried back to the room and found Ingrid and the intern setting Juana up for a bed delivery. I had previously assembled an infant warmer and all the resuscitation equipment typically available in the delivery room. It had been decided earlier that Juana, because of her chickenpox, should be delivered in place in the labor area, sparing her the disruptive trip back to the delivery area isolation room.

Even though one could see the baby's head ready to come out, Juana seemed to be in the throes of a terrible lethargy, seemingly beyond exhaustion. All of us in the room continued to coax and encourage her to give that final effort required to expel her baby. Hector was at her side, watching anxiously and helping as he could. Finally, believing that resident help was called for, I had the clerk summon Dr. Chan.

He watched Juana push ineffectively through her next contraction. Then he did something that I had not seen before. With his gloved hand, he inserted several fingers into her rectum, and Juana had an immediate and overwhelming urge to push. With a superhuman effort, she bore her infant.

The baby let out a preliminary and very muted cry. Then the little newborn boy was quiet, and I hurried over to the warmer where Dr. Chan carried the limp and silent newborn. The pediatrician began to dry off the baby and stimulate him, trying to get a good cry. Nothing. He started to give the baby oxygen. After I gripped the umbilical cord and could feel only the barest pulsation, I began chest compressions on the barely moving chest wall. I told Ingrid in a tense voice, "Get some help for this guy. We need the Ped's Fellow here."

Within twenty seconds of our call, this expert neonatologist came into the room. Just then, Juana's baby let out his first decent cry. Within a minute, he pinked up and was crying fitfully. I began to relax a bit and turned away from the scene of this infant resuscitation effort to let Juana and Hector know that things were beginning to resolve for their son.

What I saw troubled me. Dr. Chan and the intern were watching Juana's bottom, as the placenta was not quite on the point of delivering. Juana's husband, back in the corner by her head, was bent over and calling quietly to her. I circled around the bed to see what was happening and was horrified by what I observed. Juana was lying with eyes rolled back in her head, and her hands were clenching in a very ominous way that we call "posturing." I realized that Juana must have suffered some tremendous cerebral incident in those final seconds preceding or, indeed, in the very act of giving birth. I ran out of the room and almost barreled into Dr. Kirkpatrick.

"Please come quick," I exhorted her. "Juana is not with us."

In the room, Janet went to Juana's side while I called on the overhead page for anesthesia assistance. Within seconds, all the medical team had assembled. I handed an airway to Dr. Boitano, the anesthesiology resident, who was concerned about Juana's respiratory status. Dr. Kirkpatrick asked me to put a urinary drain into Juana's bladder. I did so hastily, and there was an immediate flushing back of about a cup and a half of urine. Janet had been right about there being a mechanical impedance to Juana's urinary system rather than kidneys that were shut down.

Juana was breathing on her own, but she was in no way conscious of any of the events occurring around her. I was sick at heart but had no chance to sit and ponder the awful chain of events leading up to this catastrophe. I went out of the isolation room to find Hector, Juana's sensitive and caring husband, who had been escorted earlier from the room by Ingrid while we were working so intensely over his insentient wife.

Out in the corridor, Hector was seated, bent over and crying. I knelt down beside him and gave what comfort I could, putting my arm around the eighteen-year-old's shoulder. I could not reassure him with news that his wife was out of trouble. In fact, somehow in my heart, I knew that the last moments he and I had spent with the vital young woman whom we knew as Juana had taken place minutes before her delivery.

In a bit, Hector pulled himself together. I asked him if he had any family or friends we could call to be with him. He said that he wanted his uncle but that he would have to go himself and get the gentleman. He seemed calm enough to go safely on this mission. I watched him walk down the hallway with a terrible sense of defeat and sorrow. This calamity simply could not be happening to this sweet, young couple that should even now be experiencing the joy of meeting their little son.

Back in the room, a team of neurologists had arrived emergently. They did all the tests designed to define the problem that was occurring in Juana's head. She remained unconscious through all, her hands still contorted in that way that describes an awful insult to the human brain. She was so very, very compromised. Within an hour, she was transported to the neuro intensive care unit in the main hospital.

Later in the day, Juana had a CAT scan that revealed the grim truth. Her hypertensive disorder had created horrific intracranial pressure. She had eventually squeezed the lower part of her brain through the small notch at the base of the head through which the spinal cord passes (herniation of the brain stem). The pain she complained of at the base of her skull was a forewarning of the critical pressure that ultimately was her death sentence.

Juana Benitez expired later the next day, one day after having given birth, on her eighteenth birthday as well as the one-year anniversary of her marriage to Hector. She never saw her infant son, and I never saw the young and grieving husband again. Two weeks later, the baby went home in good shape with his widowed father.

"Vaya con Dios."

CHAPTER FORTY-SEVEN

"Now caught up in my own personal funk, I felt like a trapped animal."

October 21

I CAME TO WORK tonight with a bad attitude. I brought irritations and squabbles from home with me and did not manage to leave them in the dressing room where I changed into scrubs. My assignment was to a labor room with two patients in early labor. I introduced myself in Spanish and told the two women to let me know if they needed anything. I hoped they didn't ask me for much because my heart simply wasn't in it tonight.

As the night progressed, our chronic short-staffing left all the labor nurses confined to their rooms. Merilee, who was making a valiant effort to get to each of us for a half-hour respite, was repeatedly called back to cover emergency deliveries. Usually, I accept this situation with grace. It's the reality of working here. Now caught up in my own personal funk, I felt like a trapped animal.

So it was no smiling angel of mercy who greeted a sixteen-year-old brought to my labor room at about 2:00 a.m. The transporter informed me that the ER resident had checked this young lady and found her to be four centimeters dilated. I asked Jackie, my new patient, to move from the stretcher onto the labor bed. Cursing furiously in Spanish-inflected English, she inched over onto the bed. That about ended her cooperative spirit. It seemed I had a patient with about the same temperament as her nurse, only Jackie felt freer to express her emotions.

I tried to get the leads for the fetal monitor attached to Jackie's tight little abdomen. She thrashed about and could not, or would not, cooperate. At the same moment, Vanessa Cordova arrived to see our new patient. The beautiful Latina resident observed the trouble I was having eliciting any cooperation from the fidgeting teenager and did not lose a moment in getting tough.

"Now look at me, young lady. You're going to stop that kind of behavior. You're going to let the nurse put those things on your belly so we can see how your baby is doing. In a minute, an intern is going to come and put an IV line in your arm. Right now, I'm going to examine you to see how far along you are. If we can, we'll give you some pain medicine. If you're old enough to get pregnant, you're old enough to behave like a grown-up."

Accepting a glove from me, Vanessa approached the bed to do a vaginal exam. Jackie continued to pitch and toss in the bed. She would not open her legs to allow the slender, raven-haired resident to do the exam. Vanessa put her free hand on Jackie's knee to nudge the girl's legs apart. Jackie proceeded to smack her hand away.

That did it.

"I don't have to put up with this, you know," Vanessa informed her new patient in a disgusted tone.

"I didn't want to come to this dump anyway," responded Jackie contemptuously. "I'll get my boyfriend to take me down the street to _____ Memorial."

"Fine," commented Vanessa sarcastically. "Let _____ Memorial have the pleasure of your company. We've got all the business we can handle without you." She then stripped off her glove and left the labor room without a backward glance.

My former irritability had fled somehow in the midst of this little drama. I scanned the room to exchange saddened looks with Angelique, the midwife on duty this night. Vanessa's behavior was not helpful or therapeutic in this situation. I wished that she could have scraped up a little psychological savvy in dealing with this admittedly difficult teenage patient. We were all a lot older and a lot better educated than this tough young woman.

I waited for a bit until a nasty contraction subsided and then, in a calm voice, I coaxed her.

"Look, Jackie, I know you're in a great deal of pain. You can go to _____ Memorial if you like. But realistically, they won't be able to do anything different for you. You're in hard labor now, and if I am right, things are moving along pretty quickly. Won't you let us help you?"

The now teary-eyed Latina looked up at me through a tumble of dark curls. All her former bratty attitude appeared to crumble.

"I'm just so-o-o scared," she wailed, again gripped by a whopping contraction.

I went out to the resident desk where Vanessa was working on charts. I told her about the turnabout in our patient's sentiments. Vanessa had calmed down by now too.

"OK." She sighed. "Get an intern to do her IV. I'll come back to check her in a bit. If she's far enough along, I'll order some Demerol. Maybe an epidural would even be better."

Things were to proceed along distinctly different lines from that point on. There was to be no IV, no Demerol, no epidural. Unlike most first-time labors, Jackie was dilating almost by the minute. When I checked her, I could feel no cervix in the way of a hard little head. Instead of the hour-long period of pushing one might expect with a first baby, Jackie went on to bring her baby down in three to four contractions. Soon, a fifty-cent-sized view of baby's dark hair was visible.

As the intern and I were pushing Jackie's bed out of the door to take her back to delivery, her boyfriend arrived. Informed that only minutes remained before he was to become a father, he complimented Jackie affectionately:

"*M'ija* (my dear little one), you done good!"

Jackie looked at me with self-conscious eyes, and we both laughed.

"Yes," I commented to both, "she did great."

CHAPTER FORTY-EIGHT

"Women having complex problems during labor and delivery need an extraordinary degree of tender, loving, skilled care from their doctors and nurses."

November 2

I WANT TO REFLECT a bit on my career to date as a moonlighter at the local hospital. It is amazing to me that I can be working at my job at the city hospital like a stevedore, handling an ever-increasing workload of maternity patients, participating in intensely stressful emergencies night after night. The next night I am at this place and find myself often with not a single patient to look after, or at the most, one or two.

Instead of running between multiples of laboring women, at the beck and call of equally harassed interns and residents, the deliveries here take place in a calm and quiet atmosphere with dad always present. Two nurses attend each delivery, one to care for the newborn infant and one to help with the needs of both the delivering mother and the obstetrician. Dad is many times occupied with making a photographic journal of his baby's birth, and expensive camcorders or digital cameras are practically *de rigueur*.

After the birth occurs, we keep the whole new family unit in a private place where a lovely period of bonding goes on. More photos or videos are created. We work with the mom to initiate breastfeeding if so desired. The whole family of siblings, grandparents, and godparents can come in and share in the immediate postpartum euphoria. When the couple is ready, we move them to the maternity ward where they finish their hospital stay in a private or sometimes a two-bed room. A lactation nurse visits later to give coaching and support to the newly breastfeeding mother.

Since there are so few patients at a time, it is almost always possible to give intensive individualized care as a nurse. Most couples have gone to childbirth preparation classes, so come equipped with good coping skills. Conversing in English, there are many delightful and extended chances to get to know the patients and their spouses well. The basic work is the same, babies coming in the same manner whether the patient is a well-heeled, middle-class insured woman or my indigent patients at the city hospital. Here, however, the emphasis is on birth as a healthy function of womanhood, with a generally happy and positive outcome.

So with everything rosy here, why am I not thinking of resigning my full-time position at the med center to come to this nirvana of obstetrical departments? Not so fast. There are things going on here that give me a great deal of pause, much of it having to do with the way the physicians and nurses operate. There is a beehive of activity and undercurrents lying beneath the placid surface that patients see when they come here.

There are about ten obstetricians on staff who divide up the eighty to ninety deliveries each month. (At City Hospital, we deliver this same number in less than three days.) Several of these private docs belong to a four-man group practice, so they have the luxury of being on call no more than once or twice a week. There is always a second physician from the practice for backup when a cesarean section becomes necessary. There is another group of three with the same advantages. Then there are several docs who practice by themselves. They often help each other out by responding to the other's need for assistance if a C-section is called. Sometimes they can look for help in an emergency from the trauma surgeon who is on call here twenty-four hours a day for serious situations coming into the ER.

There is one obstetrician on staff who is the delight of the nurses and has their total affection and respect. Frank LeBand is their personal choice for their pregnancy care. I worked with this nice gentleman for three years when he was completing his residency at City. He is the same calm, decent, and knowledgeable person in private practice as he was as a physician in training.

One of the things that most wins him approval from the nurses is that he does not treat them like they are his servants. When his patients have delivered, he assists them onto the stretcher from the delivery table. Then he bends down to collect the debris that has accumulated from the birth process instead of leaving this mess for the nurses to clean up. It is small gestures like these that win friends and influence people.

The rest of the docs, however, are a collection of prima donnas and oddballs about whom the nurses, disposed as they are to want to like and respect the people with whom they work so closely, have a hard time finding much to say of a positive nature. One in particular, who is paradoxically the busiest and most successful of the obstetricians on staff, really gets on my nerves. Wesley Allen, a bright, energetic, spoiled man who really loves the adulation and power he has as a much-in-demand practitioner in this community, has the manners of a . . . well, I'm not sure to what I can compare the man. He pretty much ignores me as a newcomer but takes every opportunity he can to make me look small and foolish in front of the patients and their families. Dr. Allen is an emotional thug with a stethoscope.

The other evening he came in to see Mrs. Bellamy, a patient of his who was about midway through her labor. He decided to place an internal monitoring system—a scalp wire to track the baby's heart rate—and a pressure catheter to measure the strength of contractions. I had been caring for Mrs. Bellamy, and this was my first time assisting Dr. Allen with this routine procedure. He made a lot of dramatic gestures while putting these things inside his patient. Then it was my turn to attach the thin wires from the scalp lead to the fetal monitor plate. He became excessively irked when I fumbled for a second with the Velcro strap that secures the device to the patient's leg. Instead of giving me a few more seconds to get it right, he let out an exasperated sigh as if to say, "Imbecile!" He grabbed the stuff out of my hands and did it himself. Then he smiled at Mrs. Bellamy and her husband, as if waiting for their applause. They looked at him in confusion.

I have noticed that when things like this happen in front of patients, they may appear momentarily taken aback but never say anything. This passivity prevails, even when Dr. Allen exclaims to them, as he routinely does in deliveries that turn out to be male births,

"Hey, look at this kid. He's hung like a bull!"

I have seen the appalled look on the faces of couples who are far better mannered than their physician, yet they ignore such crudity. There is even in this affluent population of patients a feeling of being intimidated in the presence of their physician. Dr. Allen could better expend his energy explaining to his moms and dads that the scrotal swelling that sometimes occurs in male babies is physiologic and will subside fairly quickly after birth.

As for the nurses here, they have no ability to say what they like to financial powerhouses who are providing the hospital with much-desired income. Typically, their judgments do prevail, but they must do their all to manipulate the obstetricians in a way that leaves these docs' egos in ascendance. Sickening. And these are very skilled and intelligent nurses I find myself paired with here. From stories they tell me of situations they have been in when an emergency takes place, with the physician still at the office or home in bed, I have to marvel at their presence of mind, courage even.

I have a rather low threshold for anxiety and wonder how I would have handled the situation that occurred here a few nights ago when a woman came into the emergency room ready to deliver. Sandy, one of the OB nurses, was summoned hurriedly to the ER, while their staff paged the on-call obstetrician at home. Arriving in the ER, she found that the baby was breech and ready to come out. Sandy proceeded to deliver the baby because the ER physicians won't touch this kind of complex birth if they can avoid it. Everything went well, and Sandy was the heroine of the day.

Sometimes it is their very skill and knowledge that makes for problems for these excellent nurses. Two years ago, a young mother was admitted here for management of premature labor. She was receiving a rather new drug to stop contractions, a powerful drug that had a lot of unpleasant side effects for the woman. The medication sped up mom's heart rate furiously, as well as baby's. Ritodrine also had one potential complication for which nurses were taught to be observant; namely, pulmonary edema. Such an adverse reaction to the drug is a serious situation and must be addressed promptly.

Stephanie, a very sharp and capable nurse who has a background in intensive care nursing, detected that the young woman in premature labor was beginning to exhibit signs of pulmonary edema. She called the physician from the group practice who was covering inpatients that day and asked him to come in to have a look. Dr. McFarland arrived, checked things out, and dismissed the notion of pulmonary edema. Stephanie reiterated all her findings to Dr. McFarland, who thereupon told her not to worry her pretty little head and proceeded to leave the hospital.

Uncomfortable as she was, Stephanie felt she had no recourse but to call another member of Dr. McFarland's practice, explain what was occurring, and ask for his intervention. Dr. Harvey Klein came in to evaluate the patient, with both mother and baby showing marked signs of deterioration. In minutes, he was convinced of the seriousness of the situation, and he had to call Dr. McFarland to return and assist with an emergency cesarean section. They delivered a tiny and very fragile newborn that ended up needing transfer to a regional hospital with an excellent neonatal intensive care unit. Mom also had to spend time in the adult ICU to recover from her complications.

Did Stephanie win accolades for her intelligence and persistence in both diagnosing the patient's problem and obtaining the necessary help to prevent a disaster from occurring? No. Instead, Dr. McFarland, incensed by what he felt was Stephanie's insubordination, tried to have the hospital fire her. When he was thwarted on this front, he simply began a childish campaign to freeze Stephanie out. He has not spoken to her in several years and lets her know that she is pond scum to him. If someone treated me so in my primary job, it would be easy to ignore in the mill of so many other congenial people. Here, such contempt and isolation stands out because of the small size and intimacy of the physician and nursing staff.

One other problem I have here is that there isn't the same collegiality between the medical and nursing staff that I enjoy at the city hospital. Sometimes I don't care for the manners of a few young physicians in training I deal with nightly, but I certainly feel able to give input and opinions on what is happening to a patient. By and large, I feel that my thoughts are entertained respectfully. Here, nurses are not ever to get in the way of a physician's decisions or management of a case.

An example: Last week I was caring for a laboring patient who was known to be a diabetic. A nurse by profession, she had worked very hard to keep her blood sugar in strict control and had had a very benign prenatal course. Her labor was progressing well, and at around 10:00 p.m., Mrs. Burnett was dilated to six centimeters. Having delivered successfully in the past, and likely to proceed quickly to delivery, I called her physician, Dr. Chi, and let him know to come in from home.

After I hung up, Adelaide, the nurse I was partnered with, began to stamp up surgical paperwork for Mrs. Burnett.

"What are you doing?" I quizzed her. "She's making great progress."

"You watch" was Adelaide's knowing reply. "Dr. Chi will walk in the room, feel around a bit on Mrs. Burnett's stomach, and then he'll say something like, 'Hmm-m. Big baby. Mo betta C-section.'"

And that is exactly what happened. Dr. Chi arrived moments later, and within fifteen minutes, we were in surgery. Later, I asked Adelaide what the justification for this surgery could be.

"They all give the same reason if you look on their operative reports: cephalopelvic disproportion."

Meaning that the doctor judged the baby's head as too big to pass through mom's pelvis. That's a hard sell when Mrs. Burnett's history stated that she had previously been able to deliver a nine-pound baby vaginally without event. At the teaching hospital where I primarily work, every cesarean section, other than those done emergently for either maternal or fetal distress, must have careful consideration and documentation for legitimacy. I have never, never seen surgery done for a frivolous, fuzzy, or downright misleading rationale.

Adelaide went on to tell me that the C-section rate in this obstetrical department was near 50 percent. My god. Our rate at City Hospital is something like 12 percent, even with quantities of high-risk moms receiving care. These patients here are almost all healthy young women, yet I had only seen one patient protest mildly when the private doc informed her he thought surgery was the way to go. If you asked most women in the midst of their painful labor if they were agreeable to having their torture ended by the surgical option, many would prove willing. It has been a big part of my job as a nurse to support women in labor by encouraging them that they will survive the ordeal of labor and will not die from the pain.

Here, everyone is complicit in this expensive, wasteful process of delivering half of their pregnant patients by cesarean section. The physicians get a tidy sum for the much-costlier surgical procedure. They also circumvent the possibility of complications from birth injury, thus precluding any potential lawsuits. However, they are subjecting patients to the chance of a surgical complication from what is a major abdominal operation. They also get to go home for dinner or get an uninterrupted night's sleep.

I am not kidding about this. Most of the surgical deliveries, other than the prescheduled ones, take place at five thirty in the evening or ten o'clock at night. The MDs are not the only ones to push for these timely (for them) operative births. Once the woman has had her cesarean section and is shuffled off to the recovery room, the nurses are often back to one, or none, as far as patient load stands. And they like that, so thus often appear delighted with the move for a surgical option. Shame on them.

All these things have caused me to feel great dismay, although I had somehow anticipated such issues when I took on this new job. I didn't want to have my misgivings confirmed. Maybe I simply chose the wrong place, although Caroline, my friend at City who has many years of experience in private OB units to her credit, tells me that she encountered identical problems. I'll have to ask her if she has ever been asked to strap on some incredibly chauvinistic doctor's gold bracelets after a delivery, as the nurses here have to ritually do for one of the docs. Thank God he doesn't think I rate yet, so I have not been called upon to render this nauseatingly obsequious service. Doesn't he know?

I'm beginning to think that the only way I can find a spot where the patient is the recipient of consistently decent, compassionate, humanistic obstetrical care is to go back to school and study midwifery. I've never yet been in a situation where a midwife failed to render knowledgeable, interested, and personable care to a laboring or delivering woman. Their focus is on assisting women through what is an intense, painful, but natural process. Their C-section rates are miniscule, so excellent are they at risking out problem pregnancies to medical management and keeping those women with prospects for benign births.

I'm going to have to do some real soul-searching around this issue. I do know that I would have a really hard time leaving high-risk obstetrics. Women having complex problems during labor and delivery need an extraordinary degree of tender, loving, and skilled care from both their doctors and nurses.

If it was not for this understanding, and the fact that I think I am darn good at work I love, then, hey, I'm outta here.

Addendum: Later in my experience at this private hospital, I was able to perform a huge service for the L & D nurses. They had never been able to tell the physician how they loathed his ritualistic choosing of one of them to strap on his gold bracelets after completing his deliveries. Finally, one informed him, in a joking way, of how that "nurse from City laughs at us for doing this." Thereafter, he left his jewelry at home.

CHAPTER FORTY-NINE

"They were not in the habit of taking any guff from young Nicaraguan immigrant girls."

November 9

A N INCIDENT OCCURRED today that left me wondering just what to think about the ethical implications of taking care of this poor, largely immigrant patient population. It was a funny, whacky adventure on one level, a medical-legal dilemma on another. So you make the call.

A young Latina came in to have her first baby this morning. I was not taking care of her, but the nurse into whose labor room they admitted Daisy Cano kept coming to me to ask for guidance. By exam, the girl was only a few centimeters dilated. She was in early labor, and since an average labor for first-time mothers is about twelve hours, there was quite a while to go.

After an uneventful period, Daisy's baby's heart rate took a sudden, ominous, and lengthy dip. Sheila, my young nurse friend, called for the residents to come and intervene. The team went about the business of turning off the Pitocin infusion, turning the mother on her side, starting some oxygen by face mask, and increasing the IV fluids. These are all measures we take to send some extra oxygen support to a distressed infant. The fetal heart rate problem lasted about three minutes and then made a slow recovery to normal.

When a baby gets into trouble in this early phase of labor, we take this to be a signal to be hyper attentive. The stress will only increase as mother gets into the more intense, active stage of labor. This young woman was not sophisticated enough to understand what all the fuss was about. Clearly, she was unsettled by the abrupt surrounding of her bed by a bevy of medical staff and the various manipulations of her body they implemented.

Things returned to an acceptable state for perhaps another hour. Then a repetition of the same sort of dangerous lowering of the baby's heart rate occurred. The senior resident Dr. Powell arrived this time to look at the situation. By then, the heart rate was again back to normal, though this deceleration was equally as impressive as in the first instance.

"Well, it's likely to happen again. If it does, we're not going to mess around. We'll just take her back to surgery and free up this kid. Get her consented, and we'll watch and wait." With this pronouncement, Dr. Powell left Sheila's labor room.

Minutes later, an intern appeared with the consent form. He started to go through the usual canned speech designed to help the patient understand the possible benefits and risks of surgery, in general, and cesarean section in particular. Before Dr. Mackay even got to the good stuff about possibly having her uterus removed, or never being able to have children again, Daisy began to remonstrate. In rapid-fire Spanish, she indicated to Sheila that she was refusing surgery. Sheila, an Asian nurse who grew up in South America, was trilingual. She responded to Daisy's protestations by carefully explaining that the intern needed to obtain her consent for surgery in case there was any further evidence that her baby was in trouble.

This speech didn't seem to compute with our young mom. When Daisy continued to argue with Sheila and Dr. Mackay, insisting that no one was going to operate on her, the baffled intern asked her for her reason.

"If the Virgin Mary had her baby without surgery, then that is the way heaven intended babies to be born" was Daisy's novel reply.

Now the medical staff had a good laugh for a minute, but then it was back to the same quandary. What was going to happen if the baby took another bad turn? The senior resident Dr. Powell came back to Sheila's labor room and was blunt with our teenage mother. He lent his efforts to impress her with the possible fatal outcome for her child if she refused to let the medical staff intervene surgically. Daisy responded to this hardball speech by stating that she didn't want to have a scar on her stomach for life.

Although Daisy didn't seem to be mentally unbalanced, merely quite naive, unsophisticated, and stubborn, she had succeeded in baffling and raising the ire of a great many high-powered and extremely intelligent medical folks. They were not in the habit of taking any guff from young Nicaraguan immigrant girls.

Next, Dr. Powell told Sheila to inform the patient that, in the interest of ensuring a safe outcome for her baby, he was going to request a court order to allow surgery. Sheila, her small body swollen with her first pregnancy, continued to try and persuade Daisy to acquiesce with our plan for her. Meanwhile, Dr. Powell went out to the desk and began to make the appropriate calls. The first was to his attending staff who cautioned him to wait a minute before pursuing the court order.

Dr. Matsuki, a gentle-mannered and extremely humane sort of fellow, went in to talk to the troubled young woman. Instead of taking a hard line, he employed a different approach. Talking in a soft voice and using simple terms, he attempted to obtain Daisy's compliance. The result was exactly the same. Daisy continued to adamantly refuse any surgical intervention.

Dr. Powell was back on the phone, talking to the chief of perinatal medicine to get concurrence for a court order. It was at this point that another player came on stage. Dr. Bielenson, a rather cold and cerebral third-year resident who pretty much disdained too-close contact with patients, happened to be just then coming back to the labor area after completing a surgical case. He heard Dr. Powell's end of the phone conversation about a "court order" and asked me about the strange chain of events that precipitated such an unusual intervention. I related the odd things that were coming out of our stubborn labor patient. Dr. Bielenson picked up the surgical consent form and lost not a beat in walking briskly in the direction of Sheila's labor room.

Coming up to Daisy's bed, Dr. Bielenson directed Sheila to translate for him.

"Señora," he addressed her sternly, "if you continue to refuse surgery and your baby dies because of it, that's a mortal sin. You'll go to hell for that. You understand? *Big fire!*"

Daisy turned terrified and abashed eyes toward Sheila. She took the consent form and signed her name. Dr. Bielenson walked out. Less than half an hour later, another episode of a dramatic plunge in the baby's heart rate occurred, and the patient was rushed to the operating room for surgery.

Upon examination, the umbilical cord was found to have a true tight knot. To have continued Daisy's labor was a presumptive death sentence for her tiny and vulnerable baby, minus the surgical option. In the world of theory, Dr. Bielenson had committed an outrageous moral circumvention of the patient's right to make an unpressured, informed consent to treatment. Yet he had intervened in a way that likely saved her baby's life. So again, you make the ethical call.

CHAPTER FIFTY

"It is common practice in the drug-dependent community to prepare for the agony of labor by indulging in "speedballing," a delightful cocktail of cocaine and heroin."

November 15

I HAD A RARE night off last evening because I was attending class today. Traffic was light on my way to the hospital. As I had an extra half hour to squander, I went upstairs to the unit instead of heading to the basement auditorium. What I found there was a chilling reminder of the escalating crisis we face with the ever-increasing numbers of women being brought here for care.

As I walked down the long corridor toward the desk in my street clothes, I wove between a forest of beds and stretchers. Women were in labor on both sides of the hallway, portable fetal monitors at every station where an electrical outlet was available. The women in these beds looked at me dolefully, as if to ask, "Why must I be going through this agony out here?"

At intervals, screens were placed around a stretcher where an intern or resident was doing an exam or procedure. The faces of all the nurses and doctors looked gray and numb, as if in shock. What hell this night must have been, particularly for the physicians who had been on duty since early in the morning yesterday. Surely with the enormity of numbers of patients, not one of them had been able to rest for a second.

At the desk, I looked for Merilee or Anita, wanting to help in whatever small way I could for the last forty minutes until the day staff arrived to take over. However, neither of these experienced and steady women were present. Instead, Ruth told me that the nurse in charge of this nightmarish situation was Adam.

One of the rare men in nursing to choose obstetrics as a specialty, Adam is not very experienced as a team leader but is a calm and very giving member of the nursing staff. He likes to take the charge role. As he extends himself to be helpful to the nurses he is directing and is a pretty good problem solver, Merilee has been an encouraging mentor in acclimating Adam to the leadership role. It was soon apparent to me that, as willing as Adam was to take the charge position, he was not veteran enough to handle this incredible situation. There were twelve women who needed care and only had the hallway for their labor experience. I saw Adam down one wing, taking care of three women on beds strung out along the wall. He looked a bit dazed as I approached him.

"Adam, what's the most pressing thing you need me to do right now?" I asked him.

"Hey, not much I can do but just keep on trucking," he responded in a subdued voice. "I'm OK here."

But what about those three women on gurneys lined up down the opposite wing? These were three patients who were not having their babies monitored. How long had they been like that, unattended? How long had they been waiting for some patient to go to delivery so that they could have their little plot of land along the corridor walls or in some labor room? When I queried him, Adam could not speculate as to when these women had arrived. He turned away from me, obviously determined to stick to the job at hand. He had no mean task, caring for three high-risk obstetric patients under such conditions.

To me, this was a mark of both his youth and his inexperience, or even more probable, a reaction to the seemingly impossible job of trying to lead the nursing staff under such brutal conditions. When in charge of this unit, both the senior resident and the nursing team leader are especially responsible for all that goes on. Somehow, Adam should have developed a plan to deal with those three unattended women. He could have assigned the nurses in the labor rooms down that corridor to take a handheld Doppler out in the hallway and establish that the babies had a normal heart rate. Such an intervention would at least ensure that we were not endangering these vulnerable little ones by our inability to provide space, equipment, and staff to do the job.

I was pondering how to set something in motion while still in my street clothes, not even part of the working staff at the moment, when, abruptly, the woman in the bed next to me began to display the agitation I have come to associate with imminent birth.

"Delivery!" I called out, attempting to attract the attention of a passing resident. Dr. Agnew did not even glance my way as she brushed past me. I knew that this birth was going to inevitably become the work of this mother and me.

Janice Patrick, an exquisitely fine woman both in terms of her dark-skinned beauty and her nursing professionalism, came out of her busy labor room with a delivery pack and began to assist me. I proceeded to deliver a healthy, pink, and dark-haired son for this veteran mother. Without waiting for the appearance of the placenta, I quickly moved this couple to the delivery area. I handed them over to the very much overwhelmed delivery area staff. Then I hastened back to choose a new player for the vacated spot from the three orphan patients who had been tickling my conscience.

I looked at the three women, each lying flat on their narrow stretchers, their bellies mounded high under the sheets. I made a fateful decision to take the first in line. She was a thin, light-complected black woman in her early twenties who appeared almost as agitated as my recently delivered mother had moments before birth. I was hoping to get this woman's baby on the monitor and do a vaginal exam, fully expecting to find this patient nearing her time. Then I could perhaps see her back to the delivery area and get back to the next waiting patient. So much for well-laid plans.

As I moved the writhing and crying woman into the newly emptied spot along the wall, I found that a female sheriff's deputy was shadowing us. It was only then that I spotted the handcuff that secured the patient to the bed rail. I ignored the shackling issue temporarily because Luanna Edwards was screaming lustily now, too beside herself for me to attach the fetal monitors. I got a glove, sure that when I checked Luanna, I would find the head of her baby meeting my hand on the way out. Luanna stopped vocalizing long enough to say two things: "Don't stick your hand in my coochie," and "That's an awesome dress you is wearin'."

I was wrong about Luanna. When I felt inside, instead of meeting a hard little head, I had to reach deeply to find the cervix, the mark of a labor that is in the very earliest stages. *Hmmm,* I thought. I supposed that the reason Luanda was screeching with such fury was that she was probably incarcerated for a drug problem and wasn't able to tolerate even beginning labor pains.

But as I brought out my gloved hand, with it came a fistful of clotted blood and a gushing stream of red behind it. All this from a cervix whose opening was no greater than my fingertip. I knew we were in trouble. I stepped a few feet away to the resident desk where I tapped the shoulder of that exhausted resident, Dr. Agnew, the one who had recently ignored me.

"I know you aren't in the mood for even one more problem," I said to her sympathetically, "but you better come over here quickly." I told her about the impressive bleeding I had found. Dr. Agnew wearily pulled herself up and followed me to our hallway bed.

"She *is* having a healthy amount of bleeding," Dr. Agnew agreed as I went about trying to pick up the baby's heartbeat with the cardiac monitor lead. Scratchy noise was my only reward. Dr. Agnew seemed rooted to her post by the bedside, unable to decide on the next step to take in dealing with one more possibly life-threatening obstetrical emergency since it was occurring in the hallway.

"Dr. Agnew, I think we're in the soup here, so let's somehow get this woman into a room where there's oxygen, where you can do an ultrasound," I told her. I then had to negotiate with Janice to bring her least-active labor patient out into the hallway and slip Luanna into the vacated space. Dr. Agnew had gone to get the ultrasound machine. I got some oxygen going, resumed my attempt to locate the baby's heartbeat, and thanked Janice for her cooperative spirit as she set about starting an IV line in Luanna's arm.

Dr. Agnew returned and did another exam, this time producing an even more significant gush of bright red blood and clots.

"Can you try to get a scalp lead on?" I asked her. "I can't find this baby's heartbeat, and time is passing."

I handed her the equipment to put a tiny wire on the baby's head to allow us to have a direct and continuous readout of the baby's heart rate. An experienced resident can get this device on through a barely dilated cervix. Dr. Agnew struggled but finally said she thought she had gotten the scalp wire attached. I hooked it up to the fetal monitor, and after some seconds of scratchy interference, it began to trace out a fetal heart rate of eighty beats per minute straight across the graph paper. That is not what we want to see. It can mean one of two things: either the baby is dead and the scalp wire is picking up the mother's heartbeat, or the baby is very compromised and potentially moribund.

I motioned to the deputy sheriff to come to the bedside. She'd been watching events silently from the corner of the labor room and she didn't hesitate a moment in unshackling Luanna from the bedframe. Dr. Agnew stepped into the hallway. "Call delivery!" she yelled at the desk clerks. "Crash coming back, and it's a bad one."

Still in my green dress, I helped run the stretcher down the hallway, around the turns to the delivery area, even crossing the lines that designate the perimeter of the ORs. No thought to my stopping to put on the proper garb for entering a surgical area. The anesthesia residents were ready and waiting, and I got out of the room hastily as everyone began to assemble for the start of emergency surgery.

Pressured as surely few human beings are in this life, both by the fury of this night's work and the uncertainty of whether they could salvage this baby's life, the team of physicians and nurses got the little girl out in minutes. She was severely depressed, and it may be days before we know if she will make it.

Dr. Agnew told me later that the placenta was virtually detached from the sides of the uterine wall and that blood had spouted up like a fountain when she incised Luanna's womb. Placental abruption. We had had no time to get any information from Luanna about her health history prior to this emergency. Two primary reasons for the placenta to slough off the wall of the womb prior to delivery are severe hypertensive disease and maternal ingestion of cocaine. We have learned that it is common practice in the drug-dependent community to prepare for the trials of labor by indulging in "speedballing," a delightful cocktail of heroin and cocaine.

All this is pure speculation until the lab work comes back from both Luanna and her baby. I hope that Luanna was in jail for shoplifting or bad checks rather than for drug abuse, because even if her baby makes it, life for the little newborn girl would be so very tough as the child of a drug addict. I'd like to think that a better fate is in store for Luanna's daughter, as it had been so iffy that I had even been on the spot to pick up the problem that had led to emergency surgery. I had much to fill my thoughts as, late to class, I spent some eight hours being treated to riveting lectures on the new documentation system.

CHAPTER FIFTY-ONE

"They seemed very aware of the stir they were causing, as young female nurses and docs all found something pressing to do in the corridor."

November 20

I T'S GOTTEN SO that my friends and coworkers among the nursing staff want some answers about what those in charge are going to do about the alarming overload in the patient census. They feel as if we—the doctors, nurses, and patients—have all been abandoned to a cruel fate. When each day sees the hallways littered with poor women in labor on stretchers, the staff feels helpless to deliver a decent quality of care to our patients.

The thing is, we worker bees down here don't have any idea what those administrators up on the eleventh floor are thinking about all of this. What of those even more removed and inaccessible to us, the anonymous creatures who officiate over health care in this city whom we simply refer to as "downtown?" Maybe they are just as perplexed and feel as helpless as we about how to solve the crisis in obstetrics for the poor we serve. Maybe, even as I write, they are planning strategies to cope with the escalating demand for maternity care by the huge wave of immigrants to this area.

Meanwhile, even in the midst of the most desperately busy times, there is a bit of humor to help me endure. Recently, early in the morning I was working in the corridor with three women in labor. There were fetal monitors layered one atop another on hastily commandeered tables between stretchers lined up along the walls. To use the monitors, we have resorted to stringing long industrial-strength extension cords into nearby rooms. Sometimes we have to unplug one patient's fetal monitor so a resident can do an ultrasound on another patient.

Janelle, the nurse manager, had the head electrician here to see about getting some more wall outlets installed. It seems that the hallway patients are not going to disappear anytime soon. Ergo, we need to give the unfortunate women forced to labor in the hallway the benefit of the same technology that their fellow patients in the labor rooms enjoy. Janelle started to show the electrician where she wanted more plugs put in so as to obviate the necessity for the use of extension cords.

"I can't do that," the gentleman replied with a deadpan expression.

"Why not?" asked Janelle.

"Because we can't put more outlets in the hallways. Patients can't be cared for in the hallway," he said solemnly.

Janelle glanced up and caught my eye. We exchanged a wide-eyed look.

"Mr. Stokes," the ever-politique Janelle continued, "as you can see, we are indeed taking care of patients in the hallway. We need more electrical outlets to do a decent job by these women."

"I hear you," he responded, his expression unchanged, "but we don't take care of patients in the hallway."

OK, so we aren't going to be able to look for solutions from the electrical department. Shortly after report last night, with the usual shortage of nurses and overage of patients, one of the nurses had another idea. Laura brought up the fact that having the halls crammed with beds and equipment was surely a terrific fire hazard. Before we had to resort to giving obstetrical care in the corridors, we used to be repeatedly dinged for the few bits of paraphernalia left outside patient rooms when the fire inspectors came to survey us. What would the fire department say if they were to come now when we can barely thread a bed through the obstructed hallways when we have to get a woman back to the delivery area?

Laura, tiny little bundle of energy that she is, was all for calling the fire marshal anonymously and reporting us, just to see what the resultant fallout would be. Her thought was that such action would force the brass to deal more expeditiously with the situation.

Soon I was caught up in the effort to care for so many laboring and delivering women and their babies. I forgot all about the fire department and Laura's plotting, which I took to be mostly bluff. At about 1:00 a.m., she came to my post in the LICU and told me that she had gone through with her innovative plan. She described making ten separate phone calls to get to someone with administrative responsibility in the fire department. At that point, she was told to "call back a week from Tuesday, 'cause that guy's on vacation." I laughed about this bureaucratic dystocia and then rapidly forgot the whole thing in my busy care area.

At about 4:00 a.m., Merilee came to me. "I need someone to help me put a Foley in a girl who is going for C-section." Hmmm. Nurses who work in Labor and Delivery are probably some of the foremost experts in putting tubes in women's bladders. I have inserted a catheter in a patient while crouched under the heavy linen drapes in the operating room with almost zero visibility. The fact that Merilee needed help with this procedure alerted me to the fact that something unusual was going on.

I followed Merilee to the isolation room where she had been taking care of a sixteen-year-old girl who had come to us this night from her present address at Juvenile Hall. Becky Kallins was a thin, blonde, troubled-looking teenager. I put on a pair of sterile gloves, and Merilee began to open up a sterile field in the bed between Becky's doubled-up legs. I tried to make casual conversation with our young patient, as I could only begin to imagine Becky's embarrassment at this intrusion on her privacy. She answered my simple questions with monosyllables, her facial expression wooden.

"What I need you to do is help me find the opening," Merilee informed me with a very conscious look.

I finally stared down at Becky's exposed vulva and was met by one of the strangest sights I've ever encountered. Becky had a condyloma, more commonly known as a genital wart. This wart was seated right between this poor girl's legs, growing apparently out of her labia. It had the size and appearance of a medium-size head of cauliflower. I do not see how Becky had been able to walk with this huge growth between her legs. I guessed that, under the influence of pregnancy-related hormones, the condyloma had increased in size dramatically. So much did the huge wart cover Becky's genitalia that it could have meant big trauma to the area if a vaginal delivery was attempted. Still, it would be the first time I had ever seen "wart" as an indication for a cesarean section.

Merilee had me put just a bit of traction on this growth so that she could visualize the small dimple that directs us to the opening into the bladder. With my maintaining the gentle traction, she could locate the entry point through which she could then thread the drainage tube. We were attempting to do this procedure with an eye to preserving the teenager's dignity as much as possible. We acted as nonchalant about working around the huge warty structure as if this was the most everyday sort of occurrence for us. Of course, we had the doors to the room shut tight for privacy.

Even with the doors closed, our ears were suddenly assaulted with a loud, insistent voice demanding to know "Where's Merilee? Get her out here now!" That voice sure sounded like that of Karen Wrightsman, one of the night nursing supervisors. But Merilee was still in the midst of threading the catheter past Becky's wart, so I stepped out into the hallway to find out what was up.

There came Ms. Wrightsman, looking most terribly peeved, with a collection of four stunningly handsome young gentlemen from the fire department. The eye-candy crew was all decked out in their asbestos trousers, boots and helmets, and were looking about them interestedly. They seemed very aware of the stir they were causing, as young female nurses and docs all found something pressing to do in the corridor.

I walked over to Karen and told her that Merilee was tied up for a few minutes but would be with her shortly. "You tell her to get out here *now!*"

I had never seen the usually affable supervisor in such a state. I guess she doesn't like surprises. I guess she received her surprise midnight visitors in response to "some nurse from Labor and Delivery calling to say the place was a firetrap."

As I looked about me, most of the patients who had previously been in labor in the hallway had been fortunate in finding spaces in rooms vacated by women going to delivery. Other than one or two remaining women on stretchers, and the clutter of equipment left behind in the aftermath of doing hallway care, the place did not look nearly as congested as it had when the night began.

"Really, it's not so bad here," remarked one of the strapping fire hunks. "You should visit the emergency room up the hill sometime. Now there's a scene!"

Merilee, totally innocent of complicity in the plot to call the fire department, nevertheless agreed with the consensus of opinion on the floor that we ought to be working much more closely with these fine young men to solve our deficiencies in the area of fire safety. Yes, indeedy. Let's get those excellent fellows back, and soon!

CHAPTER FIFTY-TWO

". . .limp to the dressing room with bladders full to bursting, their underwear stained with menstrual flow they could not even take one minute to attend to."

November 23

IT CAME TO me tonight that this unit is dying. Its physical structure endures. The medical staff remains, compelled to stay to complete their training program at this prestigious university hospital with its national reputation for obstetrics. The nursing staff, however, is floundering. And this unit is dead without its nurses.

Each week sees the submission of the resignations of several nurses. They turn them in defiantly to Janelle, the nurse manager. To their fellow nurses, they express regret, guilt, and then profound relief that they are escaping the impossible situation here. Veterans. Newcomers. All are victims of the ever-increasing workload and a stress level that becomes nearly intolerable on any given day, absolutely intolerable as a steady diet.

More and more we find ourselves working with a skeleton crew. Every bed in the labor rooms, antepartum problems/PAR, LICU, and mother-baby assessment is occupied. It is now customary, not unusual, to see women brought up from the emergency room and left on stretchers to labor and deliver in the hallway. There is no extra nurse to assume care for these unfortunate patients. The unlucky nurse who is in charge has to either take on their care herself or beg the assistance of nurses already straining to deal with the needs of the four women they are managing. I was told of a recent date when we hit the record for most patients receiving care on stretchers in the corridors—eighteen.

In a typical twelve-hour shift, no nurse assumes that he or she will have even five minutes to eat a hurried meal, get off tired and battered feet, or even go to the bathroom. As we move our labor patient to the delivery area, some transporter is moving a new patient into the vacated space before we are even able to tidy the equipment-strewn, often blood-spattered area.

Increasingly we hear the short-tempered and strained voices of doctors and nurses trying to prevail on each other for assistance when there is simply none to be had. The nurses have become accustomed to delivering patients in their labor beds, as the sheer volume of patients ensures that all medical staff is tied up at the moment a birth becomes inevitable. "Do the best you can," responds the weary senior resident to a nurse who is panicky about the prospect of delivering a baby whose mother is at risk for complications like seizures or shoulder dystocia. I was faced with this very situation recently when a mom in the LICU had a stuck infant trying to emerge. In the past, the cry of "shoulder dystocia" would have elicited an immediate response from several residents. On that night, I feel that only the expertise and experience of Anita Ewald, who came to my assistance, saved this mom and baby from a terrible outcome.

We could not possibly complain to Merilee about such a state of affairs. She is far more overworked than any other nurse on the unit, and moreover, her responsibility is so great. She worries that she can only staff the mother-baby assessment room with one student nurse worker, who may end up admitting more than twenty mother-baby couplets during the night. She worries that she has only one nurse and two surgical techs to staff the delivery area in an era when we are delivering what is the equivalent of two kindergarten classes a day. She knows that if a crash cesarean section takes place, she will inevitably have to drop whatever she is doing to go back and assist.

The other morning, from my stand in the hallway, I watched as this amazing woman was walking out after an unspeakably difficult night with at least the prospect of escaping to home and sleep. Past her rushed two docs taking a patient back to the OR for an emergency C-section. She knew that the team of oncoming nurses numbered less than our meager quota, and no one was responding to the demand for nursing assistance. Her conscience would not let her walk out on this scene, and I noted the overwhelmed and exhausted expression on her face as she hurried to catch up with the physicians.

And thus do we run without pause for twelve hours straight. Sometimes one sees a nurse munching on an apple or sipping a cup of coffee in the hallway outside his or her labor room. We have stopped asking Merilee when she will be able to give us a rest break. If she gets to us, fine. We know that respite time for her nurses is becoming an impossibility for her to provide. And the patients cannot be left alone.

The day shift charge nurse Gloria, having only recently assumed the charge position, comes on about six thirty in the morning. She sees the patients littered on stretchers in the hallways, sees that she has a paltry six nurses coming on duty when she knows that she should have twenty, and promptly bursts into tears. She calls the nursing supervisor to relate the crisis, who responds with the inevitable: "There's no one to send." We know that this is the truth, that there are no nurses in the hospital trained or willing to brave the trials served up here. Gloria knows that she will be the principal repository of an excruciating load of stress for the next eight hours.

I feel for her, as Gloria was one of the first nurses I met here as a graduate nurse, and she was kind and supportive to me as a newcomer. We ended up coming to Labor and Delivery together and have been good friends ever since. She has a problem with high blood pressure, and there is no doubt that the current circumstances will impact on her health. How long can she endure in this frightfully scary, stress-laden position?

Our night shift nurses, including me, are too emotionally and physically worn to deal with the plight of our peers on the day shift who are at least entering the fray after a full night's sleep. We limp to the dressing room with bladders full to bursting, our underwear sometimes stained with menstrual flow we could not even take one minute to attend to. We are too strained and distraught to have the energy to complain. As I drive home from these unbearable nights, I am so exhausted that I have to keep pinching my cheeks and slapping my legs to prevent falling asleep at the wheel. I wonder who will be the next casualty in the gutting of our nursing staff by the obscene demands placed on us nightly?

One of the worst features of this state of affairs is that those of us who remain do not elicit one drop of admiration or sympathy from the residents, interns, and medical students with whom we work. They too are under an intolerable burden. They know that the nursing staff is stretched far beyond its capacity to watch our patients minute to minute as, ideally, we must. The physicians feel an added sense of responsibility for the well-being of all these high-risk mothers and their infants. What has become commonplace is to see the medical staff venting their anger, frustration, and sometimes even panic on the heroic nurses who still show up for work. We have grown accustomed to being yelled at, not for what we accomplish with our pitiful numbers but for our inability to clone ourselves and provide even minimally acceptable personnel to assist with this workload.

What about me? I am just one of the few remaining nurses who asks herself before every shift, "Can I survive another turn at this bone-dissolving mental, physical, and emotional pressure cooker?" I have so many times lately wanted to succumb to the temptation to call in sick, to avoid even one night of the enormity of trouble that greets the nurse who elects to show up. I know that I will be working like a packhorse, worrying the whole time about how to cope if even one more emergency comes through the door, dreading the times I will preside over this craziness as the nurse in charge. Yet I cannot bear to make harder the plight of such valiant friends as Merilee and Anita, who have never once chickened out of what they must know will become their personal nightly hell.

And still I love this place. I dearly love the nurses who remain–their idealism, their skill and wit, their sense of commitment and deeply giving spirit. I love our patients, who look on with dismay as they struggle with their pain and fears, watching helplessly as their nurses and doctors strain to give care under these appalling circumstances. If there was only some way to begin to build our staff again–a seemingly impossible task in light of our desperate situation.

Our preceptors–those who train the nurses orienting to Labor and Delivery–have also fled. The one preceptor who remains on staff trains three to four nurses at a time. Lately, half of this teensy number of recruits do not stay the course. The newcomers in training either leave partway through their orientation or within months of joining the staff. What they see of the treatment nurses receive here, what they see of the phenomenal workload and excruciating responsibility, terrifies them.

After agonizing for months about what I should do, feeling myself teetering on the edge of resigning, I've come to the point where I can see only two choices. Either I must renew my commitment to my work here or decide to quit in the simple effort to preserve my health and sanity. I have been wracking my brain for any possible solution to the staffing crisis here, based on my abiding love for this work. Untypically for me, I have been mulling over the possibility of taking on a teaching role myself, here on the night shift. What has held me back is the knowledge that I don't like teaching as a steady diet. My heart lies with the work I do with my patients, and I wonder how fulfilling it would be if I were not taking direct personal responsibility for my patients' care. Moreover, I did once have a teaching role here, with some quite painful results.

My one previous experience with acting as nurse preceptor was a miserable failure. It all boiled down to the irreconcilable differences I had with another peer. David and I started out together on this unit in the same orientation group four years ago. He was an interesting fellow who was frank and open about his homosexual lifestyle. His sexual orientation was a nonissue with me. I was, however, a little shocked at hearing from other nurses about his regaling them with very explicit stories of his adventures cruising the local gay scene.

Beginning to hear of the devastating consequences of HIV infection for the gay population, I marveled at his bragging about his risky behavior.

A very bright and capable OB nurse, David left patient care about eighteen months after coming on staff to accept the role of preceptor for this unit. When the lead instructor left as her husband made a job change, David began to recruit me to become his teaching partner. He was most encouraging about his assessment of my skills for being an effective preceptor. Reluctantly, not as sure of my suitability as he was, I agreed to give the new role a try.

A mere few weeks into our working together as I assumed my first students, it became apparent to me that David and I disagreed wholeheartedly about styles of teaching. His belief was that nurses training for the work here needed to deal with the reality of the stress they would be experiencing. He tried to subject his nurse trainees rapidly to increasing levels of responsibility during their orientation so as to evaluate their ability to stand up under pressure.

I took a different path. I never kidded my students about the intensity of the work here. I tried, though, to give my students a gradual adjustment to the full pace. I was supportive and encouraging, rather than confrontational and critical. I tried always to give my nervous and struggling students a sense that this work was doable, but that each would have to take their baby steps before becoming an accomplished high-risk OB nurse.

After a few weeks of working together, David began to berate me for not putting enough pressure on my students. He would demand that I assign one to care for a critically ill patient on a ventilator before he or she was sure of the labor process itself. He would force an orientee to scrub in on a crash C-section while still unsure which instruments were appropriate to the flow of the case. This ploy would subject the learner to the ire of the surgeons for slowing the pace of surgery in a time-intensive emergency.

Finally, things came to a head. He insisted that I set up a placebo medicine on an infusion pump at some unwitting patient's bedside. Then I was to set the pump to an incorrect rate to see if my student would catch the mistake. I was pretty sure that this plan was not even legal or ethical practice, and was fundamentally opposed to such weasel-y tactics as an instructor. I refused quietly, firmly.

This imbroglio occurred on a fateful Friday afternoon. As we left together on the elevator, David's face was nearly purple with anger as he lit into me for my obstinacy. Although I did feel a deal of anxiety about this confrontation with a peer, I probably could have handled his anger better. Quivering on the inside but maintaining a nonchalant attitude, I responded in an offhand tone, advising him "not to stroke out over our difference of opinion." First thing Monday morning, he reported me to the nurse manager and the education department for incompetency.

They got us together to discuss the issue of my "problem." As David was considered the senior educator, I could sense that the bigwigs present felt his negative evaluation of me could not be dismissed. I stated my beliefs, and they listened intently. The upshot was that I could continue, but would in a sense be on probation, forced to stay on the day shift with David evaluating my competency.

I responded, "No thanks." I explained that I had been very happy taking care of patients. I both wanted and needed to work at night for family and financial reasons. I was also adamantly in disagreement with any plan to have David in a position to evaluate my work. I felt that almost anyone else would be perfectly capable of assessing my teaching competency in a neutral manner—the charge nurse, someone from the education department—but not David. We would never be in agreement on the proper method for training nurses for this unit, and I was not personally able to espouse his belief system.

I will never forget the animosity in David's eyes, the cold stare he directed at me while I was reduced to tears when the management folks in that meeting said they felt unable to comply with my request to have someone else evaluate my teaching practice. I would have to continue with David. I stood my ground and said that when I finished with my current students, I wished to return to night duty as a staff nurse. Somehow, though I was proud that I had stuck up for my convictions, I felt a sense of failure, a sense that I was admitting some inability to perform as an instructor. I struggled for many months to renew my self-esteem after this difficult and painful experience.

The irony was that David was gone within six months, driven by the complaints of nurse orientees who reported what they felt were his abusive methods. Not one of the big shots present at the meeting to thrash out my fate as a preceptor ever had the decency to say to me, "Maybe we were wrong. Maybe you were given a bad deal." Oh well. I was happier rejoining my friends on the night shift and returning to my patients.

But that is all history. If this unit is to survive, a rapid infusion of nurses is needed. I no longer have doubts about my abilities and skills, and feel that only a supportive and highly motivated person like myself could successfully get nurses through the minefield that training to this unit at present would be. Since the training program takes three months, we have to get going. If I were to volunteer and be accepted, if we could get another nurse to precept on the evening shift, we might score twelve new nurses on staff early in the New Year. I'm going to approach Janelle, the nurse manager, tomorrow morning and see what she thinks.

Addendum: I caught Janelle as she was turning her key in her office door this morning. She agreed that the unit was in terrible jeopardy. I could sense her lining up her defenses, sure that I was another in a long queue of complainers.

When I told her of my idea to run three simultaneous orientation groups on three shifts, I could virtually see the wheels turning in her oh-so-intelligent head. If she could pull this off, she would surely score some big career points. As things stood, her job had to be on the line, though the horrid state of affairs here could not in fairness be laid at her door.

So guess what? I'm to be the new nurse preceptor on the night shift. I'll be starting four nurses through the difficult three-month orientation to high-risk obstetrics in just two weeks' time. Dear God, help me. And help them too.

EPILOGUE

I BEGAN MY CAREER as nurse preceptor and trained about twenty new nurses over the next two years, many of whom remain on staff today. Their skill and prowess as high-risk obstetrical nurses is a constant source of gratification to me. Now some of these nurses have become our instructors.

Conditions in the high-risk obstetrical unit did not become fully tolerable for several years after the conclusion of this journal. Today, we still have a persistently high census and many challenging patient situations. However, certain changes took place that succeeded in making our unit a much more humane place for both physicians and nurses to train and work, and for patients to receive care.

One of the more consistently difficult features of working in this unit was the overcrowded status of the labor rooms. Reading back over the entries in this journal, I am repeatedly struck by the struggle I went through to preserve my calm in the face of the staggering workload involved in caring for four high-risk mothers and their vulnerable infants in these cramped little boxes. One day, Janelle sought me out and proposed the novel idea of having the nurses go on record as refusing to treat more than three patients in these labor rooms. "I can't put my stamp on this idea because I'd be fired."

Never mind. A few activist nurses circulated a petition. After the initial outrage of those with medical and administrative responsibility for this department and their threats to "fire every last one of them" ran their course, the new policy became a reality. The chief hospital administrator told the physicians, "How can we deny these nurses when what they are proposing is in the interest of safety for our patients?"

The change in the workload proved to have a beneficent effect on the morale of the nursing staff. This nurse-patient ratio still did not meet the standards recommended by national organizations governing obstetrical inpatient care. But the somewhat decreased number of patients and the improved space in the labor rooms did a great deal to decrease burnout among the nurses.

Though we did not know what was going on behind the scenes, the city health gurus were aware that this hospital could not sustain the entire burden for the maternity care of our indigent, immigrant, and uninsured patients. They worked to implement a system in which they contracted with hospitals in the community to take our less complicated, less high-risk mothers for care. If a woman with no health or obstetric issues was a candidate for cesarean section, they would be preadmitted to these hospitals and present for their surgery at the appointed time. An ambulance sat at the emergency room entrance twenty-four hours a day, solely for the purpose of transporting low-risk pregnant women in early labor to private hospitals in the community.

This program was slow to get going, as there was a lot of initial resistance to assuming care for our "city" patients. In time, hospitals sitting with unoccupied beds in costly maternity units came to see that taking some of our patients on a regular basis was good for business. Now instead of helping fifty to sixty new citizens into the world each day, we increase the census by a much more reasonable number. We still care for the sickest mothers and babies in the city's pregnant population, which continues to provide quality education for both the nurses and doctors who embrace the challenge of such cases. Slowly but surely, the need to render care to patients in the corridors became a thing of the past.

As for myself, I finally got tired of seeing the revolving-door effect of training nurses, only to see them leave in less than six months. Once more, I reflected on the situation and thought about some creative ideas for massaging the problems we experienced in retaining nursing staff. I made an appointment with the nursing director, a woman I had never met and who was obviously reluctant to listen to what she anticipated was another bitch session. When she heard me out, she was enthusiastic about my suggestions. She'd implemented one of my ideas by the time I returned to my unit the next night.

She asked me if I would take a new role as the unit staffer and work to actualize some of my notions of what might improve things. My only difficulty with agreeing to this change was the prospect of moving to the day shift, but I reluctantly assented. I discovered a much-improved sense of physical and mental well-being working in daylight hours, after years of subjecting my poor body by forcing it to stay up when it wanted to be asleep in a warm bed. I did get approval to come in at five in the morning to network and advocate for the valiant night staff.

One of my ideas was to contact every nurse who had left service in the wake of our crisis. The health department, realizing that our overcrowded and understaffed situation was putting our patients in peril, had authorized a hefty budget for registry nurses. Yet the typical experienced registry nurse would not brave the conditions they had heard of at the city hospital. Letting our nurses who'd abandoned ship know that there was a princely monetary reward for coming to a place they were familiar with proved helpful. We began to see these already-trained vets start to plump up our numbers. Men and women going through our orientation program were not so daunted by the challenges of the work here when they observed that our patients had much safer numbers of caregivers.

In the two years following my accepting the new position, we went from carrying a staff of twenty-four nurses to over eighty. My ideas were by no means the only factor in our trek back to better conditions. Rather, there was a coming together of strategies from many different sectors, resulting in gradual improvement which sustained those willing to stay the course. Things have improved to the point that newcomers cannot completely envision the situation as described by nurses who lived through the dark days.

I think that this story of a revitalized unit proves my belief that nurses have enormous power for good when they choose to exercise it. There are still some nagging issues that, if resolved, would make my unit a much better place to practice the art and science of obstetrics. A start has been made and has allowed me to remain working in a place that is still intense in atmosphere but rife with possibilities for personal growth and satisfaction. Not a week goes by that I do not put aside my administrative duties to get into scrubs and perform the work that brought me into nursing, giving what I hope is knowledgeable, skillful, and sensitive care to the childbearing woman.

Addendum: Veteran labor and delivery nurses who read this journal will realize that these events took place some years ago, based on treatments and procedures that are now outdated (i.e., scalp sampling, Ritodrine). It's my belief that the events recorded here nevertheless remain timely, as birth still occurs in the same manner as it has from time immemorial. I do not think that human nature has been transformed to the degree that the behaviors described herein are not relevant and illustrative of the dynamics one could find in any setting fraught with such stress, such challenges, and also so many incredible rewards.